D1496443

SETTING OUT TO
BEGIN A NEW WORLD

The Cherokees from the River Savannah, 1762 (detail)
University of Georgia Library

SETTING OUT TO BEGIN A NEW WORLD

Colonial Georgia

A DOCUMENTARY HISTORY
EDITED BY EDWARD J. CASHIN

A Beehive Press Book
LIBRARY OF GEORGIA
SAVANNAH · 1995

LIBRARY OF GEORGIA
c/o The Beehive Foundation
321 BARNARD STREET · SAVANNAH · GEORGIA 31401

Contents

THE ROYAL PROVINCE

REVOLUTION

Introduction

EARLY GEORGIA was caught up in the game of international competition for territory. Spain had a head start when Ponce de Leon claimed the southeastern part of the continent as La Florida. A short-lived settlement was planted on the Georgia coast near present-day Darien. Hernando de Soto strengthened the Spanish claim by marching across the region in his search for Cofitachiqui, the fabled town ruled by a beautiful princess. The village was probably on the Saluda River in South Carolina. The Spanish authorities lost interest in La Florida when de Soto failed to find gold. A group of French Huguenots, under the famous captain Jean Ribault, thought to try their luck in Florida. Their mistake was not so much that they were Protestants trespassing on territory claimed by a fiercely Catholic king but that they could not resist the temptation to attack the Spanish gold galleons following the gulf stream just off their coast. So the fiercely Catholic king sent his best pirate catcher, Menendez des Aviles, to remove the French interlopers. Menendez put Ribault and a number of the Huguenots to the sword and turned to the task of establishing St. Augustine as a permanent settlement.

Menendez invited missionaries to introduce Christianity to the native inhabitants. Those ardent sons of Ignatius of Loyola, the Jesuits, answered his call and established the first missions. Franciscan friars succeeded the Jesuits and started missions along the Georgia sea islands and coast, and across the neck of Florida into Apalache and up the Chattahoochee nearly to the site of today's Columbus, Georgia. The mission chain took the shape of the letter U, cradling the region which became

Georgia. The Spanish and their Indian allies occupied the land for a century.

Georgia might have remained Spanish, except that the British colony in Barbados became overcrowded. Some of the prominent planters decided to ask King Charles II for a land grant, and shrewdly included the king's closest councilors in their petition. The king gave them land that wasn't his, the northern reaches of La Florida, from Virginia into Florida and from the Atlantic to the Pacific. The Barbadians sent out explorers who mapped the coast and selected the site of Charleston. Knowing that the Spanish would be annoyed, they hid behind a barricade up the Ashley River. When the King of Spain informed the King of England that they might stay there provided they came no further South, the Carolinians built Charleston and put a wall around it just in case. Soon, adventurers from Charleston penetrated the interior and followed the old trails to the Chattahoochee, where they found eager customers for the rich red cloth called strouds for the Cotswold town where it was made. In 1680 the Carolinians destroyed the northernmost Spanish mission on St. Catherine's Island, and in 1702 they destroyed everything else along the Atlantic coast except for the fortress of San Marcos in St. Augustine. Two years later the English put an end to the missions along the Chattahoochee and sold over a thousand Christian Indians into slavery in the West Indies.

The French under King Louis XIV were seriously interested in expanding the boundaries of Louisiana. By 1718, the prospects were encouraging for the French. They had permanent settlements at Biloxi, Mobile and New Orleans, and in that year built a fort in the heart of Muskogee Indian country where the Coosa and Tallapoosa rivers met to form the Alabama and called it Fort Toulouse of the Alabamas. The Muskogees, known as Creeks by the Carolinians, had been alienated by the venality of the Charleston traders. The Yamassee tribe took to the warpath, killing all the traders they could find. The Yamassee War delighted the French, who posed as the only true friend of the Muskogees. As a token of friendship, they laid claim to everything the Muskogees claimed. A map made in 1719 by Louis's cartographer put the border of Louisiana at the Savannah River and, until the English could do something about it, the region was French.

Meanwhile, a group of English gentlemen began a discussion which influenced the destiny of Georgia. A member of Parliament from Haslemere in Surrey, James Edward Oglethorpe, and some of his friends were inspired by the Rev. Thomas Bray to undertake some worthwhile humanitarian project. They raised funds for their good work before deciding what that work would be; in fact, the good Dr. Bray died before the project was launched. Most Georgians know about Oglethorpe's investigation of prisons and some know about the death of his friend Robert Castell in debtors' prison. It is even more widely known that Oglethorpe decided to found a colony where debtors might get a fresh start. Very few, even in Georgia, realize that Parliament did not approve this idea. Oglethorpe and his associates then formulated reasons calculated to win Parliament's approval. They proposed calling the colony Georgia to please the King, sending hardworking poor people who would guard the rich rice colony of South Carolina (North and South Carolina had been separated in 1729), setting them to work growing crops useful in England. They also suggested that the colony could be a haven for the German Protestants crowding London.

The sponsors obtained a patent to conduct their experiment in social planning for a period of twenty-one years. The charter specified that the new colony would be located between the Savannah and Altamaha rivers. Oglethorpe's associates were organized as the Trustees of Georgia and charged with responsibility for governing the new colony. They can be forgiven for indulging in self-congratulation befitting noblemen who have done a good deed for their fellow men. No requirement was exacted from those who would go over at the charity's expense except that they would plant mulberry trees for silk production, be prepared to defend the colony, contribute some public labor and remain in the colony three years. For this, the colonists would be allotted fifty acres of land and no more. They need not worry about governing themselves, the Trustees would do that. The Trustees were so convinced of their good intentions and so confident that the colonists would be happy and grateful that they barred lawyers from the colony. For good measure, they barred Catholics and Jews also. The first Georgians were screened by a committee and selected on the basis of their good conduct and skills.

These were the days of the greatest optimism. Phillip Thicknesse, an early colonist, recalled: "I had been so poisoned by the glaring colors in which Oglethorpe displayed the prospects of his new colony that I was determined to go thither. This project filled me with infinite delight, for I then considered myself as one setting out to begin the forming of a new world." The colonists went to work with enthusiasm, the Carolinians cheered for Oglethorpe and Governor Robert Johnson sent skilled black carpenters from South Carolina to help build the first houses. Oglethorpe got along well with the venerable chief of the nearby Yamacraws, Tomochichi. He secured the assistance of Mary, the Creek Indian wife of the Carolina trader John Musgrove, who kept a trading house near Savannah. Oglethorpe was astonished at the amount and value of deerskins brought down the river from Savannah Town, the Carolina rendezvous near the head of navigation. His Indian friends informed him that the Carolina traders were up to their old tricks, plying the Indians with rum and then cheating them. The chiefs were restless and there was talk of cutting off the English trade in favor of the French. Already the French at Fort Toulouse were doing a brisk trading business. If he had not been aware of the French pretensions before, Oglethorpe certainly became so during the first few months in Georgia.

After settling the colony of German Salzburgers at Ebenezer, he returned to England and enlisted his fellow Trustees in lobbying Parliament for the passage of three pieces of legislation. Two of the measures were intended to reform the Indian trade. The Indian Act required traders working west of the Savannah River to obtain licenses from

Georgia and specifically from Oglethorpe who was named commissioner of the Indian trade. The second act forbade the use of rum in Georgia. The Trustees' primary objective was the elimination of rum in the Indian trade, but a second thought was that sobriety was wholesome for Georgians generally. A third law forbade Georgians the use of slave labor. As well intentioned as these three measures were, the effect was disastrous. The Carolinians were outraged; they had welcomed the neighboring colonists and now Oglethorpe attempted to steal away their lucrative Indian business.

Before he returned to Georgia in 1736, Oglethorpe engaged in a dubious bit of cartographic chicanery. The Georgia charter limited the province to the region between the Savannah and Altamaha rivers. Oglethorpe had a map made which showed a branch of the Altamaha flowing into Florida's St. Johns River, thereby extending Georgia's boundaries to the St. Johns and justifying the establishment of forts on Cumberland and Amelia Islands. Expecting trouble with Spain, Oglethorpe's agent George Dunbar recruited a colony of Scots from Invernesshire, all members of the Clan Chattan headed by the McIntoshes. The newcomers were busy building houses in Darien on the Altamaha when Oglethorpe paid them a visit, dressed like them in tartans. Oglethorpe made a second voyage to London and talked the king's minister, Robert Walpole, into giving him a regiment, the Forty-first, then stationed in Gibraltar. In 1738, Oglethorpe was back in Georgia and his regiment garrisoned in the fortified town of Frederica on St. Simon's Island.

One of Oglethorpe's best attributes was his ability to deal with Indians in a way that won their respect. Colonial governors were usually too high and mighty to undertake a tedious journey into Indian country. To his credit, Oglethorpe did just that. With an escort of rangers, he followed the trading roads to Coweta, principal town of the Lower Creeks. He signed a treaty of friendship by which the Creeks confirmed the cession of the tidewater region between the Savannah and Altamaha rivers. Oglethorpe was delighted that his efforts to regulate trading practices cemented the alliance between the Creek Nation and the British, especially at a time when the French governor in New Orleans was planning a grand offensive against the beleaguered Chickasaws. While in Augusta in September, 1739, Oglethorpe heard the news he had expected, England was at war with Spain. Like many other aspects of Georgia's early years, this war was unusual to the point of being bizarre, with elements of high comedy. For a start, this war is known in history as "the war of Jenkins Ear." A British sea captain by name of Robert Jenkins smuggled goods into Spanish American ports once too often, and the Garda Costa applied a routine punishment: they cut off one ear. Jenkins preserved the ear in a whiskey bottle and displayed it before a discomfited Parliament, which thereupon declared war. The major British effort in this particular war was the launching of a mighty fleet under the command of Admiral Edward Vernon, who was supposed to conquer Florida along with the rest of the Spanish Main. Unfortunately, Vernon confined his efforts to the reduction of Cartagena in South America. Florida was left to Oglethorpe.

It seemed an easy thing. Oglethorpe had his regiment, his Scottish contingent from Darien, five hundred volunteers from Charleston and nearly a thousand Indians, mostly Cherokees. The Creeks who had recently welcomed him now prudently waited upon the outcome of the contest. Their attention was distracted by Governor LeMoyne Bienville's long-awaited campaign against the Chickasaws, their near neighbors to the West. Oglethorpe was keenly aware of both enemies, and his brave message to the Trustees deserves to be remembered: "The French have attacked the Carolina Indians and the Spaniards have invaded us. I wish it may not be resolved between them to root the English out of America. We here are resolved to die hard and will not lose one inch of ground without fighting."

The Florida campaign was consistent with the other phases of Georgia's beginning; nothing went as planned. Oglethorpe and his regiment guarded one seaside approach to St. Augustine and the Carolina volunteers guarded the other. A "flying squadron" of Darien Scots and a few Carolinians were supposed to patrol the land approaches behind the town. Instead, the flying squadron went to sleep in an abandoned fort and was completely surprised and routed by a Spanish night assault. Then a Spanish ship slipped past Oglethorpe's besiegers and brought supplies to the defenders of Castillo San Marcos. Finally, the Carolinians decided to go home, grumbling that Oglethorpe had botched the siege. Oglethorpe had no choice but to follow, at least as far as Frederica, where he waited for the inevitable counterattack. Fortunately Bienville's campaign against the Chickasaws fared no better.

When the Spaniards launched their counterinvasion, it seemed unstoppable. An armada of ships carrying three thousand men, including a number of blacks, advanced up the Georgia coast in July, 1742. Carolina ignored Oglethorpe's appeals for help, so Georgia's fate depended upon the Forty-first Regiment and a few surviving Darien Scots. Happily, at this most critical moment, fortune smiled. The Spanish were greater bunglers than the Georgians. The Spanish general, Montiano, wasted his overwhelming numerical advantage by sending a small force of about two hundred probing along the military road leading to Frederica at the northern end of St. Simon's Island. Oglethorpe rushed out to meet the invaders with no more men than the enemy's advance party. A confused melée ensued, known as the Battle of Bloody Marsh, the moment of Oglethorpe's greatest glory. Montiano abandoned St. Simon's and, on the way home, attempted to redeem himself by capturing little Fort William on the south end of Cumberland Island. The gallant defenders refused to oblige him, so the mighty host slunk back to St. Augustine. Oglethorpe's success encouraged him to try another invasion of Florida. The failure of the second expedition thinned his hero's laurels.

By 1743, it seemed that everything had gone wrong. Perhaps disappointment was inevitable after the ballyhoo which launched the Georgia project. The Trustees, who remained at home chaired by John Percival, Lord Egmont, needed the encouragement of good news, and Oglethorpe hated to disappoint them. As a result, the Trustees believed that conditions were better than they actually were. When Georgians raised legitimate complaints, the Trustees called the protesters "malcontents." The complaints, slow at first, grew in intensity as they went unheeded. The Salzburgers objected to the location assigned by Oglethorpe. The Darien Scots starved for lack of supplies. The Savannahians quarrelled among themselves, complained bitterly about the storekeeper Thomas Causton and gradually focused upon the basic plan itself. The prohibition of rum cut them off from trade with the West Indies, because rum was the main product of the islands. Carolinians, with slave labor, produced everything Georgia did, and much more cheaply. The limitation on landholding was a source of frustration. Why be satisfied with a tract of fifty acres of sandy land in Georgia when one could cross the river and buy freehold land in Carolina on the installment plan? The protesters selected Thomas Stephens to convey their criticisms to Parliament, requesting a regular government for Georgia, land grants like those in Carolina, the introduction of slave labor, bounties for a variety of products and, in lieu of the above, funds to allow Georgians to settle elsewhere.

The Trustees' response was woefully inadequate. They divided Georgia into two counties, with a president and council for Savannah and another for Frederica. William Stephens, the colony's resident secretary, was named president at Savannah, but Oglethorpe failed to nominate anyone for Frederica. Parliament's loss of confidence in Trustee rule was evident in 1742 when that body declined to renew the annual subsidy to the Trustees. Oglethorpe returned to England in 1743 to face a court martial instead of a hero's welcome. Lieutenant Colonel William Cook, who had defended Fort William on Cumberland Island against the Spaniards in 1742, brought charges against Oglethorpe for maladministration of the regiment. Oglethorpe was cleared on all charges. Lord Egmont, who with Oglethorpe was the strongest advocate of Georgia, resigned as president of the governing council. The plan came unravelled thereafter. In 1742 rum was allowed; in 1750 the ban on slavery was lifted; and in 1751 the Trustees gave Georgia up to Parliament.

Before the Trustees yielded control of the colony, they called for elections to an assembly. It was the first for Georgia. Every settlement of ten families elected one deputy, Augusta and Ebenezer sent two and Savannah four. Frederica had declined with the disbanding of the Forty-first Regiment in 1749 and was not represented. Sixteen deputies met in Savannah on January 14, 1751. Their requests were more sensible than might have been expected from amateurs in government. They asked not to be annexed to South Carolina, they wanted improvements for the port of Savannah in order to challenge Charleston's dominance in trade and they required soldiers for defense. The Savannah delegates complained that the Indian merchants in Augusta ignored Savannah and did all their business with Charleston; they asked the Trustees to break up the Augusta monopoly on the Indian trade. The Augustans responded by reciting a list of good deeds done in the interests of the colony, including the preservation of the Creek alliance during the recent war. They noted the inadequacy of the facilities at Savannah and the infrequency of sailings from that port. In short, they advised the Trustees not to meddle in one of the few successful enterprises in the colony.

Georgia began a new phase of its history when the Trustees surrendered their charter in 1752. The Board of Trade replaced the Common Council of the Georgia Trust as the supervisory authority. Coincidentally, the Board itself was in the process of change. For decades, the Board was merely a clearing house for colonial correspondence, without any real control over the American colonies. Power to appoint and dismiss Royal officials was vested in the office of the secretary of state for the southern department, and since 1724 that official was Thomas Pelham-Holles, the Duke of Newcastle. Newcastle was more interested in the game of patronage than foreign policy, and the interest that he had was dedicated to maintaining a balance of power in Europe. Except for the opportunities the provinces afforded for the exercise of patronage, America received scant attention. As a result, the colonies developed differently from each other and assumed ever greater control of their governance. When George Montagu Dunk, the Earl of Halifax, was named President of the Board of Trade in 1749, he was determined to rejuvenate the Board and regain control over the American colonies. His first colonial project was the anglicization of Nova Scotia. Hundreds of English settlers were sent to that province, and the French Acadians were scattered among the other colonies. By 1754 Halifax had wrangled a seat for himself on the king's privy council and had wrested colonial patronage away from the secretary of state. He needed a model colony to serve as an example to the older errant provinces, and Georgia, he decided, would become that exemplar. His choice of the man to serve as model governor was John Reynolds, captain of the Royal navy. Halifax would not have chosen Reynolds except that the prestigious Lord Chancellor Hardwicke recommended Reynolds, and Halifax owed a favor to Hardwicke. British politics was frequently a case of favors returned for earlier favors given. Halifax handed Reynolds a lengthy commission setting forth the duties of a model governor of a model colony and gave him eleven days to board ship for Georgia. Not a quick learner, Reynolds never got the hang of the business of governing anything larger than a warship. But Georgians did not know that and welcomed Reynolds upon his arrival in Savannah on October 29, 1754. Those who lived outside Savannah were particularly pleased that the interregnum was at an end.

For two years preceding Reynolds's arrival government was in the hands of William Stephens's successors, a president and council, all of whom were from Savannah. The council discriminated against Georgians outside Savannah in land grants and other measures and built a legacy of distrust. When Reynolds reappointed the members of the interim council as his own council, he disappointed the Augusta traders as well as the planters on the lower coast. An anti-Savannah faction was organized by Edmund Gray, a recent arrival from North Carolina who affected the simple manners of a Quaker and lived near Augusta. Gray allied himself with candidates from the towns eligible to elect representatives. He and several of his friends were elected to Georgia's first assembly, which met in Savannah in January, 1755. Gray complained that some of his party were defeated by fraud. He blamed the members of the council and their Savannah friends, not the governor. Gray and his followers boycotted the assembly and were expelled by the rump assembly. Thereupon, Gray circulated flyers calling upon friends of liberty to gather in Savannah to protest the fraudulent proceedings. Governor Reynolds equated talk of liberty with rebellion and prohibited gatherings for any and all purposes. Whatever Edmund Gray was he was not a rebel, and rather than make trouble he and his followers left Georgia for the region below the Altamaha.

Governor Reynolds pleased the members of his council by siding with them against Gray but soon lost their support by withholding sinecures they expected. Instead of spreading around the appointments at his disposal, Reynolds gave seven salaried positions to his friend William Little, a naval surgeon who had come with him to Georgia. This singular example of poor judgment did not bode well for Reynolds's success. When the members of the council complained that Little was not performing his seven duties adequately, Reynolds ordered an investigation—by William Little! Little reported that perhaps he was not doing two of his jobs as well as he might, so the governor deprived him of only those two. Reynolds thus alienated the council after he had disappointed the opponents of the council, the followers of Edmund Gray. The strangest part of the story is that William Little allied himself with the Gray faction, was elected to the 1757 Commons House of Assembly and chosen Speaker of that body. The result was that the governor began to cooperate with the lower house while quarrelling with the upper house. Reynolds's most noteworthy achievement was the organization of two troops of rangers for defense of the frontiers.

Reynolds was bested by his opponents where he was most vulnerable, in London. Councilor Alexander Kellett carried the complaints of the Savannah faction to Lord Halifax and the Board of Trade with the result that Reynolds was called home to answer the charges. Halifax welcomed the excuse to remove Reynolds, because he had a better candidate at hand. Henry Ellis had first attracted Halifax's attention when he returned from a much-publicized voyage of exploration for a northwest passage and wrote a book about it. Ellis was invited to join the Royal Society, where he met Oglethorpe and consorted with England's best and brightest. He then returned to the sea as captain of *The Earl of Halifax* and was in the West Indies when Halifax first needed a model governor for Georgia. In 1756 Ellis happened to be in London, and Halifax seized upon Kellett's criticisms of Reynolds as an opportunity to name Ellis lieutenant governor and dispatch him to Georgia.

Ellis was embarrassed by the tumultuous reception he received in Savannah, particularly because Reynolds was still in town. Ellis's most difficult task was to measure up to the inflated expectations of Lord Halifax in London and to reconcile the quarrelling factions in Georgia. To his credit, he did so. Inflammatory rhetoric disappeared from Georgia with the departure of Reynolds, who was removed from office in 1758. Under Henry Ellis, now promoted to governor, Georgians learned for the first time how to govern themselves. They never had that opportunity under Trustee rule. During the interregnum, the council's partiality to Savannah did more harm than good for the province. Reynolds only demonstrated the defects of government during his tenure. Ellis appealed to the patriotism and civic responsibility of Georgians by outlining problems and asking the Assembly to recommend solutions. A budgeting system was adopted, the province was reorganized into parishes and Georgia became a constitutional colony, one which managed local affairs and left larger policy to Parliament.

Ellis impressed his friends in England with his management of Indian affairs. After Oglethorpe's departure, Governor James Glen of South Carolina claimed jurisdiction regarding all aspects of Indian policy, including trade. His successor, William Henry Lyttelton, continued to maintain that prerogative. Both Glen and Lyttelton affected that arrogance of demeanor which was one of the least attractive characteristics of the English ruling class. Ellis, like Oglethorpe before him, had the courtesy to treat the Indians with the respect they deserved. At an historic conference in Savannah in 1757 he embraced the Creek chiefs individually and invited them to take supper with him in his own house.

The French and Indian War complicated Ellis's efforts to establish Georgia's prosperity. He did all he could to prepare for the worst, prodding Augustans to rebuild their decrepit fort, paying rangers out of his own pocket, erecting fortifications around Savannah. Since Oglethorpe's departure Carolina governors claimed jurisdiction over the troops stationed at Georgia's forts Augusta, Frederica and Barrington. Ellis argued that the policy conflicted with his commission as commander of the military in Georgia. Under his own authority, he outfitted a schooner and sent it to do battle against French privateers harbored at St. Augustine. Because the French were doing it, he offered rewards to Creeks and Chickasaws who brought scalps of the enemy to Savannah. In Georgia's darkest hour, when painted Cherokees terrorized Augusta, he enlisted Creek war parties in the defense of his province. The hardy traders who lived among Indians and did business with them praised Ellis's skills in Indian diplomacy and gave him their full support. Lachlan McGillivray and George Galphin employed their enormous influence among the Upper and Lower Creeks respectively to preserve the friendship of that Nation.

Ellis left Georgia in November, 1760, to seek military assistance from General Jeffrey Amherst in New York. His physical condition deteriorated alarmingly during his last year, probably because he had contracted malaria. Even though weakened in health, he undertook the hazardous winter voyage to New York and obtained Amherst's promise to send regulars southward to subdue the Cherokees. Ellis then proceeded to London, where he learned that his patron Halifax had appointed him governor of Nova Scotia. Ellis held the position for two years but never left England.

The details of Ellis's career after he left Georgia have become known only recently. The new king, George III, disagreed with William Pitt's war policy, and Pitt resigned from the privy council in October, 1761.

Pitt's successor as secretary of state, Lord Egremont, knew very little about America. Egremont's friend Halifax introduced Ellis as one who could advise him on American affairs. London gossips soon began referring to Ellis as Egremont's "oracle." Extant memoranda written by Ellis contain advice on prosecuting the war against Spain, taking Cuba and exchanging that island for Florida in the peace treaty. Ellis wrote a draft of the famous Proclamation of 1763 which created two Floridas, a British government for Canada and an Indian reserve west of the Appalachians. Ellis suggested the St. Mary's River as Georgia's southern border and advised calling an Indian conference at Augusta in 1763. If Egremont had lived longer, Ellis would have continued to influence American policy and would have been honored with a peerage, but Egremont died in August, 1763, soon after he informed the king that he had completed his American business.

Ellis deserved the Georgians' gratitude. After false starts under the Trust and during the first royal administration, the colony was finally able to govern itself. Economic prosperity accompanied and fostered political maturity. There were similarities between Ellis and James Wright, his successor. Wright followed Ellis's example in his relations with the Assembly and was equally assiduous in cultivating the good will of Georgia's Indian neighbors. Both gave Georgia faithful service and highly competent administrations. There were also important differences between the two men. Ellis was more outgoing and charismatic. He loved a good show. Sharp of wit and glib of tongue, he sparkled in civilized society. He would not have been satisfied to remain in Georgia much longer than he did. He enjoyed the company of aristocrats, philosophers and scientists. Georgia was a way station to greater things. Wright, on the other hand, was content to be a good governor of Georgia. Born in England, he grew up in South Carolina and was more American than English. Role models for him were the merchant planters of Charleston, and he succeeded admirably in following their example. During his tenure as governor he acquired eleven plantations worked by 523 slaves.

Everything went well until 1765. Wright's major achievement was hosting the successful Indian Congress at Augusta in 1763. Pitt's successor as Secretary of State, Lord Egremont, prompted by Henry Ellis, ordered the governors of Virginia, North Carolina and South Carolina to go to Augusta to meet with chiefs of the Creeks, Cherokees, Chickasaws, Choctaws and Catawbas and tell them that the war was over, the French were banished and that King George was their true father and friend. The governors grumbled that Augusta lacked the proper amenities, but they went there because the Indians refused to go any farther. The Royal dignitaries were surprised at the outset by the Creek offer to cede land between the Savannah and the Ogeechee rivers. The Georgia Assembly later thanked Lachlan McGillivray and George Galphin for their part in persuading the Indians to make the cession. The fifty-mile-wide strip beckoned pioneer farmers to Georgia. They came by the hundreds, down the valleys of the Appalachians, into the Carolina up-country and the Georgia backcountry. Unlike the older residents of Augusta, they did not know Indians or desire to know them. They regarded Indians as potential enemies and, at best, obstacles to their possession of land. Inevitably, they began to cross over the Ogeechee River, into the Creek hunting reserve. Governor Wright ordered the treaty line of 1763 to be marked more clearly, but the aggressive frontier people were not deterred by blazed trees. Wright sponsored two townships on the boundaries, Wrightsborough on the Little River and Queensborough on the Ogeechee River, hoping that the settlements would bring order and security to the backcountry.

Efforts by Henry Ellis's high-placed friends in the British government to attend to American problems began to intrude into Georgia politics. Georgia, like Nova Scotia and the two new Florida provinces, had less to complain about than the older colonies in the matter of taxation. Georgia received an annual subsidy of about £4,000 from Parliament out of which salaries of the governor and Royal officials were paid. About one-third of that amount was raised by property taxes. The protest movement that led to the American Revolution was aimed at Parliament's efforts to raise money to pay the expenses of governing America. The older colonies took the position that they would rather pay the salaries of Royal officials themselves than be dependent on Parliament. Georgians never joined that particular chorus.

Rumbles of opposition greeted the Sugar Act of 1764, and a storm of protest followed upon the imposition of the Stamp Tax in 1765. Throughout the major port cities from Boston to Charleston, organized mobs took to the streets to demonstrate in favor of liberty and in opposition to taxation without representation. The demonstrations were supported and, in some cases, sponsored by the well-to-do merchants and lawyers who disdained public protests themselves. The reaction to the Stamp Act might be viewed as the beginning of the two traditions which have characterized American politics ever since. The conservative merchant and planter class was satisfied with the way things were; they opposed any new British intervention into their affairs. The demonstrators were not content with their lot; they wanted a share of the good things enjoyed by the conservatives. Because they favored change, they were called radicals, but essentially they were democrats interested in spreading the benefits of government. Another lingering effect of the Stamp Act riots was the legitimization of street protests as agents of change. We have been doing it ever since.

Governor Wright had the Georgia rangers to help him quell disturbances during the Stamp Act crisis, but he lost them when they were disbanded in an economy move by the government. The Royal Americans stationed in Augusta and Frederica were withdrawn to northern posts in 1768. After that Governor Wright had only his prestige and the militia to rely upon. The strength of both depended upon the vagaries of public opinion. Henry Ellis once expressed the wish that South Carolina were at a greater distance, and James Wright must have agreed. The repeal of the Stamp Act in 1766 quieted the radicals, but they rose up again when the Townshend Duties were imposed in 1768. There was no need for the conservatives to foment a reaction this time. Popular leaders, having tasted power, needed no urging to take to the streets again. Once more protests and boycotts had the desired result and the Townshend Duties were repealed by a new ministry headed by Frederick, Lord North. All were repealed, that is, with the notable exception of a tax on imported British tea.

Despite the sporadic expressions of discontent on the part of the merchants at Savannah and Sunbury, most Georgians were satisfied with their lot and respected their governor. The backcountry people thought well of Wright because of the second great land acquisition which he engineered in 1773. The Cherokee Indians offered to pay their accumulated debts to traders in land. Private land cessions were forbidden by Royal policy, but Wright worked out a scheme in conjunction with the principal traders. Let the Indians cede their land to the king, who would then sell tracts to those who could afford to pay. Governor Wright had in mind "the better sort" and "the middling sort" as he phrased it, but not the lower sort whom he called Crackers. Governor Wright applied the word to the restless vagabonds who squatted on other people's land.

William Bartram, the Philadelphia naturalist, happened to be in Augusta for the treaty signing in May, 1773, and observed that the Creeks objected strenuously to the transaction. Governor Wright had hoped to persuade them to give up the strip between the Ogeechee and Oconee rivers, but the Creeks refused. Only reluctantly they consented to give up the area above the Little River and east of the Ogeechee River, which they jointly claimed with the Cherokees. Although the Creeks left Augusta in a disgruntled mood, all other parties were pleased. The Cherokees, the Augusta traders, their London suppliers and the backcountry settlers generally hailed the treaty and cheered for Governor Wright. When we recall that the treaty was signed the same year the Boston Tea Party occurred, it is obvious how different the mood was in the two places. In fact, Governor Wright advertised in England for purchasers of estates on the newly ceded lands, promising that the fertile region was far removed from the tumult in Massachusetts.

The young warriors among the Creeks decided that their elders had given away too much of their hunting ground at Augusta. In December, 1773, war parties attacked the frontier settlements along the Little River. The Augusta militia marched out to repel the invaders, but fled in a panic at the appearance of painted warriors. People from all over the backcountry flocked into Augusta. Some of the wealthier citizens put stockades around their houses in the expectation of an attack. Governor Wright had only one weapon in his arsenal after the failure of the militia. He put a stop to the Indian trade. To his surprise the tactic worked. Chastened chiefs came to Savannah begging for a resumption of trade. Wright arranged a meeting with the headmen in October, 1774. The frontier people had never been so loyal. When the Savannah merchants protested the British measures that punished Massachusetts for dumping tea into Boston Harbor, men from all the backcountry settlements signed petitions of loyalty to Wright and King George. The Savannahians did not speak for them, they said. They expected that Governor Wright would use the occasion to obtain the land he failed to get in 1773, the Oconee strip.

Wright was caught in the most critical dilemma of his long career. The Indian traders urged him not to force the Indians back to the Oconee or else Georgia would lose the trade to Mobile and Pensacola. John Stuart, the Indian superintendent, objected to any land cessions, citing the Proclamation of 1763 which guaranteed an Indian reserve and the line established by the 1763 Treaty of Augusta which was supposed to be permanent. On the other hand, the settlers maintained that they needed the Oconee as an outlet for their produce, that Wright had been willing to ask for the Oconee in 1773 and that the Indians were disposed to give their consent as the result of the trade boycott. Wright made his decision. He required the guilty chiefs to be put to death and then resumed trade as usual. Because nothing was said about territory, the people felt betrayed. Wright had cast his lot with Indians and Indian merchants. After the October treaty, backcountry radicals joined their low-country counterparts in a coalition which moved Georgia toward revolution.

During the year 1775, Wright gradually lost control of affairs. A provincial congress replaced the Royal assembly, and Georgia joined the other colonies in an association against trade with England. Radical leaders like George Wells and Button Gwinnett gained the ascendancy while moderates hung back. The provincial congress elected delegates to the Continental Congress, established an executive agency called a Council of Safety and authorized local committees to enforce the trade boycott. These committees assumed the name "Sons of Liberty" and set about ferreting out people who disagreed with them. One prominent opponent in the backcountry was Thomas Brown, who had established Brownsborough outside Augusta. He refused to join the association and urged all who would listen to form a counterassociation of men loyal to the king. In August, 1775, the Liberty Boys made an example of Brown. A blow to the head fractured his skull, he was scalped, his feet burned, and, more dead than alive, he was trundled through the streets of Augusta in a cart, an object lesson to those whose notions of liberty differed from the majority.

After Brown recovered he joined sympathizers in the South Carolina up-country and helped organize them in support of the king. A civil war nearly broke out between the loyalists and the whigs, but neither side was properly armed and equipped. The loyalist leaders, one of whom was Thomas Brown, formulated a plan which was eventually adopted by the British ministry. They would bring Indians down on the frontiers in conjunction with the landing of British troops on the coast and catch the whigs between the enemies they feared most, Indian warriors and redcoats. With the approval of the Royal governors of South Carolina and Georgia, Brown went to St. Augustine, where Governor Patrick Tonyn became an enthusiastic convert to the plan. Tonyn commissioned Brown a lieutenant colonel of the Florida rangers and sent him into Creek country to enlist Indian allies. Georgia's military activity during the entire Revolutionary War involved Thomas Brown. For each of the first three years, Georgians attempted to invade Florida to put a stop to harassment by Brown's rangers and

Indians. For the rest of the war, they fought to drive Brown and his friends out of Georgia.

Even though he had lost control of events, James Wright remained in Savannah throughout 1775. On January 18, 1776, several British warships sailed into the Savannah River. The Georgia Council of Safety put Governor Wright and the leading loyalists under arrest. However, Wright and his friends took advantage of their opportunity to escape aboard the British vessels. Georgia's first battle of the war occurred when the British warships ventured upriver to Savannah and captured several merchant ships loaded with rice. The Georgia militia, under Lachlan McIntosh, claimed victory because the British ships failed to capture Savannah. The idea was good for morale, but the British were after the rice, not the town.

On April 15, while the warships still threatened Savannah, the provincial congress sought the safety of Augusta and issued a constitution, a short and simple document called Rules and Regulations. The dominant radical faction vested authority in a one-house legislature with a weak, plural executive body. Two radical leaders, Button Gwinnett and Lyman Hall, were in Philadelphia to vote independence, and George Walton, a conservative who later joined the radicals, arrived in time to sign the Declaration of Independence. Button Gwinnett returned to Georgia to be elected to a constitutional convention which met late in 1776 and early 1777. Radicals controlled the convention and wrote the constitution, one of the most democratic of all those drawn up in the new states. Authority was vested in a one-house legislature which elected the governor. Of course, victory was not won in the writing; the loyalists backed by the British military had to be beaten and the conservative faction held at bay.

At times, the radicals seemed more at odds with the conservative faction of whigs than with the loyalists. Before the constitutional Convention adjourned, the leaders decided upon another foray into Florida. As president of the convention, Gwinnett claimed military command of state forces, but Colonel Lachlan McIntosh, commander of Georgia's continental battalion, took his orders from George Washington. The result was that both Gwinnett and McIntosh asserted the right of command, neither would cooperate with the other and the expedition ended in failure. The radical-dominated assembly investigated the affair and upheld Gwinnett's version of what happened. McIntosh blurted out for all to hear that Gwinnett was "a Scoundrel and lying Rascal." The two engaged in a duel only a few paces from each other, so close that neither missed his shot. Both were wounded, McIntosh recovered, Gwinnett died three days later.

McIntosh's friends became so discouraged that they considered asking South Carolina to annex Georgia. Carolinians liked the idea and sent William Henry Drayton to explain to the Georgia Assembly how much better off they would be under the government of South Carolina. The Georgians knew that Drayton regarded them as bumbling rustics; they rejected his offer and offered a reward for his arrest if he dared come again to Georgia.

In 1778 a third invasion of Florida was attempted with General Robert Howe playing the part of McIntosh and Governor John Houstoun that of Gwinnett, and each refusing to cooperate with the other. This was a larger effort. South Carolina contributed militia under Andrew Williamson, and there was some skirmishing with Thomas Brown and his rangers, but in the end the invasion accomplished no more than the first two. By late 1778, the war in the North had become a stalemate and Lord George Germain, the war minister in London, turned his attention to the southern theater. In a gesture toward reconciliation, Parliament promised that any colony which rejoined the mother country would be spared of taxation.

During the last days of December a British army, under Lieutenant Colonel Archibald Campbell, landed below Savannah and routed General Robert Howe's defenders. They were joined by British troops from Florida, including Brown's rangers. Campbell's orders were to march quickly to the backcountry where he would meet Indian allies. Campbell's forces met little opposition on their march to Augusta. At first, it appeared that the strategy was successful as people flocked in to Augusta to swear allegiance to the king. But after two weeks an army of North Carolinians appeared across the river from Augusta. At the same time whigs under Andrew Pickens and Elijah Clarke defeated a loyalist band at Kettle Creek. Campbell decided not to wait any longer for his Indian friends and abandoned Augusta, to the dismay of those who had so recently declared their loyalty to the king. The whig army followed the British downriver, careless in the assumption of victory. While encamped at the junction of Briar Creek and the Savannah River, the North Carolinians and Georgians were surprised and defeated by the British. The Battle of Briar Creek, March 3, 1779, ensured British control of Georgia below Briar Creek. Archibald Campbell ordered civil government restored in that part of the province. Governor Wright and other exiled officials returned to Savannah, and Georgia was officially declared a royal province exempt from taxation. Georgia was the only colony accorded that dubious distinction.

Goverment in the region above Briar Creek suffered from the renewal of conservative-radical contention. John Wereat, a close friend of Lachlan McIntosh who never approved of Georgia's constitution, took the lead in convening a Supreme Executive Council and was elected its president. During the emergency, he announced that the constitution would be suspended and the Council would rule. This was too much for George Wells, who served under Button Gwinnett on the committee which drafted the constitution and who acted as Gwinnett's second in the fatal duel with McIntosh. He called for elections to form a constitutional government. Before the year was over, a radical government operated in Augusta in opposition to Wereat's Council. Thus Georgia had three governments, two in Augusta and one in Savannah.

The major military event of the year was the sudden arrival off the coast of Tybee of a French fleet of twenty-two ships of war with four thousand troops aboard. Count Charles Henri d'Estaing answered

George Washington's request to stop off on his way back to France and recapture Georgia. He believed that the errand would delay him only a few days. Instead, the operation consumed almost two months and accomplished nothing except sound, fury and a great amount of bloodshed. The combined French and American forces launched a grand assault on the British lines on October 9, 1779. Prominent among the fatalities was Polish Count Casimir Pulaski, killed leading the American charge, and Sergeant William Jasper, hero of the Battle of Fort Moultrie in 1776. As a consequence of the defense of Savannah the British decided to pay greater attention to the southern theater. Sir Henry Clinton, commander of British forces in America, led a major invasion of South Carolina from a base on Tybee Island.

Meanwhile, American General Benjamin Lincoln sent George Walton to establish a constitutional government in Augusta. George Wells and the radical faction gave Walton their support and, in November, Walton was elected governor. The factional feud was fueled by the appearance in Augusta of General Lachlan McIntosh at the head of a small body of light horse from Virginia. McIntosh, understandably confused by the political division in Augusta, consorted with the Wereat conservatives. Therefore, the Walton regime sent a letter to the Continental Congress requesting that McIntosh be transferred out of Georgia. McIntosh's friends were furious at Walton and later accused him of forging the name of the Speaker to the letter. The Walton party remained in power in 1780. Among other pieces of legislation the Assembly established free land grants for heads of families with additional grants to those who would erect sawmills, gristmills or ironworks. The same legislation established a government and town plan for Augusta and created a new town in the backcountry, Washington in Wilkes County. These novices in government showed an unusual degree of sophistication in their brief tenure.

When Charleston fell to Henry Clinton's besieging forces on May 12, 1780, it seemed that the war was over in the South. Whig resistance collapsed all over South Carolina. Georgia Governor Stephen Heard preserved a figment of government by refusing to surrender and retiring to the North Carolina mountains along with Elijah Clarke and a valiant few. The new British commander in Augusta was none other than Thomas Brown, whose Florida Rangers were now called the King's Rangers. Brown's work with Indians earned him the position of British Superintendent of the Creek and Cherokee nations.

The Indian supplies stored in Augusta lured Elijah Clarke out of the mountains. Clarke's raiders surprised Brown and besieged him in a fortified house on the outskirts of town. British reinforcements from Ninety-six rescued Brown and chased Clarke back toward the mountains. Another British contingent, under Patrick Ferguson, attempted to cut Clarke's line of retreat. Clarke's friends, the "Over-the-Mountain Men" under seven different officers, swarmed out of the mountain passes and caught Ferguson atop Kings Mountain. Kings Mountain was a turning point in the war in the South. Stung by Kings Mountain, Cornwallis brought his army out of Charleston into the up-country. After an indecisive battle against General Nathanael Greene at Guilford Courthouse, Cornwallis marched into Virginia. Isolated British garrisons were left to hold the Carolinas and Georgia, a fact which General Greene did not fail to notice. Greene began picking off those posts, dispatching "Light Horse Harry" Lee to take Augusta. A classic two-week battle followed, with Lee pitted against Brown whose rangers were fortified in the newly constructed Fort Cornwallis. Night after night Lee's engineers dug trenches ever closer to the walls of the fort. Finally, they constructed a thirty-foot tower and mounted a six-pounder cannon which raked the interior of Fort Cornwallis. Brown surrendered on June 5, 1781.

The recapture of Augusta permitted a resumption of whig government later in the year with Nathan Brownson elected governor. Cornwallis's surrender at Yorktown on October 18 effectively ended the war, but the British stubbornly clung to the southern strongholds of Savannah and Charleston. Greene assigned "Mad Anthony" Wayne to take charge of the reduction of Savannah. The last battle in Georgia was fought outside Savannah by Thomas Brown's newly recruited rangers and Lieutenant Colonel James Jackson's Georgia Legion. Over Governor Wright's protests, the British military abandoned Savannah on July 12, 1782. The honor of leading the victorious whigs into the capital was given by Wayne to James Jackson. Parliament ratified the Treaty of Paris in 1783. Soon thereafter, James Edward Oglethorpe, who had lived too long to be bitter, shook the hand of John Adams, the first United States minister to the Court of St. James.

Georgia's history, colored by improbabilities and punctuated with false starts, assumed a focus and direction it never had before. The old political and economic links which bound colony to mother country were broken as Georgians took control of their destiny. The infant state turned toward the limitless promise of its vast frontier, a hinterland which stretched to the Mississippi River. No matter that the still powerful Creek Nation occupied most of the territory, Georgia claimed it all as the trophy of war and set about making the most of it. The capital moved inland from the coast, to Augusta, Louisville and Milledgeville, following the westward pioneers.

Founding and Settlement

IN FEBRUARY, 1731, James Oglethorpe suggested a modest philanthropic project to his friend Lord Egmont. They had served together on a Parliamentary committee investigating the condition of debtor prisons and both were concerned about the starving, unemployed poor in London. Egmont would become the president of the Georgia Trustees, and Oglethorpe would go with the first settlers. [Document One] The Trustees hired a secretary, Benjamin Martyn, who produced a tract to solicit contributions, in which he advertised Georgia as a noble experiment that would be unique among Britain's colonial ventures. [Document Two] The Trustees leased a ship, the *Anne*, to carry the first colonists to America in late 1732. One of the colonists, Thomas Christie, described the voyage and his arrival at Savannah. [Document Three]

Oglethorpe and his shipload of colonists reached Savannah in early 1733. The first Georgians, assisted by some skilled black carpenters from South Carolina, were busy clearing land, planting crops, fortifying the settlement and building houses. [Document Four] Another early colonist, Peter Gordon, furnishes us with engaging glimpses of daily life during the first months: the Indian eagle dance of welcome, the elderly Doctor Lyons in drink and cavorting with the Indians, the servant girl sentenced to be whipped for disorderly behavior and the Irishman suspected of being a Spanish spy. [Document Five] By the time Francis Moore came to Georgia in 1735 the Trustees had better organized their recruitment and logistics. [Document Six] Moore states specifically that any debtor who applied must have permission of his creditor in order to be considered. There is no documentary evidence for the popular myth that Georgia was a haven for jailed debtors.

The scheme: to procure a quantity of acres in the West Indies and to plant thereon a hundred miserable wretches who, being let out of jail, are now starving about the town for want of employment.

LORD EGMONT, 1731

JOHN PERCIVAL, the first Earl of Egmont (1683–1748), was an Irish peer who served on Oglethorpe's jails committee and, with him, was one of the founders of the colony of Georgia. Egmont served as the president of the Georgia Trustees during the early years. In his diary, crowded into his busy life at court, he narrated Georgia's modest beginnings. These selections are extracted from R. A. Roberts, *Diary of the First Viscount Percival* (London, 1920–23).

Friday, 13 February [1731]. I met Mr. Oglethorpe, who informed me that he had found out a very considerable charity which lay in trustees' hands, that the two old men were very honest and desirous to be discharged of their burden. The trustees had consented that the trust should be annexed to some trusteeship already in being, and that, being informed that I was a trustee of Mr. Dalone's legacy, who left about £1000 pounds to convert Negroes, he had proposed me and my associates as proper persons to be made trustees of this new affair, that the old gentlemen approved of us, and he hoped I would accept it in conjunction with himself and several of our Committee of Jails and some other gentlemen of worth. The old trustees of the £15,000 would as yet allow but £5000 to be under our management, which sum would answer the scheme: to procure a quantity of acres either from the government or by gift or purchase in the West Indies and to plant thereon a hundred miserable wretches who, being let out of jail by the last year's act, are now starving about the town for want of employment; that they should be settled all together by way of colony and be subject to subordinate rulers, who should inspect their behavior and labor under one chief head; that in time they with their families would increase so fast as to become a security and defence of our possessions against the French and Indians of those parts; that they should be employed in cultivating flax and hemp which, being allowed to make into yarn, would be returned to England and Ireland and greatly promote our manufacturing.

Wednesday, April 1. I called on Mr. Oglethorpe, who kept me three hours and more in explaining his project of sending a colony of poor and honest, industrious debtors to the West Indies by means of a charitable legacy left by one King, a haberdasher, to be disposed of as his executors should please. Those executors have agreed that £5000 of the money shall be employed to such a purpose, and our business is to get a patent or charter for incorporating a number of honest and reputable persons to pursue this good work, and, as those executors desired the persons entrusted with that sum might be annexed to some trust already in being, I am desired to consent to admit such as are to manage that money into my trust for disposing of the legacy left by Mr. Dalone for converting Negroes to Christianity, to which I very readily have consented. Mr. Oglethorpe told me that the number relieved by the last year's act out of prison for debt are 10,000.

Thursday, 30 July. We agreed on a petition to the King and Council for obtaining a grant of lands on the southwest of Carolina for settling poor persons of London and, having ordered it to be engrossed fair, we signed it.

6 [February 1732]. In the evening Mr. Oglethorpe came again to talk over the Carolina settlement. The Board of Trade have reported in favor of it, and we, the undertakers or managers, have the government of the people we send thither for twenty-one years with a large tract of land granted that lies between two rivers.

Friday, 18 [February]. Perceiving an unaccountable delay in the putting His Majesty's seal to the Carolina charter and that it sticks with the Duke of Newcastle, all our gentlemen concerned as trustees are much out of humor and some are for flinging it up and restoring the money given for the advantage of the colony.

Sunday, 23 [April]. Mr. Sharp, Clerk of the Council, told me that our Carolina Charter had been signed by His Majesty last Friday. The chief of our business for a twelvemonth will be only to get in subscriptions and settle schemes for our proceeding. It will be a great while before we can proceed to anything of good purpose, because without a necessary fund of money we can do nothing, and I said that under £12,000 we could not undertake to send families over lest we should starve them. Every family will stand us in £100 at £20 a head the bare fitting out with tools, clothes and transporting, besides which we were to maintain them in provisions a year when arrived, to build houses, &c. and erect a sort of fort, &c.

Friday, 12 May. This day several petitions were offered to the House complaining of the great abuses and mischief arising from vagrants and beggars. It was intended by Mr. Oglethorpe and the other gentlemen concerned in the new intended settlement of colonies in South Carolina to ground thereupon a motion for addressing the King to grant £10,000 to us for transporting those vagrants and beggars under the age of sixteen to South Carolina and bind them apprentices to masters we should send over.

Thursday, 29 [June]. In the evening, met as usual the Trustees of the Georgia Colony, where Mr. Oglethorpe brought us the charter, which was signed the 9th instant but did not pass all the offices till this week.

Thursday, 20 [July]. In the evening went to our [Georgia] office, it being the day on which I summoned all the trustees to meet. I swore those who were present to their oath of office. We also agreed upon a printed letter to be sent to such persons as we thought would advance subscriptions.

Friday, 28 July. I went to Court, where the Queen told me I had a good deal of business on my hands on account of the new colony of Georgia. She wished it might succeed.

Thursday, 3 August. In the evening went to our Georgia Colony office. We agreed on several commissioners for collecting gifts towards the promoting the settlement of the colony. We also directed that Mr. Martyn's short account of the design of the Georgia Colony and the advantages accruing from it to England should be printed with the names of the trustees at the end of it. We appointed Mr. Martyn our secretary. He is a very ingenious young man and writ a tragedy last year.

Wednesday, 18 [October]. I had an account from Captain Coram that the trustees of the Georgia Colony had concluded to send a small number of persons over and that Mr. Oglethorpe resolved to go with them. Though I am not of opinion they should send any away so soon, yet it rejoiced me that Mr. Oglethorpe would go.

Wednesday, 1 November. After dinner I went to town to attend the meeting of the Georgia trustees. We resolved a civil government should be established in Georgia and the town to be erected should be named Savannah, the government to be by bailiffs, constables and tythingmen, a court to be erected of Oyer and Terminer, with a judge, jurats, justice of peace, &c. We were not particular in establishing the constitution, because till we come to that the laws of

England take place. We nominated our bailiffs, judge, recorder, storekeeper and justice of peace and added some persons to the number that are to go in the first embarkation, which is now designed 100 whole persons. They are now but ninety-eight, of which persons about forty are able, sensible men, the rest women and children. To Mr. Oglethorpe (who has the public spirit to go over with them) we gave several powers under our seal. And all who go signed a form that they would submit to the laws we should make and be dutiful to the government set over them, that they would stay three years in the country, mutually assist each other in clearing the land and building their settlements the first year, &c. There goes with them a surgeon and apothecary, and Mr. Herbert goes voluntarily chaplain to the colony for a time. I hope with the blessing of God this noble, charitable, disinterested and profitable design to the nation will take root and flourish.

Wednesday, 8 [November]. I went to town on a summons from the Georgia Society. We dined at the Horn Tavern and afterwards returned to our office. I took my leave of Mr. Oglethorpe and Mr. Herbert, who go on board at Gravesend on Wednesday next in order to proceed on their journey, the persons they conduct being already on board, about forty men able to bear arms, besides women and children. Mr. Oglethorpe acquainted us that an able engineer goes generously with him, a volunteer, to erect the fort we design to build.

Thursday, 23 November. In the evening went to the Georgia Board at 4 o'clock and stayed till 9. We noted down some poor persons who attended and desired very urgently to go over, but we dismissed several who were able to earn their bread in England and are careful not to send any who do not satisfy us that they have their creditors' leave to go and that they do not run away from their wives and families to leave them a burden on the parish.

Thursday, 30 [November]. We dined at Pontack's, after which I went to the Georgia Board. We examined several poor people who appeared and some of them were noted down, others who could get their bread at home we rejected. I proposed that for the future when we sent any persons over, we should publish their names in some public paper a fortnight before, that their creditors might not be defeated of their debts, which was approved.

7 December. I went to the Georgia Board. We examined about thirty poor persons who applied to go over, which held us till 9 at night. Most of them we rejected as able to live, though poorly, in England, but we noted down about four of them who cannot subsist at all for future consideration.

⌈ 2 ⌋

The time and occasion calls out upon the rich and generous people of England! A great number of small benefactions will amount to a sum capable of doing a great deal of good. Beyond the ocean, you may increase the wealth, the strength and the honor of the kingdom!

BENJAMIN MARTYN, 1732

BENJAMIN MARTYN (1699–1763) was appointed their secretary by the Trustees of Georgia, principally because Martyn, born in Wiltshire, was known as a literary gentleman who had written a play. He was the first person to promote a plan of erecting a monument to Shakespeare in Westminster Abbey. As the Trustees' secretary, Martyn kept records, penned correspondence and wrote promotional tracts to raise money. This appeal for public support is extracted from "Some Account of the Designs of the Trustees for establishing Colonys in America," a manuscript which has been attributed to either Martyn or James Oglethorpe. The present whereabouts of the manuscript is unknown.

Many poor families are reduced to the utmost necessity by inevitable misfortunes, as tradesmen who have suffered losses, artificers and manufacturers of such branches of trade as are decayed or overstocked, fathers of numerous families by sickness thrown behindhand so as they cannot retrieve it, laboring men who having served in the army or in private families when discharged are rendered by disuse incapable of returning to their former occupations. The insolvent who is turned naked out of a prison and has not a friend to trust him with work reaps but the privilege of starving at large. The want of friends, want of credit or a false shame of working in a lower degree prevents several honest men from being useful in England and makes them either perish for want, fly their country or seek for bread by unlawful means. Want first reduces them to sickness or to prison, and, when the man's industry is useless, the wife and wretched children must either perish or ask relief.

Besides the honest and unfortunate, there is another species, the idle poor, the disposing of whom may be considered not only as a charity to them but a benefit to ourselves, since it is the removing of so many enemies to the public tranquility. These may be divided into convicts and vagrants. He who is committed to Bridewell is not reformed but initiated in all the secrets of roguery and comes out ten times wickeder than before! It is a reflection both upon the charity and policy of a Christian city to see numbers of boys, healthy and strong, idling about the streets, breeding up recruits for the street robbers. The putting them and such persons as have no legal settlements into a method of earning their bread, the rescuing them from vice, necessity and idleness and training them up to labor would be a real charity.

As there are numbers of poor in England who are of no use to themselves and of little to the public, there are other parts of the world where men are as much wanting as lands are here, places in which fertile tracts of land are of no value because there is none to cultivate them. The countries lying between the Savannah and Altamaha which are granted by His Majesty to the Trust are little known to the English, they never having extended their plantations so far. This tract of land lies in the same latitude with Persia and Jerusalem in Palestine. The climate is hot in summer but the heat is much abated and the air cooled by northwest winds and running streams. The winters are short and the frosts, though not severe, are sufficient to kill the insects and purify the air. Many rivers and brooks fall into the sea between the Savannah and Altamaha.

Towns for trade might be conveniently situated along the sides of the navigable rivers. For the subsistence and employment of the inhabitants of each town there might be allotted a particular produce particular to that place, natural to that climate and such as England is now obliged to buy from foreigners. Some towns, besides the provisions of corn and cattle, may raise hemp and flax, and, considering that they will be free from the burdens of superstition, taxes and high rents which the countries from whence those families are brought groan under and considering the fertility of soils never yet broke up, it is to be believed that they may furnish flax and hemp much cheaper than any of the continents of Europe can. Other towns may be employed on raising vines and mulberry trees for the silk worms. Where the soil is more proper for it, olive yards may be the support of the adjoining town. Various other productions will maintain various towns, and the exchanging of them for English commodities or for each other will create an intercourse and traffic.

The lands near the sea will produce flax, hemp, mulberry trees for the silk worms, cotton, indigo, olives, dates, raisins, pitch, tar and rice, the two last of which are needless, there being enough of them produced in the present settlements. Higher up the rivers and in hilly countries, good wine might be made and perhaps the Mohair goat might keep the fineness of its fleece there as well as in Angria. Gums, barks and woods fit for dyeing all kinds of colors might be also there raised and indeed every kind of produce with which England is now supplied from countries lying in the same latitude. That the mulberry trees may be planted at equal distances, vines may be reared against them and wheat sowed between, that the shadows of the trees may defend the corn and grapes from the too parching heats of the sun, that the leaves may be gathered by the women and children to feed the silk worms.

This tract of land not only wants people for the cultivation of it but also for the preservation of South Carolina. The English carelessly dispersed themselves in single families through the country as if it had been entirely subjected, relying wholly upon the Indian faith and at the same time injured and refused justice to those brave, well-armed and revengeful nations upon whose faith they relied. In the year 1715 the Yamasee Indians, having called to their aid a large body of other nations from beyond the Savannah River, destroyed all the English unfortified houses to within five miles of Charles Town! But a number of towns established along the rivers Savannah and Altamaha would prevent any future massacre and make a strong barrier to the present settlement and keep the Negro slaves of South Carolina in awe, who are now so numerous as to be dreadful even to their masters.

As there are some in England whom misfortunes may force abroad, there are infinite numbers in other parts of Europe to whom tyranny and persecution have made banishment less dreadful than the residing in their native countries. It is surprising to think that, notwithstanding in America there are fertile lands sufficient to subsist all the useless poor in England and distressed Protestants in Europe, yet that thousands should starve here for want of mere sustenance. His Majesty for inducing colonies into America hath incorporated Trustees with the powers to gather such people as are proper to be sent over and to take care that they shall be there established in a regular manner.

In choosing the first colony regard should be had to the preventing those evils by which infant colonies have frequently been destroyed. The English attempts in America have often miscarried by desertion, sickness, famine, mutiny or force of an enemy. The first colony should consist not of single men but of families, for a wife and children are security of a man's not abandoning the settlement and the presence of those dear pledges who will reap the advantage of it will the more strongly incite him to labor. Even in the beginning, women and children will not be useless mouths, since there will always be some business which they may do and save so much labor to the men, such as preparing their food, cleaning and mending their clothes, gathering wild fruits, roots or shellfish, &c.

The families should be laborious and honest people whose motive for leaving their country should not be crimes but misfortunes. The manner of collecting them may be first by publishing proposals of the terms they are to go upon in some such manner as this: "This is to give notice that all persons whose necessities render them desirous of reaping the benefit of the intended colony may send in writing their names, place of abode at present and for three years last past, what trades or occupations they understand, their own ages and, if they are married, the ages of their wives and number and ages of their children, to the Secretary of the Trustees and after ten days in which their characters shall be inquired into, if the Trustees find them to their satisfaction, they will be admitted of the colony with the following advantages. First, they will be subsisted till the ships are ready to sail at the house belonging to the Trustees, where they will have an allowance of salt provisions in order to accustom them to what they are to meet with at sea. Secondly, on their being embarked, they, their wives and children are to be clothed from head to foot at the expense of the Society. Thirdly, they are to have bedding and hammocks sufficient for themselves and families given unto each of them. Fourthly, each family is to have kitchen utensils, working tools, seed or other necessaries given gratis on their landing. Each person who hath an apprentice will be allowed to take him with him provided the same is above fourteen and under twenty years of age. Fifthly, each family is to have provisions for one year.

"In return of all these benefits and for the preservation of themselves and of the colony, they are to conform to the following regulations. First, they are to be obedient to their directors. Secondly, they are to assist each other and by joint endeavors fortify such place as their chief commander shall think proper to establish their town in. Thirdly, they are by joint endeavors to build houses for themselves and cultivate and sow lands for their next year's provision. Fourthly, after that is done, the houses that are built and the land that is cultivated are to be divided amongst themselves, each man to have a house and twenty acres of land to himself and to his heirs male forever. Each man is to pay for his house and land one day's labor in the week, which labor is to be employed in the service of the public. Fifthly, all persons that have three children alive at the same time shall during the time of their three childrens being alive at once be exempted from the rent of labor. Sixthly, all persons above sixty years of age shall be exempt from labor. Seventhly, no person shall leave the country in two years without license obtained, which shall not be refused anyone who will repay to the commander in chief the expense which the Trustees have been at on his account. Eighthly, all persons that go are themselves and families to be free and no labor taxes, tythes nor money under any pretence whatsoever is to be exacted from them save only the above-mentioned labor, which is to be the rent for their lands, the produce of which labor is to be laid out for the support of the colony in time of war, sickness or famine and for the sending over more poor families to increase it. Lastly, all the males from seventeen years of age to forty-five shall be obliged to take up arms in defense of the colony and shall be exercised for that purpose."

Of the persons who shall give in their names to the Secretary, the Trustees will choose such as are sober, healthy and able to labor, whose families are not too numerous in young children and provide a house to subsist them in till they can be embarked, where they may be accustomed to that discipline which they are to preserve when abroad. Those who are impatient of orderly government may be dismissed, and the wheat winnowed from the chaff, for it is infinitely better to lose expense some weeks than to carry over a mutinous or effeminate fellow.

The next thing is the embarkation, on which they should have their new clothes and bedding delivered unto them and be reviewed by such of the Trustees and benefactors as are willing to see the fruits of their charity. For preserving them in their passage it will be necessary that the ship should not be crowded, that they should be brought up frequently on deck for the benefit of the fresh air and that in the meantime the places where they lie should be washed with vinegar and proper things burnt therein to take away all nauseous smells, cleanliness being of great consequence to health, whilst the men might be taught the use of the musket. These things belong to the leader of the colony to execute, and he must look upon the colony as his family.

The utmost endeavors should be used to instill a spirit of labor into the poor people, for extreme necessity generally breaks the minds of the distressed and throws them into a habit of idleness very difficult to be cured. For the remedying of this ill habit the method would be that such of the poor as seem most industrious should be encouraged and that out of them should be appointed Tythingmen and Foremen. The Constables ought to be men that should understand the nature of the climate to which the colony is to be sent and to know those arts which are necessary for the first establishment. They should instruct the Tythingmen and Foremen in those things which are most necessary to be done at their landing, they should acquaint them with the nature of building houses, clearing woods, mending and making their own tools and also the seasons and manner of digging, plowing and sowing of corn, &c., raising provisions and managing hemp, silk, vines, &c.

By often conversing of these matters in the voyages, the people will grow eager to arrive in port, in order to put them in practice. The women should be inspired with the same spirit of labor, such as understand making of clothes, spinning of linen, &c. and household services should be encouraged so as to make others emulate them and be allowed something for instructing those who are ignorant. Little prizes for those who are most expert may be perhaps a good way of encouraging industry both in men and women. Great care ought to be taken in instructing them in their duty towards God and man and a wise minister might take many occasions to urge such precepts home when their minds were most inclined to receive them from storms and other accidents which frequently happen on the face of the deep! All kind of refreshments should be on board for relief of the sick, and the same care ought to be taken of the poorest colonian, if any of them should be afflicted with sickness, as of the principal officer.

The situation of the town being fixed upon, it ought first to be fortified in such a manner as may make it defensible against the insults of any enemy that can attack it in that distant quarter of the world. A ditch well flanked and pallisadoed will very probably be a sufficient fortification, which in a short space of time may be finished. At the same time that one detachment of men are cutting the trees, digging the ditch, fixing the pallisadoes and mounting of cannon, another detachment may be running up the private and public buildings, which at first for expedition's sake will be of boards, and two carpenters, considering the timber grows upon the place, may build a wooden house in a few days. In the distribution of the town the streets should be spacious and laid out by line and a large square reserved for a market place and for exercising the inhabitants on the sides of which may be the church, infirmary for the sick, an house for newcomers, town house and other public buildings. Without the town, a mile square, which amounts to 640 acres, might be reserved as a common for the pasturing of the cattle and all within musket shot of the works should be cleared. This open space will contribute greatly to the health and security of the town as well as to the conveniency of the inhabitants. Each family should have a farm in the country and an allotment sufficient for a house and garden in the town. The leader of the colony should take care with the utmost expedition to have an acre cleared and sowed upon each farm and a house built upon each allotment in the town.

After the land is divided into farms and the town into allotments and a house built upon each allotment and an acre sowed upon each farm, it may not be improper that a Thanksgiving Day be appointed, on which the people should in their cleanest and best apparel assemble themselves in the great square by break of day and begin the day by prayers and thanksgiving to God for His delivering them from misery and establishing them in a happy state of life. After prayers the men should stand to their arms in the square and, the drums beating, the town and the colony may be publicly named. After the naming [of] the town and province the articles or laws under which they are to be governed should be read. They should draw lots for the lands, and the people should draw lots for their farms. After this the cannon and small shot may be fired and the rest of the day spent in manly exercises and in decent joy and gladness, a comfortable meal being provided for the whole people at the expense of the Society and the same day of that month may be kept every year as a Thanksgiving Day for the establishment of the colony.

What can be a truer charity than the giving bread to the hungry, clothes to the naked, liberty of religion to the oppressed for conscience sake? What more humane than rescuing unfortunate youth[s] or abandoned and helpless orphans from the temptations want or ill company may expose them to? What more glorious than of these to form well regulated towns, to give them houses, cattle and lands of inheritance, to instruct them how to raise all those good things which make life comfortable and how to enjoy them under such laws as tend to make them happy both here and hereafter? The persecuted and distressed Protestants will be relieved, they will gain by their sufferings; instead of the Rocky Alps or the marshes of Poland, they will have the fertile plains of Carolina, a land of corn, vines and olives, a glorious reward even in this life for their constancy! The people of England will be greatly augmented and numberless poor will be here employed for supplying of them with necessaries. For the more people are drawn off, the more room is left for others to supply their places. Every foreigner and every Englishman who cannot get work and goes to Carolina is a benefit to the nation and increases the people, for he employs the makers in England of all the English goods he consumes and the more employment there is the more manufacturers there will be.

There is an occasion now offered for everyone to help forward this design. The smallest benefactions will be received and applied with the utmost care, every little will do something and a great number of small benefactions will amount to a sum capable of doing a great deal of good. The time and occasion calls out upon the rich and generous people of England! Religion, charity and the love of our country persuade, nay even self-interest prompts, to send away those whom want may force against their own inclinations upon dangerous courses. Desperate poor never more abounded. Witness the frequent murmurs for want of employment from all parts of the kingdom. The Protestants from abroad, harrassed by the madness of Romish priests, cry out for a place of refuge and would enrich and strengthen your America. All nations are improving their trade, all eager for foreign plantations. Let not the Britons now grow indolent! Take then the benefit of the general tranquility and improve beyond the ocean. There without bloodshed or the hazard of a battle you may increase the wealth, the strength and the honor of the kingdom more than the Edwards or the Henrys did by their glorious but destructive victories. They burnt towns, you will build them! They ravaged, you will cultivate large dominions! They destroyed, you will preserve and increase mankind!

[3]

John Thomas, master of the ship Anne, *now in the River of Thames, shall take on board passengers not exceeding one hundred whole heads and sail to Beaufort Town in South Carolina.*

LEASE OF THE "ANNE," 1732

IN NOVEMBER, 1732, the Georgia Trustees hired the ship *Anne* to carry the first colonists to Georgia. A copy of their agreement with John Thomas, shipmaster, is in the Egmont Papers at the University of Georgia Library.

This charter party of affreightment indented and made the 6th day of November *Anno Domini* 1732 and in the sixth year of the reign of George II, King of Great Britain &c., between Samuel Wragg of London, merchant, part owner, and John Thomas, master of the ship *Anne*, burden 200 tons or thereabouts now in the River of Thames, of the one part and the Common Council of the Trustees for establishing the Colony of Georgia in America of the other part. Witnesseth that the said part owner and master have letten and the said Common Council hired the said ship for a voyage with her to be made from London to Beaufort Town in South Carolina in America on the terms and condition following:

First, the said part owner and master for themselves, their executors and administrators do covenant, promise and agree to and with the said Common Council and their successors and assigns by these presents that the said ship, being tight and strong and well manned, tackled and provided fit for merchant's service, shall on or before the 7th day of November instant depart from Gravesend with all such goods and merchandizes as the said freightors or their assigns shall in the interim think fit to load and put on board her not exceeding what she may reasonably stow and carry in her, except reasonable and convenient room for the said ship's crew, her stores and the stowage of eight tons of goods which is reserved for the use of the said master and owners of the said ship; and before such her departure from Gravesend shall receive and take on board her from the said freightors or their assigns passengers, not exceeding 100 whole heads, and with the said goods and passengers directly, as wind and weather will permit, proceed and sail to Beaufort Town in South Carolina (or as near thereto as she can safely get) and then stay four days (if not sooner discharged) to deliver the goods taken in at London and set on shore the said passengers with all and singular their baggage and so end her voyage, the perils and dangers of the seas and restraint of princes and rulers during the voyage always excepted.

And further the said part owner and master do covenant and agree to and with the said freightors that the said passengers shall have four beef days, two pork days and one fish day in every week during their being on their passage and that they, the said part owner and master, will, before the said ship's departure out of the River of Thames, put on board her for the use of the said passengers a convenient and sufficient quantity of provisions, viz: 84 butts of water, eight tons of beer, 40 hundredweight of beef, 19 hundredweight of pork, 60 hundredweight of bread with a sufficient quantity of fish, flour, peas, butter, suet and plums and shall cause the said passengers during all the time of their being on board the said ship to be served out daily their allowance of provisions in this manner, to wit: on the four beef days, four pounds of beef for every mess of five men and two pounds and an half of flour and half a pound of suet or plums; on the two pork days, five pounds of pork and two pints and an half of peas for every five men; and on the fish day, two pounds and an half of fish and half a pound of butter for every five men, the whole at sixteen ounces to the pound; and allow each man seven pound of bread of fourteen ounces to the pound per week and two quarts of beer per man per diem for the space of six weeks and, moreover, that the said part owner and master shall, before the said ship's departure from London, cause thirty-five cradles to be built and fixed between the said ship's decks with boarded bottoms, the cradles to be each five feet eight inches in the clear in the inside and that there shall be a canvas curtain fixed to hang four feet below the beam from the bulkhead of the lazeretta to the bulkhead of the gun room on both sides and, further, the said part owner and master do covenant and agree to deliver the said thirty-five cradles at the said ship's side within four days after the said ship's arrival at Beaufort Town aforesaid, being paid and allowed for the same at the rate of seven shillings per cradle.

In consideration whereof the said freightors for themselves and their successors, do covenant, promise and agree to and with the said part owner and master, their executors, administrators and assigns by these presents that they, the said freightors, their successors or assigns shall and will, not only put on board the said ship at Gravesend seventy whole heads certain and dispatch her from thence by the 7th day of November instant and upon her arrival at Beaufort Town aforesaid unload and take out all the goods and passengers belonging unto them together with the said thirty-five cradles and that within the four days above limited for doing thereof, but also shall and will well and truly pay or cause to be paid unto the said part owner or master or their or one of their assigns in London the sum of £4 sterling per head for each of the said seventy whole heads certain and £2 of like money per head for the remaining thirty heads if they shall not be shipped; but if shipped or any part of them, then the sum of £2 per head more for as many of the said thirty as shall be shipped. The heads to be accounted in this manner, viz: Every person shipped above the age of twelve years to be accounted a whole head and for all persons shipped of the age of seven years and under the age of twelve to be accounted two-for-one and for passengers shipped above the age of two years and under the age of seven to be accounted three-for-one, but no freight for any passenger under the age of two years. The aforementioned freight to be paid upon the embarkation of the said passengers and their goods, provided always that it shall be lawful for the said freightors, their successors or assigns to keep the said ship on demurrage in the River of Thames and at South Carolina by the space of fifteen days at each place besides the days above limited for her stay at the same or so many of them as need shall require. They, the said freightors or their as-signs, paying to the said master, his executors or assigns for every day of such detention the sum or value of £2–10 per day and 8 pence sterling per day per whole head for victuals day by day, as the same shall grow due, anything afore-said to the contrary notwithstanding.

And to the performance hereof the said master bindeth himself, his executors, administrators and ship and the said Common Council of the Trustees hereby bind and oblige themselves and their successors the either to the other in the penal sum of £600 sterling firmly hereby. In witness whereof the said Common Council of the Trustees for Establishing the Colony of Georgia in America have affixed the common seal of the corporation of the said Trustees to these presents and the said Samuel Wragg and John Thomas have severally set their hands and seals to another part thereof, remaining in the hands of the said Trustees the day and year first above written.

Mrs. Warren's child christened Georgius Marinus, Mr. Oglethorpe godfather. Three quarts of flip given to every mess, the people were merry. Missed and lost a black bitch belong[ing] to Mr. Oglethorpe. Supposed to be flung overboard by some of the sailors.

THOMAS CHRISTIE, 1732

THOMAS CHRISTIE was thirty-two years old when he sailed to Georgia on the *Anne* and scribbled this brief journal of the voyage. Though later accused of living in adultery, Christie served as Recorder and First Bailiff of the town of Savannah. The journal is preserved in the Gilcrease Museum of Tulsa, Oklahoma. Observations of weather and tides have been deleted and abbreviations expanded, and one or two additional small deletions have been made to improve readability in the version printed here.

Thursday, the 16 November. This day several of the Trustees with James Oglethorpe, Esq. dined at Gravesend. Came afterwards aboard. Were saluted from the ship with four guns. Mustered all the people. A petition was presented, signed by the people aboard, giving the Trustees thanks for all their favors and indefatigable pains, protesting an entire obedience and desiring a list of their benefactors in order to raise a pyramid to their memory on arrival in Georgia. The Trustees being informed that there was a woman aboard lately lain in with her child not christened gave two guineas to make the company merry the day of the christening. Took their leave that evening. The pilot being in liquor was set ashore and another ordered in his room.

November 18. Ordered several dozen of fowls, ducks and geese, three sheep, four hogs, six quarters of mutton, two quarters of beef and several sorts of roots which came aboard. Several boats came aboard with brandy.

November 19. Ordered those that were able to come to prayers, and those that were sick were ordered water gruel with sugar and white wine in it. Ordered every Thursday and Sunday pork and peas, Saturday stockfish with butter and every other day beef and suet pudding for the people belonging to the colony.

November 20. All hands aboard assisted to get her anchor up which they did with expedition and sailed that night.

November 21. Found ourselves this day abreast of the Isle of Wight. Mr. Oglethorpe came down in the hold and visited every cradle with the doctors. Gave some wine, others sage tea and others ordered some chicken broth.

November 23. Mrs. Warren's child christened Georgius Marinus, Mr. Oglethorpe godfather. Three quarts of flip given to every mess and a handsome supper. The people, very much refreshed this day, were merry. Drank the Trustees' health and success to the colony.

November 24. No candle to be burnt but in lantern and ordered Mr. Kilbury to go 'round everybody's cradle and see all the lights put out by eight. Missed and lost a black lurching bitch belong[ing] to Mr. Oglethorpe. Supposed to be flung overboard by some of the sailors.

November 25. Ordered eight of our men to keep watch and watch all night, four in a watch, one to visit the cradles [to] see all things orderly and quietly disposed and to have an eye to the dogs and fowls and that no candle be burnt after eight except for those who are very sick and that in lanterns. Defended [prohibited] everybody from smoking unless with a cap on the pipe and then on the deck.

November 26. James Cannon, an infant, departed this life. This day prayers were read in the cabin with an exhortation suitable to the present undertaking. A strange bird came aboard and was caught.

November 27. This day ordered several of our people to see water, flour, beer, bread, &c. given out by eight in the morning.

November 28. Divided the people in four tythings and every tything man to order the people under him to take it by turns, one out of each tything, to assist the ship's people in the hole to get up what was wanted.

November 29. A great many of the fowls died, either because they was too close together or through neglect in not giving them water.

November 30. Observed that almost all the water on board had been put into red wine casks, which made it foul and black and gave it a very disagreeable taste, which proved a very disagreeable thing and caused a great murmuring against the Captain during the whole voyage.

December 1. Potatoes ordered amongst the people and half a pound of butter once a week to each mess consisting of five heads.

December 2. Split the main top-sail. Onions ordered to the people once a week.

December 3. The parson, Dr. Herbert, read prayers and preached a handsome sermon in the great cabin this day suitable to the present occasion.

December 4. Ordered a bottle of vinegar to be given out every eight days to every mess.

December 5. One of our hogs died and one of the sheep.

December 6. Ordered every ten days a bottle of treacle, which the people made use of in sage tea and several other ways to sweeten their water and proved of great service during the whole voyage and to be preferred before sugar.

December 7. Carrots given out to the people.

December 8. Ordered Mr. Kilbury to go between decks every week and sprinkle the side of the ship and cradles with vinegar, which proved very wholesome and refreshing.

December 9. Struck the main top gallant mast. Ordered Dr. Cox to [go down] between decks every day and visit every cradle and see how all the people did and make his report of the same to Mr. Oglethorpe, who then ordered whatever the doctor said was proper to be given out to the people by his own steward out of his own stores.

December 10. Several people have been made violently ill by the close shutting the hatches by the heat and want of air this three days past. Mr. Oglethorpe ordered a bottle of white wine to each mess.

December 11. Ordered four beds at a time to be brought upon deck and aired till all the beds was aired. Passed the Tropic [of Cancer] this morning.

December 12. Several young people were to be ducked (for not paying bottle and pound according to custom) which the Captain strenuously insisted upon. One was hauled up to the yard arm but not ducked. On their promise to keep the cradles all clean and to scrape and sweep under them, especially for those that were sick and not able to do it themselves, they were excused, and Mr. Oglethorpe compounded for all his people but promised the ship's crew to give it 'em in money when he came ashore.

December 13. Two flying fish flew aboard this night. Several tropic birds and dolphins were seen.

December 14. Our beer grew sour.

December 15. Wilson, the lawyer, tried and brought to the gangway for giving a sheep's head to the dogs but pardoned by Mr. Oglethorpe by Dr. Herbert's intercession.

December 17. Prayers with a very good sermon. Several persons was let blood, being very much indisposed. Mr. Milledge bruised his leg by a fall, Mr. Hughes had several fits and Mr. Gordon was desperately ill of the cholic.

December 18. Mr. Oglethorpe caught a dolphin and being apprised of some big-bellied women longing [for it] gave it all amongst them without tasting any himself.

December 19. The ship's crew tarred the ship's sides this day.

December 20. The long boat was hoisted out and Mr. Oglethorpe, Dr. Herbert, Captain Thomas and some others went dolphin fishing with fish gig all 'round the ship but under an umbrella, the weather being very hot.

December 21. Mr. Oglethorpe's birthday. Mutton and broth ordered, as also a pint of punch to each head. The people were very merry and drank the success of the colony and the trustees' health. There was cudgel playing this day for a pair of shoes.

December 22. Samuel Clark, an infant, departed this life. Clark's child was thrown overboard this day and the ceremony decently performed by Dr. Herbert. When it was over and the doctor got on the quarter deck but before the people were separated the [illegible] offered to throw water on them, when Mr. Oglethorpe came behind him and gave him a good kick on the arse.

December 24. A great deal of gulf weed came by the ship this day. Took some of it up to save it for curiosity sake. Prayers with a very good sermon.

December 25. Squalls carried away mizzen top-mast, sprung the fore top-sail and studding sail boom. This day there was prayers with a sermon in the cabin suitable to the day. Mutton, beef broth and pudding with a pint of flip to each head given to the people. Exceeding hot weather.

December 26. A fresh gale carried away the main top gallant yard in the slings. Our allowance of water and beer shortened about a pint a head.

December 28. A sack or two of wheat ordered up and spread on a sail to sweeten and dry.

December 29. Ordered several people to perform the exercise with firelock and bayonet upon deck. Brought up several arms and cleaned 'em. Our suet for our pudding falling short, ordered plums in the room of it.

December 30. Exercised several of the most knowing men with firelock and bayonet.

December 31. Ordered four papers with the same words of command as at present used by His Majesty's Guards to be writ out and used by four men of the most expert who were to teach the others. Prayers with a good sermon on deck.

January 2. Mr. Oglethorpe came between decks himself and visited several people that were sick.

January 3d. Mr. Oglethorpe ordered every woman a glass of wine and Dr. Herbert visited several people that were sick.

January 5. Exercised several of the people with firelock and bayonet.

January 6. Broached two barrels of carrots which were so rotten for want of packing up in sand or something else that they were obliged to fling 'em away.

January 7. Prayers with a very good sermon this day suitable to our present circumstances.

January 8. Some of the people falling out altogether, Mr. Oglethorpe ordered 'em to be friends and gave all our people a pint of bumbo each head to drink and be friends together.

January 10. Saw abundance of garnets and small birds. Supposed to be near land.

January 12. Found ground at 21 fathom.

January 13. Found ourselves very luckily over against Charles Town, when upon firing four guns a pilot came aboard. P.S. I beg you will excuse this scribble, being all in a hurry and with no manner of conveniency.

[4]

We just now discover the coast of America. We can, from the deck with the naked eye, discover the trees just above the horizon, no disagreeable sight to those who for seven weeks have seen nothing but sea and sky.

JAMES OGLETHORPE, 1733

THE FIRST colonists landed at Beaufort, South Carolina, and then made their way to Savannah. Their leader, James Oglethorpe (1696–1785), was a London-born general, parliamentarian and philanthropist, who sent regular reports back to the Trustees on the thrilling events of the first few months in Georgia. Other letters were sent by Thomas Causton, one of the first colonists who became the official storekeeper, and Samuel Eveleigh (1672–1738), a Charleston merchant who spent much time at Savannah during the first two years. These letters are in the Egmont Papers at the University of Georgia. These letters and many others from the early colony were published by The Beehive Press/Beehive Foundation in *General Oglethorpe's Georgia* (Savannah, 1975, reprinted 1990). Some deletions have been made.

JAMES OGLETHORPE TO THE TRUSTEES

On board the Ship *Anne*
8 of the Clock
January 13, 1733

Gentlemen: We just now discover the coast of America and it proves to be the land which lies off Charles Town. We are now within nine miles distant and can, from the deck with the naked eye, discover the trees just above the horizon, no disagreeable sight to those who for seven weeks have seen nothing but sea and sky. We have had a very favourable passage, considering that we passed the Tropic of Cancer and stood to the southward 'till we came into 20 Degrees and then stood back again to 32 where we now are. By this means we lengthened our navigation from England above a third, which was done to avoid the fury of the northwest winds that generally rage in the winter season on the coast of America. We have lost none of our people except the youngest son of Richard Cannon, aged eight months, and the youngest son of Robert Clarke, aged one year and an half, both of whom were very weakly when I came on board and had indeed been half starved through want before they left London as many others were who are recovered with food and care. But these were so far gone that all our efforts to save them were in vain. Doctor Herbert and all on board are in perfect health except Mr. Scott who was bruised with a fall in the last storm. At present we are all in a hurry so must beg leave to refer you for a fuller account to my next letters. We intend to take in a pilot at this place for to conduct us to Port Royal where we shall hire embarkations to carry us to Georgia.

From Camp near Savannah
February 10, 1733

Gentlemen: I gave you an account in my last of our arrival at Charles Town. The Governour and Assembly have given us all possible encouragement. Our people arrived at Beaufort on the 20th of January, where I lodged them in some new barracks built for the soldiers whilst I went myself to view the Savannah River. I fixed upon a healthy situation about ten miles from the sea. The river there forms a half moon, along the south side of which the banks are about 40 foot high and upon the top a flat which they call a bluff. The plain high ground extends into the country five or six miles and along the riverside about a mile. Ships that draw twelve foot water can ride within ten yards of the bank. Upon the riverside in the center of this plain, I have laid out the town. Over against it is an island of very rich land fit for pasturage, which I think should be kept for the Trustees' cattle. The river is pretty wide, the water fresh. And from the quay of the town you see its whole course to the sea with the Island of Tybee, which forms the mouth of the river; and the other way you may see the river for about six miles up into the country. The landscape is very agreeable, the stream being wide and bordered with high woods on both sides.

The whole people arrived on the first of February. At night their tents were got up. 'Till the 7th we were taken up in unloading and making a crane, which I even then could not get finished, so took off the hands and set some to the fortification and begun to fell the woods. I marked out the town and common. Half of the former is already cleared, and the first house was begun yesterday in the afternoon. Not being able to get Negroes, I have taken ten of the Independent Company to work for us, for which I make them an allowance. Our people are all alive, but ten are ill with the bloody flux, which I take to proceed from the cold and their not being accustomed to lie in tents. I am so taken up in looking after a hundred necessary things that I write now short but shall give you a more particular account hereafter.

A little Indian Nation, the only one within fifty miles, is not only at amity but desire to be subject of the Trustees, to have land given them and to breed their children at our schools. Their chief and his beloved man, who is the second man in the Nation, desire to be instructed in the Christian religion.

Savannah
March 12, 1733

Gentlemen: This province is much larger than we thought it, being 120 miles from this river to the Altamaha. This river has a very long course, and a great trade is carried on by it to the Indians, there having above twelve trading boats passed by since I have been here.

There are in Georgia on this side of the mountains three considerable Nations of Indians, one called the Lower Creeks consisting of nine towns or rather cantons making about 1000 men able to bear arms. One of these is within half a mile of us and has concluded a peace with us giving up their right to all this part of the country, and I have marked out the lands which they have reserved to themselves. The king comes constantly to church and is desirous to be instructed in the Christian religion and has given to me his nephew, a boy who is his next heir, to educate.

The other two Nations are the Uchees and the Upper Creeks, the first consisting of 200, the latter of 1100 men. We agree so well with the Indians that the Creeks and Uchees have referred a difference to me to determine which otherwise would occasion a war, and one of them has informed me of a silver mine on the riverside, the earth of which being washed away the ore lies bare, of which he promised to bring me a sample.

Our people still lie in tents, there being only two clapboard houses built and three sawed houses framed, our crane, our battery of cannon and magazine finished. This is all we have been able to do by reason of the smallness of our number, of which many have been sick and others unused to labour, though thank God they are now pretty well and we have not lost one soul since our arrival here.

THOMAS CAUSTON TO HIS WIFE

Savannah
March 12, 1733

My Dearest: We were just a week in our passage from Charles Town to Port Royal, where we landed and were lodged at some new barracks that are intended for a new fortification about three miles from Beaufort Town. At our landing Mr. Oglethorpe ordered me to take all the stores into my care and to keep an account of them. And in that office I shall continue which takes up my whole time. Some of our company who went to the town were entertained in a very elegant manner and everyone found somebody to entertain them in some shape or other. We have five or six families amongst us that are deserving a gentleman's conversation. We continued in those barracks ten days, sailed from thence in six large boats, and the country scout boat and the garrison boat with twelve soldiers attending us. We had a very fair wind and safe passage, being two days, and then arrived at this place, then called Yamacraw and now Savannah.

This place is very high ground, being about thirty yards upright from low water mark, about ten miles from the sea, and I believe that ships of 200 ton will be able to come within three miles of us. It is impossible to give a true description of the place, because we are in a wood; but I can't forbear saying it is a very pleasant one. We have about 100 Indians just by us, and a trader with them that speaks English and sells almost everything to them at what rates he pleases. Mr. Oglethorpe has behaved towards them with so much good conduct and prudent generosity that, though some amongst them were ready to grumble at our coming, yet he has both gained their love and increased their fearful apprehensions of us. They have always parties out in hunting and they bring us venison, for which Mr. Oglethorpe pays at a very moderate rate. They seem to be sober judicious men, straight and strong, almost naked. But the king and the chiefs wear coats and drawers and a piece of cloth tied about their legs like boots. The queen and her daughters wear common printed calico jacket and petticoat without any head clothes. They maintain very little distinction.

At our first landing, they came to bid us welcome, and before them came a man dancing in antic postures with a spread fan of white feathers in each hand as a token of friendship, which were fixed to small rods about four foot long, set from top to bottom with small bells like Morrice dancers, which made a jingling, whilst the king and others followed making a very uncouth hollering. When they came near, Mr. Oglethorpe walked about ten steps from his tent to meet them; then the man with his feathers came forward dancing and talking, which I am informed was repeating a speech, the acts of their chief warriors, and at times came close and waved his fans over him and stroked him on every side with them. This continued more than a quarter of an hour. Then the king and all the men came in a regular manner and shook him by the hand. After that the queen came and all the women did the like. Then Mr. Oglethorpe conducted them to his tent and made them sit down. The next day he made them some presents to make them clothing. This being the 1st of February and of our landing here. We began to pitch our tents the same evening and set four large tents sufficient to hold the greatest part.

We have had very little illness amongst us, having buried none. We are plentifully provided with victuals, and the men have a pint of strong beer every night after work besides other frequent refreshments, as Mr. Oglethorpe sees occasion. Indeed he is both great and good, and I am certain our success is owing to his good conduct only. There is no room to doubt but that we shall be a flourishing people and hope to be a thousand men before the year is ended. We have had very great assistance from the gentlemen of Charles Town, have always some of them with us who bring us workmen to help forward with our works. They have assisted Mr. Oglethorpe in laying out most of the lands already. We are, according to a plan directed to be drawn by Mr. Oglethorpe as I mentioned in my last, building the town, have got up three houses, are planting and sowing, and have sowed about ten acres in all of different kinds of seeds. The houses are made of timber of one floor, only a cock loft over it sufficient to hold two beds, the lower part will make one large room and two small ones and stands in a piece of ground which with the intended garden is 20 yards broad in front and 30 yards long in depth. We shall have a fine prospect when the woods are clear.

As to our government we are divided into four tythings, each maintaining eleven men able to bear arms, of which one is Tythingman. I am one of them and according with my ten other men keep guard every fourth night. Our situation is indeed very pleasant, and though we want for nothing we have some grumbletonians here also.

You may bring any furniture with you, and we may have two or more apprentices. I shall want thread or cotton stockings, some good checkered linen of a dark blue and strong linen for waistcoats and trousers. We are much pestered with a little fly they call a sand fly. But every insect here is stronger than in England. The ants are half an inch long and they say will bite desperately. As for alligators I have seen several but they are by the sides of rivers. Our town is too high ground for them to clamber up. We have killed one. I find the camphor very good against the stings of the flies. I now begin to be somewhat hardened against them. The gentlemen of Charles Town have given us fifty head of cattle. We had some hogs but they are run wild and left us.

SAMUEL EVELEIGH TO THE TRUSTEES

South Carolina
April 6, 1733

Gentlemen: About three weeks since I did myself the honour to go down and visit Mr. Oglethorpe. What I here remarked I caused to be published in the *Carolina Gazette* and sent it to Mr. Samuel Baker, merchant in London, and desired him to get it inserted in the London newspapers, which suppose by this time you have had the sight of.

"On Tuesday the 13th instant, I went on board a canoe, with four Negroes, and about 10 o'clock we set off from Mr. Loyd's Bridge for Georgia, and passing by Port Royal on Wednesday night, we arrived on Friday morning, an hour before day, at Yamacraw, a place so called by the Indians, but now Savannah, in the colony of Georgia. Some time before we came to the landing, the sentinel challenged us and, understanding who we were, admitted us ashore. This is a very high bluff, forty feet perpendicular from the high water mark. It's distant from Charles Town, southwest, according to the course and windings of the rivers and creeks, about 140 miles, but by a direct course seventy-seven.

"This bluff is distant ten miles from the mouth of the rivers on the south side; and Purrysburg is twenty-four miles above it on the north, and is so situated that you have a beautiful prospect. Both up and down the river it's very sandy and barren, and consequently a wholesome place for a town or city. There is on it 130-odd souls; and from the time they embarked at London, to the time I left the place, there died but two sucking children, and they at sea. When they arrived, there was standing on it a great quantity of the best sorts of pine, most of which is already cut down on the spot where the town is laid out to be built.

"Mr. Oglethorpe is indefatigable, takes a great deal of pains; his fare is but indifferent, having little else at present but salt provisions; he's extremely well beloved by all his people; the general title they give him is Father. If any of them is sick, he immediately visits them and takes a great deal of care of them. If any difference arises, he's the person that decides it. Two happened while I was there and in my presence, and all the parties went away to outward appearance satisfied and contented with his determination. He keeps a strict discipline. I neither saw one of his people drunk, or heard one swear, all the time I was there. He does not allow them rum, but in lieu gives them English beer.

"It's surprising to see how cheerfully the men goes to work, considering they have not been bred to it. There's no idlers there, even the boys and girls do their parts. There are four houses already up, but none finished; and he hopes, when he has got more sawyers, which I suppose he will have in a short time, to finish two houses a week. He has ploughed up some land, part of which he sowed with wheat, which is come up, and looks promising. He has two or three gardens, which he has sowed with divers sorts of seeds, and planted thyme, with other sorts of pot-herbs, sage, leeks, scallions, celery, licorice, &c. and several sorts of fruit trees. He was palisading the town 'round, including some part of the common, which I do suppose may be finished in a fortnight's time. In short, he has done a vast deal of work for the time, and, I think his name justly deserves to be immortalized."

There are several other things which the printer for want of room could not put in. I carried down with me a great bundle of asparagus and as soon as he received it he ordered it to be given [to] the women with child, without reserving any for himself. While I was there Mr. Oglethorpe gave Captain's commissions to two of the chief Indian warriors together with some presents, at which they seemed well satisfied and promised to do him what service they could.

Excuse me, Gentlemen, if I take the liberty to make one remark: Mr. Oglethorpe told me that by their constitution they were to have no Negroes amongst them, which I think will be a great prejudice if not a means to overset your noble design. For there is a vast quantity of extraordinary fine land which [is] plentifully stored with large trees which I can't think can be felled by persons that are not used to work. Besides, it will be very difficult for white people to hoe and tend their corn in the hot weather.

Mr. Oglethorpe once a week puts up a turkey or some other thing of value to be shot for by his men, which has already had good effect, bringing them acquainted with arms which some of them before were ignorant of.

JAMES OGLETHORPE TO THE TRUSTEES

Charles Town
June 9, 1733

Gentlemen: When I left your new town of Savannah there were then nine framed houses finished, the sides covered with feather-edged board and the tops with shingles, besides the smith forge and two other clapboard houses. The framed houses are twenty-four foot in length upon sixteen foot in breadth. They have one story eight foot high with garrets over them. They are raised upon logs two foot above the ground and are floored with inch and half plank. There was upon the place when I left it 160 heads, of whom seventy bear arms. There are two blockhouses, musket shell proof and very defensible, with four portholes for cannon and one piece of cannon ready to be put into each. There was a battery of six pieces of cannon upon the water side and a guard house of thirty-six foot long upon twenty-four foot wide, the sides covered with thick slat and the top with bark. There was also a large stout crane, four ground saw pits, supported all 'round with timber, and 140 yards on the East side of the town was fortified with palisadoes seventeen foot long. The trees all 'round the town, within an hundred yards thereof, was cleared. Before I came away there were fifty head of cattle, the gift of John Whitaker and his friend, and fifty head more, the gift of Mr. Odingsell and the people of Edisto. Landed several of them, being wild, run away into the woods. The remainder were decided by lot amongst the people. Every family in which there was a woman had a milch cow and every single man a heifer or steer. I have left with them also four horses and two canoes which I left with them on account of the Trust.

27

With respect to the Indian affairs, I had also two companies of Tomochichi's men and gave at their desire a commission to Tuskenca Istinnocecheby the name of the Captain of the First Militia Company of the Indian Allies and at their desire also appointed Skee Captain of the Second Militia Company of the Indian Allies. The two companies consisted of forty very clever men. Their pay is one bushel of corn per month for each man while we employ them in war or hunting, a gun at their first listing and a blanket per annum. We have concluded a peace with the Lower Creeks who were the most dangerous enemies to South Carolina and formerly friend to the French and Spaniards.

The land in Georgia becoming to grow valuable by reason of our settlement, several have applied to me for grants and those who have served the colony and are willing to take them upon the Trustees' terms I have promised to recommend to you for 500 acres of land: First, Mr. Walter Augustine who has been long in this country and behaved well in the Indian war. He with four men is already settled upon a lot six miles distant [from] the town. Up the river he has built a house and cleared seven acres of land which he has planted with Indian corn, a little barley and other European grain, which comes up finely. For the next lot above him I promised to recommend Lieutenant Wells; for the next above, Mr. Fennygall; and for the next lot behind them Mr. Reves, all of them being officers of His Majesty's Independent Company. I have promised to recommend Mr. Bryan, a very brave young man, who himself with four of his Negroes worked for us gratis some months. I also promised to recommend Ensign Farrington and Captain Thomas for lots upon the seacoast. Besides these, as I said before, upon finding the land grew valuable, others applied to me for large tracts of land from 3000 to 12,000 acres each, in order to monopolize the country, and offered to give me considerable presents for to bring the Trustees into making these grants and to continue at their putting Negroes upon them. I treated [them], as you may think, with contempt, and had it not been necessary to carry things with great temper here I should [have] kicked the proposers into the bargain.

Savannah

August 12, 1733

Gentlemen: I have not been able to write at length since I left Charles Town. When I returned hither from thence I found the people were grown very mutinous and impatient of labour and discipline. This petulancy was owing chiefly to several of them having got into drinking of rum and some more artful, who had a mind to buy the little things they had for liquor, and, in order to bring that about, stirred them up to desire that they might have all their provisions delivered into their own hands and then to have bought that provision from them. Some of the silly people desired their provisions that they might be able to gratify their palates by selling a large quantity of wholesome food for a little rum punch.

I found that Gray, who pretended to understand the silk, had been one of the busiest in preaching up mutiny and, whilst I was at Charles Town, had in a barefaced manner insulted all order and threatened the chief people here. For which Mr. Scott, a Justice of the Peace for this place, whom he insulted in the execution of his office ordered him to be set in the stocks. He complained to me when I came back again and told me that amongst our people he had a great many friends and a great many enemies who had sworn his destruction and would have had me have brought them face to face to have sworn against each other, and told me that if I would not give him satisfaction he desired leave to go out of the colony. I told him I would give him leave provided he went away within twelve hours, which he accordingly did.

By degrees I brought the people to discipline but could not revive the spirit of labour. Idleness and drunkenness were succeeded by sickness. To remedy the first I sent away the Negroes who sawed for us, for so long as they continued here our men were encouraged in idleness by their working for them. To remedy drunkenness I gave a moderate allowance of wine, prohibited rum and staved such as I could find in the town. But found that the Indian trading house about one-half a mile from us, in spite of all my prohibitions, sold rum to our people. I did not care to disoblige them, because they are the only interpreters we have to the Indians. However at present I must either suppress them or our people must be destroyed, we having lost twenty people within a month since the drinking of rum was come into fashion; whereas we lost but one person in five months whilst I was here and kept the people from excessive drinking.

Millidge, our best carpenter, is dead of a burning fever which on his deathbed he confessed he contracted at the Indian trading house. He drank there rum punch on the Wednesday, on Thursday was taken ill of a burning fever and on the seventh day, the crisis of that distemper, died. Poor Overend, who was recommended by Mr. LaRoche, is also dead with rum, to which most of the rest owe their deaths. But the illness being once frequent became contagious. It appeared chiefly in burning fevers or else in bloody fluxes attended by convulsions and other terrible symptoms. Dr. Cox being dead, Jones looked after the sick. The Indian root diascordium, rhubarb, laudanum and all other applications usually used on that occasion were of no effect. Almost everyone that was taken ill at first died. Jones himself fell sick and some of the women (most handy about the sick) died. So that we had neither doctor, surgeon nor nurse, and about the 15th of July we had above sixty people sick, many of whose lives we despaired of. At which time Captain Horton arrived here with some Jews and amongst them a doctor of physick, who immediately undertook our people and refused to take any pay for it. He proceeded by cold baths, cooling drinks and other cooling applications. Since which the sick have wonderfully recovered, and we have not lost one who would follow his prescriptions. By my constant watching of them I have restrained the drinking of rum. I intended to have left this place long ago, but the general sickness of the people made me think that if I abandoned them in that condition it would throw them into despair and make the distemper fatal, so that I thought it was better to neglect my own affairs and take my chance of standing the sickness here than, by quitting the people at such a time, expose them almost to certain death.

I have agreed with Mr. MacPherson, Captain of the Rangers, to build a fort upon Ogeechee River, which I have named Argyle. It is already begun and in good forwardness and I have supplied him from hence with provision, cannon and ammunition. Hetherington and Bishop with their servants have undertook to build a fort upon a creek called Thunderbolt, upon which they are to begin to work on Tuesday next. And Ferguson, Captain of the Carolina scout boat, has undertaken to do the same at Skidaway Island. The two latter in consideration of lands and the former of £200 Currency. So that by this means all the passages to this town both by land and water are covered.

On the 7th of July I held the first Court and administered the Oaths of Allegiance, Supremacy and Abjuration, named the several wards and streets and put each family into possession of an house lot, on twenty-one of which framed houses are built. The other nineteen the carpenters undertook to build for themselves. But alas! five of them died within one week. The lots of those who have no children are put into the hands of other working men who are capable to assist in building the remaining houses. We proceed first on the houses of those who have widows or children here.

Savannah
September 17, 1733

Gentlemen: I received the agreeable news of the approbation your designs have met with from Parliament, by the *Georgia Pink*, Captain Daubus Commander. The people on board him are all arrived safe, Daniel Preston excepted who was washed overboard in a storm. His widow, the day after she landed, was taken picking of the pockets of a drunken man of eight Shillings Sterling. The man was put into the stocks for being drunk, and a bill was found by the Grand Jury against her for felony. Upon her being examined before a Justice of Peace, her defense was that she was drunk and did not know that she took the money nor did intend to keep it. Upon petition and proving that she was with child, the trial before the Petty Jury was put off 'till her delivery and in the meanwhile she was admitted to bail.

In a former I gave you an account of my having agreed with Captain Mac-Pherson for him to build Fort Argyle for £200 Currency. The trees that fell into the river and were carried down by great floods stopped the passage below the fort in such a manner as to prevent any possibility of getting up there by water without immense labour in cutting away the trees. The fort being about half-finished when he represented this, I ordered him to begin another ten miles lower and allowed him £50 Currency for the work already done. He has finished the new fort, the guns are mounted, the houses built and six families settled there besides the garrison. Boats of fifteen ton burden have been there. I have settled Mr. Bishop, Hetherington &c. on a point called Thunderbolt, which commands the channel that comes up from Saint Augustine to this place. They have some guns there and a fort in pretty good forwardness. I have ordered ten men to be settled upon the Island of Tybee which commands the other passage from Augustine, and when that is fortified I take this place will be pretty safe. A beacon upon Tybee for to direct ships on their making land is very necessary. I have therefore thought that you would not be displeased at my ordering one to be begun which I hope will be finished at an expense which will be but small, if compared to the great usefulness of it.

Many of the newcomers, in spite of all I can do, drink very hard, so that I fear a mortality will soon happen amongst them. We have now four hundred people upon the place.

Savannah

December, 1733

Gentlemen: I cannot but congratulate you upon the great success your designs have met with, being not only approved of by all America but so strongly supported by His Majesty and the Parliament of Great Britain. Providence itself seems visible in all things to prosper your designs calculated for the protection of the persecuted, the relief of the poor and the benefit of mankind.

A year being above expired since I set out from England I believe you will be impatient to have a short account of what has been done towards the settlement of this colony, which seems to have been conducted to its present successful situation by the manifest interposition of God.

We landed here on the 1st of February last with but forty persons able to bear arms. Notwithstanding our weakness the Spaniards did not attack us. The Indians were most surprisingly inclined towards friendship with us. The people of Carolina assisted us with the Rangers and scout boat, the guards of that province, and sent up cattle. Colonel Bull, a man of extraordinary abilities, came up himself with a number of his Negro servants and not only instructed the people in the nature of the seasons and the manner of clearing, building and cultivating but laid out the timber and made his slaves work for us. We were some time before we could get any other assistance from Carolina, the people refusing to hire out their Negroes, though we offered security for them.

When I was obliged to go to Charles Town to meet the Assembly, who generously gave £8000 Currency towards maintaining our people a second year, some of the people begun to be intemperate and then disobedient, so that at my return I hardly knew them. Their excessive drinking was followed with sickness which raged for some time most terribly amongst us. But though individuals suffered, the colony itself increased and flourished by your supplying them continually with timely succours from Europe and the accession of many people which the reputation of this undertaking drew from several parts of America to settle here, insomuch that the colony increased notwithstanding our sickness and we were very well supplied with all necessaries for our money from Charles Town. For we had also twenty pair of sawyers from Carolina for hire and Colonel Bull and Mr. Bryan came up again in the midst of the sickness to assist us with twenty slaves whose labour they gave as a free gift to the colony.

Finding our people increase fast I enlarged our quarters by new settlements and covered this place to the southward by building Fort Argyle at about twenty miles distance. Mr. Bishop and his people were settled at Thunderbolt five miles to the southeast and by that means guarded the most dangerous water passage from the Spaniards. About six miles farther to the southward on another water passage is settled a colony of ten families to keep open the passage with Fort Argyle, whilst by land from that fort we marked a road about 40 miles in length to Pallackucola Garrison in Carolina.

The colony of Abercorn, consisting of ten families, is settled. Within land at three miles distant from the town upon two hills are situated Hampstead and Highgate, two villages of ten families each. Over against the town lies Hutchinson's Island, one of the most delightful spots of ground I ever saw, about three miles in length and one wide. A great part of it is natural meadow, the rest covered with tall trees, many of which are bays above four score foot high. In that island on the farther side, which commands the northern branch of this river opposite to the town, there is a house built and an overseer lodged with four servants belonging to you with orders to cut a walk through the wood in a straight line the breadth of this town, which will serve as a meadow for feeding of cattle and give a beautiful prospect of the other river.

A sloop loaded with [indentured] servants was forced in here through stress of weather and want of victuals. Many of them were dead. Forty only remained as they were likewise ready to perish through misery. I thought it an act of charity to buy them, which I did giving £5 a head. I gave one of them to each of the widows, which will render them able to cultivate their lands and maintain their families. I let each of the Magistrates have one at prime cost, that they might not be behind hand in their gardens and plantations by reason of their spending much of their time in the public service. Of the rest I have allotted Mr. Lafond five to help him in building a sawmill, four to the gardens and four to the island.

We go on with building the beacon at Tybee. The people who work upon it have two Shillings per diem and Blythman, the master workman, has the same wages as he could have in Carolina. The timber is already cut and squared and the upper and lower floor framed. They reckon it will be finished in March. It is an octagon of ninety feet high, twenty-five feet wide at bottom and $12\frac{1}{2}$ feet wide at top, weatherboarded twenty-six feet high and the rest open. It is all framed here of the best of light wood and to be carried down and set upon the point of Tybee. The foundation will be secured with cedar piles.

There are fifty houses of framed timber and covered with shingles, which are tiles made of wood and tarred over, already built. Three wards and an half are taken up and the people to whom they belong are all at present at work either at building their houses or clearing their lands, so that before the year is 'round there must be 120 houses built in the town or their lots forfeited. The bricks you sent were partly employed in building the smith's forge, an oven and a well twenty feet deep, which affords excellent water, the rest in the chimneys belonging to the widows.

The orphans are fed and clothed from the Public Stores and the care of them is entrusted to three of our best persons appointed for that purpose. The militia is exercised and commanded by Tythingmen and Constables. The civil government is in the Court appointed by the grant under your seal and property as regularly recovered and criminals punished as in any court in Europe. Every man pleads his own cause. The fact is tried by the Jury and sentence pronounced by the Court. We feed 259 souls in town, in Hampstead and Highgate; in the four colonies 184 besides Indians and strangers.

[5]

March the 1st, the first house in the square was framed and raised, Mr. Oglethorpe driving the first pin. We are now divided into different gangs and each gang had their labor assigned to them, four sets of carpenters, a set of shingle-makers and Negro sawyers who were hired from Carolina.

PETER GORDON, 1733

PETER GORDON (1698–1740) had been an upholsterer in England before coming to Georgia in 1733 with his twenty-eight-year-old wife Catherine. He was appointed Bailiff of the new town of Savannah but left Georgia after only two years. Gordon's journal, in the University of Georgia Library, was published by The Beehive Press in 1974 in Trevor Reese, *Our First Visit in America*. This following version has been lightly abridged.

We arrived the 1st of February at Yamacraw Bluff in Georgia, the place which Mr. Oglethorpe had pitched upon for our intended settlement. As soon as we came near the bluff, we were saluted by Captain Scott and his party with their small arms, which we returned. And as soon as we landed, we set immediately about getting our tents fixed and our goods brought ashore and carried up the bluff, which is forty foot perpendicular [in] height above by water mark. This, by reason of the loose sand and great height, would have been extremely troublesome had not Captain Scott and his party built stairs for us before our arrival, which we found of very great use to us in bringing up our goods.

About an hour after our landing, the Indians came with their king, queen and Mr. Musgrove, the Indian trader and interpreter, along with him to pay their compliments to Mr. Oglethorpe and to welcome us to Yamacraw. The manner of their approach was thus. At a little distance they saluted us with a volley of their small arms, which was returned by our guard, and then the king, queen and chiefs and other Indians advanced and before them walked one of their generals with his head adorned with white feathers with rattles in his hands (something like our castanets) to which he danced, observing just time, singing and throwing his body into a thousand different and antic postures. In this manner they advanced to pay their obedience to Mr. Oglethorpe, who stood at a small distance from his tent to receive them and then conducted them into his tent, seating Tomochichi upon his right hand [and] Mr. Musgrove, the interpreter, standing between them. They continued in conference about a quarter of an hour and then returned to their town, which was about a quarter of a mile distant from the place where we pitched our camp, in the same order as they came. Not being able to complete the pitching of our tents this night and I being but lately recovered from my illness, [I] went to lie at the Indian town at Mr. Musgrove, the interpreter's, house with Doctor Cox and his family and Lieutenant Farrington.

As soon as the Indians were informed that we were come to Musgrove's house, they began to entertain us with dancing 'round a large fire which they made upon the ground opposite to the king's house. Their manner of dancing is in a circle, 'round the fire, following each other close with many antic gestures, singing and beating time with their feet and hands to admiration. One of the oldest of our people, Dr. Lyons, having slept away from our camp and got a little in drink, found his way up to the Indian town and joined with the Indians in their dance, endeavoring to mimic and ape them in their antic gestures, which I being informed of sent for him and desired that he would immediately repair home to our camp. Otherwise I assured him I would acquaint Mr. Oglethorpe with his folly. He promised me that he would, but being so much in liquor he returned again to the Indians and danced with them as before, which being told to me I ordered several white men who were there to carry him home by force, it being of a very bad consequence that the Indians should see any follies or indiscretions in our old men, by which they judge that our young men must be still guilty of greater, for they measure men's understanding and judgement according to their years.

Friday, the 2nd, we finished our tents and got some of our stores on shore. The 3rd we got the pettiaguas unloaded and all the goods brought up to the bluff. Sunday, the 4th, we had divine service performed in Mr. Oglethorpe's tent by Rev. Dr. Herbert with thanksgiving for our safe arrival. Mr. Musgrove, the Indian trader, and his wife were present, and Tomochichi, the Indian king, desired to be admitted, which Mr. Oglethorpe readily consented to, and he with his queen were seated in the tent. During the time of divine service, several of the Indian warriors and others sat at a small distance from the tent upon trees and behaved very decently.

Wednesday, the 7th, we began to dig trenches for fixing palisadoes 'round the place of our intended settlement as a fence in case we should be attacked by the Indians, while others of us were employed in clearing of the lines and cutting trees to the proper lengths, which was fourteen foot for the palisadoes. About noon a fire broke out in the guard room, which instantly consumed the same and burnt several chests that were in it belonging to our people and likewise a hut adjoining to it belonging to Mr. Warren, whose things were likewise burned. It was with much difficulty we got the powder out of Mr. Oglethorpe's tent, which stood almost 'joining to the fire and which we preserved by taking it immediately down. After we had got the fire pretty near extinguished, one of the large pine trees near 100 foot high took fire and to prevent further damage we were obliged to cut it down and in the fall it broke two barrels of beef and one barrel of strong beer in pieces and damaged the end of one of our tents. The whole damage amounted to about £20 sterling.

Thursday, the 8th, each family had given out of the stores an iron pot, frying pan and three wooden bowls, a Bible, common prayer book and *Whole Duty of Man*. This day we were taken off from the palisadoes and set about sawing and splitting boards eight foot long in order to build clapboard houses to get us under better cover till our framed houses could be built.

Friday, our arms were delivered to us from the store, viz. a musket and bayonet, cartridge box and belt to each person able to carry arms. Sunday, we were drawn up under our arms for the first time, being divided into four tythings, each tything consisting of ten men, of which I was appointed to command the first, Mr. Causton, the second, Mr. Jones, the third, and Mr. Goddard, the fourth. I mounted the first guard at 8 o'clock at night, received orders from Mr. Oglethorpe to fix two sentinels at the extreme parts of the town, who were to be relieved every two hours and then returning to the guard house, which we had built of clapboards, upon the most convenient part of the bluff for commanding the river both ways. The next night at 8 o'clock I was relieved by Mr. Causton, who marched to the guard house with his tything under arms, where I received him with my tything drawn up before the guard with their arms rested.

Notwithstanding that our guard duty was every fourth night, yet we went directly from the guard to work in the woods after our names were called, which was done every morning at 6 o'clock before Mr. Oglethorpe's tent. And if any person did not at that time answer to his name, except hindered by sickness, [he] was cut off from his day's allowance of a pint of Madeira wine, which was allowed to every working man. About this time we had excessive hard rains and almost continued thunder and lightning to a most astonishing degree. The rains were so violent and came with such force that it beat through our tents to that degree that we have been wet to the skin in them several times in a day. And to prevent our bedding from being wet, [we] had no other method but by covering them with plates, dishes, bowls and what other conveniency we had to catch the rain in, which has often been so heavy that several gallons has been catched in those vessels upon one bed in the space of an hour.

As the country all 'round us was a continued forest and nothing to be seen but wood and water, the rains were very frequent and very severe. But as our people who were daily employed in cutting down trees and clearing the place which was intended for the town advanced in their work and had cleared a pretty large space of ground, we could perceive the rains not to be so frequent, nor so violent. Monday, Mr. Oglethorpe being informed that two fellows who had broke out of Charles Town jail were in our neighborhood and had killed several cattle at Musgrove, the Indian trader's, cowpen, ordered two men with a large swivel gun to watch near the side of the river all night to stop their canoe in case they should attempt to pass and if apprehended each man was to have a reward of £10 currency from Mr. Oglethorpe.

The 18th, a servant maid belonging to Mr. Hughes was ordered to be brought before Captain Scott, Conservator of the Peace, where she was accused of a loose disorderly behavior and endeavoring to seduce several other young women in the colony, upon which she was ordered to be whipped at the cart's tail and returned to England to her friends and in the meantime she was given in charge to the Constable. The 19th, Mr. Oglethorpe went in the scout boat to the Island Tybee in the mouth of our river to pitch upon a proper place for a small settlement for some people from Carolina who desired to be admitted under his protection and to serve as a look-out for our settlement. About 4 in the afternoon, Colonel Purry arrived at the Indian town in a canoe from Purrysburg. I was ordered to take four of my guard with their arms and wait upon the Colonel with the compliments of the gentlemen and to give him an invitation to our camp. The Colonel returned their compliments with great civility and desired me to acquaint the gentlemen that he would wait upon them presently. We were then ordered all under arms, and when the Colonel arrived we saluted him with a general discharge of our small arms. About 7 in the evening, Mr. Oglethorpe returned in the scout boat from Tybee. This day our new crane was put up.

Tuesday, the 20th, a warrant from Captain Scott came directed to me to see the sentence executed on the servant maid who some days before was ordered to [be] whipped, upon which I ordered four of my guard under arms to bring her out, a Negro being appointed to whip her. As soon as she was brought to the cart, several of our people interceded with Mr. Oglethorpe in her behalf, who remitted that part of her sentence and sent her the same day out of the colony on board a pettiagua bound for Charles Town in the care of Mr. Osborne, the patroon. The 21st about 2 in the morning, Dr. Herbert set out for Charles Town in the scout boat, accompanied by Colonel Purry and some of his people. The same day Mr. Kilbery set out with a small party and an Indian guide to apprehend the fellows who were in the woods and had been discovered by the Indians. About 11 at night he returned with the prisoners, who were immediately examined before Mr. Oglethorpe. One of them was English and the other a Frenchman. The Frenchman denied all he was charged with, of having broke out of Charles Town jail and having committed several robberies and killed several cattle in our neighborhood. The Englishman confessed most of what he was charged with, alleging that what cattle they killed was only for their own subsistence, they having been in a most miserable way, destitute of any manner of food in the woods, and must have inevitably perished had they not done it. The Frenchman was ordered into custody of the guard belonging to Captain Massy's Independent Company, ten of whom with a Sergeant were ordered to be assisting us in Georgia. The other was ordered into custody of our guard.

The 22nd, Mr. Fitzwalter, one of our people, arrived with fifty head of cattle and other stores from Carolina. This cattle was part of the hundred which Mr. Whitaker and his friends had made a present of to us. The 23rd, the bell was hung at the end of the crane. The 25th, the two prisoners were put on board Captain Anderson's pettiagua to be sent to Beaufort and there to be delivered to Captain Watts, who was the commanding officer, and to be by him forwarded to Charles Town. The same day Mr. Oglethorpe, Colonel Bull and Tomochichi went up the river in order to give the Indians possession of the lands allotted for their settlement lying between the creeks six miles above us. About 7 in the evening they returned to the camp.

March the 1st, the first house in the square was framed and raised, Mr. Oglethorpe driving the first pin. Before this we had proceeded in a very unsettled manner, having been employed in several different things such as cutting down trees and cross-cutting them to proper lengths for clapboards and afterwards splitting them in order to build us clapboard houses, which was the first design, but that not answering the expectations, we were now divided into different gangs and each gang had their proper labor assigned to them and to be under the direction of one person of each gang, so that we proceeded in our labor much more regular than before, there being four sets of carpenters who had each of them a quarter of the first ward allotted to them to build, a set of shingle-makers with proper people to cross cut and split and a sufficient number of Negro sawyers who were hired from Carolina to be assisting to us. The same night one Redmen, an Irishman, was ordered into custody of the guard on suspicion of his being a spy and intending to go to St. Augustine, a Spanish settlement, to inform them of the situation of our affairs. But after frequent examinations and nothing appearing against him, he was discharged.

Sunday, the 4th, after divine service, we were ordered under arms, and the tythings marched regularly into the wood, a small distance from the town, where Mr. Oglethorpe ordered a mark to be fixed up at a hundred yards distance to be shot at by all the men and whoever shot nearest the mark to have a small prize of seven or eight shillings value. This custom, which was intended to train the people up to firing and to make them good marksmen, was generally observed for many Sundays afterwards, that being the only day we could be possibly spared from labor and with some success.

Thursday, the 7th, the Indian king and chiefs desired a talk with Mr. Oglethorpe, which he readily granted and received them at a house which was fitted up on purpose for that occasion. Mr. Oglethorpe being seated at the door, on a bench covered with blue cloth with Captain Scott on his right hand and Mr. Jonathan Bryan on his left, the Indians advancing with Mr. Musgrove, their interpreter, before them. Most of them had their heads adorned with white feathers in token of peace and friendship. Before the king and other chiefs marched two warriors carrying long white tubes adorned with white feathers in their left hands and rattles in their right hands, which was coconut shells with shot in them, with which they beat time to their singing as they marched along.

But before they reached where Mr. Oglethorpe was, they made several stops and at each stop they began a new song, in which they recounted all the warlike exploits of their forefathers, which is all the records they have and the only method of handing down to posterity the history of their great men. When they came near the place where Mr. Oglethorpe was, the two warriors who carried the feathers and rattles in their hands advanced before the king and other chiefs singing and playing with their rattles and putting themselves in many antic postures. Then they came up to Mr. Oglethorpe and the other gentlemen and waved the white wings they carried in their hands over their heads, at the same time singing and putting their bodies in antic postures.

Afterwards they fixed a lighted pipe of tobacco to the tubes which they held in their hands and presented it to Mr. Oglethorpe, who having smoked several whiffs they then presented it to the other gentlemen, who observed the same method which Mr. Oglethorpe had done. Then they afterwards presented the same pipe to their king and two of their chiefs, the king and each of the chiefs smoking four whiffs, blowing the first whiff to the left, the next to the right, the third upwards and the fourth downwards. After this ceremony was over, they walked into the house, the king being seated opposite to Mr. Oglethorpe and the chiefs on his right hand.

Then Mr. Oglethorpe desired the interpreter to ask the king whether they desired to speak first. The king said they did and bid the interpreter should say to Mr. Oglethorpe that they were glad to see him and his people safely arrived in this country and bid us hearty welcome to Yamacraw. Then he said that with regard to one of his people that had been killed by the Uchis (another neighboring nation of Indians) he would not take revenge without Mr. Oglethorpe's consent and approbation. (Taking revenge is a term they use when they intend to declare war.) He then said that he was not a stranger to the English, for that his father and grandfather had been very well known to them. He afterwards presented Mr. Oglethorpe with some deer skins, which is the most valuable and indeed the only thing of value they have. Mr. Oglethorpe, after having assured them of his friendship and utmost assistance and protection, made them some presents with which they were very much pleased. They afterwards returned to their own town in the same manner as they came.

We had hitherto continued very healthy and proceeded in the public labor with as much success and dispatch as could possibly be expected. But the weather beginning to be extremely hot and our people having as yet no other water to drink but that of the river, which at high water was brackish, we did not long enjoy that happiness. For soon afterwards we began to be very sickly and lost many of our people who died very suddenly.

April, the 6th, Dr. Cox died very much lamented, being a general loss to the colony. He was a very useful and well experienced gentleman. As the first person that died and we being then under a sort of a military government, Mr. Oglethorpe ordered that he should be buried in a military manner. All our tythings were accordingly ordered to be under arms and to march regularly to the grave with the corpse, and as soon as he was interred and the funeral service performed we gave three general discharges of our small arms and during the time that we marched with the corpse and while the funeral office was performing minute guns were fired from the guard house and the bell constantly tolling. This military manner of burying was afterwards observed not only to all our men that died, but likewise to our women till the people began to die so fast that the frequent firing of the cannon and our small arms struck such terror in our sick people (who knowing the cause concluded they should be the next) that we have had three or four die in one day which being represented to Mr. Oglethorpe he ordered that it should be discontinued.

[6]

Frederica. . . . Each family had a bower of palmetto leaves, about twenty foot long and fourteen foot wide and in regular rows. The whole appeared something like a camp, for the bowers looked like tents, only being larger and covered with palmetto leaves instead of canvas.

FRANCIS MOORE, 1735

FRANCIS MOORE was already an experienced imperialist before he was employed by the Trustees of Georgia, for he had served the Royal Africa Company for five years. He made two trips to Georgia, in 1735–36 and 1738–43. This account of his first trip with a group of colonists headed for Frederica, where Moore was to be the storekeeper, is excerpted from *A Voyage to Georgia* (London, 1744). The complete text was reprinted by The Beehive Press in Trevor Reese, *Our First Visit in America* in 1974.

The Trustees examined at their office such persons as applied to them for the benefit of the charity, and out of them chose those who had the best characters and were the truest objects of compassion. They acquainted those that they had chosen that they must expect to go through great hardships at the beginning and use great industry and labor in order to acquire afterwards a comfortable subsistence for themselves and families; that they gave them lands and a year's provisions but that those lands were uninhabited woods; that they must lie without cover till they could build houses for themselves, live upon salt meat, drink water, work hard, keep guard for fear of enemies, clear and plant ground before they could reap any harvest; that the country was hot in summer and that there were flies in abundance and that thunderstorms were frequent; that sicknesses were dangerous to those who drank distilled liquors.

Several were disheartened, which discovered that they had pleaded necessity without reason and that they were able to live in England. The places of those who were deterred from going were filled up with others, for there were a great many more petitioned to go than there was room for. The whole embarkation, English and foreigners, together with the missionaries to the Indians, amounted to 227 heads, 202 people upon the Trust's account.

The Trustees will give to every man they send a watchcoat, a musket and bayonet, an hatchet, an hammer, an handsaw, a sod shovel or spade, a broad hoe, a narrow hoe, a gimlet, a drawing knife, an iron pot, a pair of pot-hooks, a frying-pan. The Trustees pay their passage from England to Georgia, and in the voyage they will have in every week four beef days, two pork days and one fish day, and bread, beer and water. There were two ships freighted, the *Symond* and the *London Merchant.*

All those who came upon the Trust's account were divided into messes and, besides the ships' provisions, the Trustees were so careful of the poor people's health that they put on board turnips, carrots, potatoes and onions, which were given out with the salt meat and contributed greatly to prevent the scurvy. The ship was divided into cabins with gangways, which we call streets, between them. The people were disposed into these by families; the single men were put by themselves. Each cabin had its door and partition. Whenever the weather would permit, the ship was cleaned between decks and washed with vinegar, which kept the place very sweet and healthy. There were Constables appointed to prevent any disorders, and there was no occasion for punishing anyone excepting a boy who was whipped for stealing of turnips. When the weather permitted, the men were exercised with small arms. There were also thread, worsted and knitting needles given to the women.

On the 6th of February, Mr. Oglethorpe was received at Savannah by the freeholders under arms and under the salute of twenty-one cannons. On the 8th, some boats with sutlers came on board with provisions to sell to the passengers. They privately brought some rum, which being discovered the officers who were left by Mr. Oglethorpe ordered the same to be staved. Mr. Oglethorpe brought fresh meat and other refreshments in plenty, which he distributed to the newcomers. Mr. Oglethorpe spoke to the people to prevent their being terrified with false reports. There seemed to be little need of it, for all zealous to settle a town of their own and, trusting entirely to him, were not at all apprehensive.

After three hours stay, he set out for Savannah and took me along with him. He lay that night at a house which he hires in Savannah. It is the same as the common freeholder's houses are, a frame of sawed timber, twenty-four by sixteen foot, floored with rough deals, the sides with feather-edged boards unplaned and the roof shingled.

I took a view of the town of Savannah. It is about a mile and quarter in circumference. It stands upon the flat of a hill. The bank of the river (which they in barbarous English call a bluff) is steep and about forty-five foot perpendicular, so that all heavy goods are brought up by a crane. From a very wide strand between the first row of houses and the river there is a very pleasant prospect.

You see the river wash the foot of the hill, which is a hard, clear, sandy beach a mile in length. The town of Savannah is built of wood. All the houses of the first forty freeholders are of the same size, but there are great numbers built since, I believe 100 or 150. Many of these are much larger, some of two or three stories high, the boards planed and painted. Some few people have palisades of turned wood before their doors, but the generality have been wise enough not to throw away their money.

Their houses are built at a pretty large distance from one another for fear of fire. The streets are very wide, and there are great squares left at proper distances for markets and other conveniences. Near the river side is a guard house enclosed with palisades a foot thick, where there are nineteen or twenty cannons mounted and a continual guard kept.

There are no lawyers allowed to plead nor attorneys to take money, but every man pleads his own cause. All brandies and distilled liquors are prohibited. No slavery is allowed, nor Negroes. All persons who go among the Indians must give security for their good behavior, because if any injury is done to them the Indians break out into war by killing the first white man they conveniently can. No victualler or alehousekeeper can give any credit. The Trustees grant the lands in tail male, that on the expiring of a male line they may regrant it to such man having no other lot as shall be married to the next female heir of the deceased.

There is near the town to the east a garden belonging to the Trustees consisting of ten acres. The garden is laid out with cross-walks planted with orange trees. In the squares between the walks were vast quantities of mulberry trees, this being a nursery for all the province, and every planter that desires it has young trees given him gratis from this nursery. Besides the mulberry trees, there are in some of the quarters in the coldest part of the garden, all kinds of fruit trees usual in England, such as apples, pears, &c. In another quarter are olives, figs, vines, pomegranates and such fruits are as natural to the warmest parts of Europe. And in the warmest part of the garden there was a collection of West India plants and trees. There is a plant of bamboo cane brought from the East Indies. There was also some tea seeds which came from the same place.

There were no public buildings in the town besides a storehouse. Their courts were held in a hut thirty-six foot long and twelve foot wide, made of split boards and erected on Mr. Oglethorpe's first arrival in the colony. In this hut also divine service was performed. As yet there was no prison.

Mr. Oglethorpe was much concerned at the delay, which was of great damage to the poor people who, by not being on their lands, were losing the best season both for building and improving. Mr. Oglethorpe called the freeholders together, acquainted them with the difficulties of 130 miles passage in open boats, which might take up fourteen days and could not be performed in less than six, that they must lie the night in woods with no other shelter than what they could get up upon their arrival and be exposed to the cold frosty nights and perhaps hard rain. Considering the difficulties of the southern settlement, he would permit them to settle at Savannah and the neighboring lands. He gave them two hours to consult their wives and families. They acquainted him that as they came to make a town and live together, they desired to go all together and settle the town of Frederica.

We wanted a great many pettiaguas to carry the families to the southward through the channels between the islands. These pettiaguas are long flat-bottomed boats. They have a kind of a forecastle and a cabin but the rest open. They have two masts and sails like schooners. They row generally with two oars, but on this occasion Mr. Oglethorpe ordered spare oars for each boat. Mr. Oglethorpe put all the strong beer on board one boat, which made the rest labor to keep up, for if they were not at the rendezvous at night they lost their beer.

On the 2d of March the pettiaguas and boats making a little fleet with the families on board, all sailed for Frederica, where I was surprised to find that there was a battery of cannon mounted and the fort almost built, the ditches dug round and the rampart raised with green sod. Within the fort a very large and convenient storehouse to be three stories high, was begun and a cellar underneath. The town was building, the streets were all laid out. The main street was twenty-five yards wide. Each family had a bower of palmetto leaves, tight in the hardest rains. They were about twenty foot long and fourteen foot wide and in regular rows. The whole appeared something like a camp, for the bowers looked like tents, only being larger and covered with palmetto leaves instead of canvas. There were three large tents, two belonging to Mr. Oglethorpe and one to Mr. Horton, pitched upon the parade near the river.

Mr. Oglethorpe had divided the colony into parties. One cut forks, poles and laths for building the bowers, another set them up, a third fetched palmetto leaves, a fourth thatched, and a Jew workman bred in the Brazil taught them to do this nimbly and in a neat manner. As soon as the bowers were finished, a party was set to hoeing and planting, and the rest were hired by him to work at the fort.

The crocodile abounds in all the rivers of Georgia. They call them alligators. I have seen some twelve foot long. They are terrible to look at, stretching open an horrible large mouth, big enough to swallow a man, with rows of dreadful large sharp teeth and feet like dragons, armed with great claws, and a long tail, which they throw about with great strength. When Mr. Oglethorpe was first at Savannah, having wounded and catched one about twelve foot long, he had him brought up to the town and set the boys to bait him with sticks, the creature gaping and blowing hard till the children pelted and beat him to death.

Next to the crocodile is the rattlesnake, a creature really dangerous. The bite is generally thought mortal. The Indians pretend to have performed wonderful cures. I have seen several of these snakes which were killed at Frederica, the largest above two yards long. The rattles are rings at the end of their tails of a horny substance. These shaking together make a noise. To prevent bites, those who walk the woods much wear what they call Indian boots, which are made of coarse woollen cloth, much too large for the legs, tied upon their thighs and hang loose on their shoes.

The 26th, the Indians arrived and camped by themselves near the town and made a war dance, to which Mr. Oglethorpe and all his people went. They made a ring, in the middle of which four sat down, having little drums made of kettles covered with deer skins upon which they beat and sung. Round them others danced, being naked to their waists and round their middles many trinkets tied with skins and some with the tails of beasts hanging down behind them. They painted their faces and bodies, and their hair was stuck with feathers. In one hand they had a rattle, in the other hand the feathers of an eagle. They shook these wings and the rattle and danced 'round the ring with high bounds and antic postures.

The people went on building the storehouse but slowly, hands being taken off for building the fort, and it was farther delayed for want of boards and stuff. Mr. Oglethorpe had the works 'round the fort palisaded with cedar posts. He also had platforms of two-inch planks laid for the cannon upon the bastions and took in a piece of marsh ground below the fort with a work called the spur to make it impossible for any boat or ship to come up or down the river without being torn to pieces. We had a well dug in the fort. There was an oven built, and Mr. Oglethorpe bought off the time of an indented servant who was a baker, and he baked bread for all the colony. The Indians also brought us in plenty of venison, which was divided as far as it would go to the sick first, then to the women and children and lastly to the strong young men.

All the hands were set to work upon the fortifications, Mr. Oglethorpe re-called several parties of Indians and kept them in the woods near the town. The people being tired of guards, to make them alert he one day landed with men and came to the farther end of the town without being discovered, having sur-prised the sentry that was without the wood and sent him into the town crying the enemy was upon them. The men who were with Mr. Oglethorpe fired a volley, falling in with a Spanish cry, the people ran to the fort, the very women took arms to help the defence of the fort and the whole colony was thoroughly alarmed. One Walker, then sick of a fever, took up his musket. Being asked what he intended to have done, he said that, thinking the town lost, he was resolved to die like a man with his arms in his hand and to kill a Spaniard before he died.

A magazine for the powder was begun under one of the bastions, made of solid thick timber with several feet of earth over it. A smith's forge also was getting up in the fort. The storehouse being raised and covered, we began to bring in provisions, &c. This house was flat-roofed and covered with boards to be laid over with turpentine and above that a composition of tar and sand. The boards were already laid, but the tar and other things were not yet come from Carolina. There was a fence sometime ago begun, designed to be carried all 'round the town by joint labor, but the alarms making it necessary to finish the fortifications and put the place into a posture of defence, the enclosure was obliged to be left unfinished, by which means most of the corn and other things that had been planted were destroyed by the cattle.

Personalities and Problems

DESPITE the idealistic intentions of the Trustees, the lesson early Georgia teaches is that institutionalized paternalism does not work very well. The gentlemen Trustees in London were divided from the deserving poor in Georgia by class as well as by an ocean, and this contributed to overadministration, poor communications and misunderstandings. The Trustees assumed that the recipients of their generosity would be gratefully content under their vines and mulberry trees, but early Georgians chafed under the benevolent but aggravating restrictions. The irony of the Georgia experiment is that when the Georgia poor were finally relieved of the burden of paternalism, they quickly adopted slavery, a paternalistic institution that carried the same seeds of destruction that ended Trustee rule.

Much of the criticism from the unhappy Georgians was focused on Thomas Causton, keeper of the public store at Savannah. He was accused of being tyrannical and arbitrary and perhaps he was. But he had an impossible job, for in a colony where too few could support themselves and most depended upon supplies from the public stores, the custodian had to make unpopular decisions, especially when there were never enough provisions and supplies to go around. Causton had no training for the job, and, besides, Georgia was unique. Causton tried to justify his conduct in a long letter to the Trustees, to which we have added selections from his fragmentary diary in 1737. [Document Seven]

Great loyalty and patience were the virtues of William Stephens, and he needed both in extra measure when the Trustees hired him to go to Georgia as their personal representative, administrative secretary and later as a provincial president. Upon his arrival at Savannah in the fall of 1737, Stephens found himself in a hornets' nest, where the citizens of Savannah were fighting among themselves and "clamorously malcontent" toward the Trustees. Stephens spent his first two months in the colony listening with less and less patience to all the complaints. [Document Eight]

For their part, the Trustees felt unfairly criticized by what they considered ungrateful recipients of their charity. Several petitions were dispatched from Savannah to London, complaining about land laws, the prohibition against slavery and a dictatorship of petty officials. [Document Nine]

In his old age, Phillip Thicknesse, who came to Georgia in 1736 to be Thomas Causton's servant, looked back on his experiences in the unhappy colony. He considered himself simply one of many foolish Georgia immigrants. [Document Ten]

⌈ 7 ⌉

Unhappily loaded with business, hearing the complaints among the inhabitants, deciding their differences, writing letters, supporting and encouraging those who gave some reasonable hopes of raising or producing manufactures employed my time.

THOMAS CAUSTON, 1739

A TEXTILE PRINTER named Thomas Causton (1692–1746) was one of the colonists who came to Georgia on the *Anne* in 1733. The Trustees appointed him as the keeper of their public storehouse, which made him the most important official in the colony when Oglethorpe returned to England between March, 1734, and February, 1736, and again between November, 1736, and September, 1738. Causton attempted to impose his will on the colony by withholding supplies and succeeded in making himself extremely unpopular. After the Trustees removed him from office in October, 1738, Causton attempted to defend his conduct in a petition to them. Selections from his "Humble Petition" of November 22, 1739, and his fragmentary 1737 diary provide us with an account of his trials and tribulations. Both documents are in the Egmont Papers at the University of Georgia.

I arrived in the colony of Georgia on the 1st day of February, 1733, and on arrival was commanded by James Oglethorpe to take charge of all Your Honors' stores. At all times I behaved myself with an implicit obedience to the commands of Oglethorpe and with such diligence as showed my earnest desire to be thought worthy of the trust reposed in me. I set down in writing the several parcels, quantities and qualities of stores which I received and delivered in the most exact manner as the great fatigue of business could with reason admit, having for the most part nobody to assist me and at the best those who either could not write or were so negligent that no dependence could be had on their actions.

Oglethorpe judged it necessary to settle Savannah and other towns and villages, viz. Tybee, Skidaway, Thunderbolt, Fort Argyle, Hampstead, Highgate, Abercorn, Ebenezer, Joseph's Town, Westbrooke and Grantham, many of which were twenty or thirty miles distant from Savannah. In the month of

March, 1734, Oglethorpe departed the colony for England. Before his departure from Georgia, [he] commit[ted] to me the sole power for supporting the settlements under any difficulties which might happen, also for preserving to them and others who might join the colony their peace, safety and lawful properties. Being also one of the Bailiffs of the town of Savannah, it was my duty to join the rest of the Magistrates in the administration of justice when occasion required. Being Your Honors' storekeeper, I was to issue the stipulated food and working tools. As I had not the opportunity to consider the difficulties which commonly arise by an employ of so high a nature as solely to hold the reins of a discretional power for the support of so great a number of people living in places so remote and guarding them against such distresses as might render the difficulties of a new colony easy to them, so I must naturally be uneasy at being obliged to bear so great a weight. As I find myself thereby plunged into difficulties, charged with presumptions and threatened with ruin.

Being thus unhappily loaded with business of the greatest moment to the being of the colony, I endeavored to acquit myself by all the honest and just means that I could devise, hoping that my endeavors to execute a trust thus reposed in me would at least excuse any mistakes which I might through inadvertency or want of judgment have made in the execution. I employed the most proper persons I could procure for keeping a just account and putting to writing the particulars of all goods and moneys received to and for the account of Your Honors or the colony, also the particulars of the issues and payments made by me. If errors of any kind has happened, they cannot with justice be imputed as a crime to me, because I can fully show that the daily attendance in providing for the emergencies of the colony in all its parts, guarding against the designs of its public and private enemies, hearing the complaints which naturally arose among the inhabitants, deciding their differences, writing letters on the affairs of the colony and supporting and encouraging those who gave some reasonable hopes of raising food by cultivating land or producing manufactures likely to contribute to the tranquility of the colony and its future happiness so far employed my time that it was impossible for me to give such an attendance on the accounts as wholly to prevent errors or omissions. The lands allotted to the settlers were for the most part incapable of suitable productions for their support, demanding a supply far exceeding the calculations made by Oglethorpe before his departure.

In the month of February, 1736, Oglethorpe returned to the colony and found it in all its parts in peace and safety and the number of its inhabitants greatly increased, and then declared to me that he was well satisfied in my good conduct and particularly with the great diligence I had used in supporting and keeping the settlers together in his absence. [He] was so well and fully convinced of the necessity for such extraordinary expense and of the difficulties which the inhabitants labored under that he ordered me to continue the support, although the time limited and quantity of species stipulated for such support had been long since expired and completed, and also caused several of the inhabitants and particularly the whole town of Ebenezer to be removed to a more fertile soil. Soon after his arrival, Oglethorpe made other settlements; viz. the town of Frederica on the Island St. Simon's, the Darien on the River Altamaha on Jekyll Island, on Cumberland Island, on Amelia Island and Fort St. George, and gave it also in charge to me to use my utmost endeavors in providing and sending sufficient stores to Frederica whereby the town and all the settlements' scout boats and vessels attending their service and security might be supplied with necessaries.

Well knowing that Your Honors' stores were near empty of provisions and that divers sums of money were due and unpaid to sundry persons for sundry stores and necessaries bought and services before that time done and also believing that it was not in the power of Oglethorpe to leave any money towards a reasonable discharge of what was so due and would very shortly be demanded and consequently could not enable me to defray the expenses of the colony either supporting the several settlements or executing his orders, I therefore thought myself obliged to acquaint Oglethorpe of all such facts in as plain a manner as I could (that is to say, of the small quantities of provisions then remaining in the store, of the state of the cash and of the most material demands that then were expected to be discharged) and expressly desired that Oglethorpe would acquaint the people at Savannah that it could not be in my power, by reason of present demands and the uncertainty of future support from England, to continue such assistance to them as they very probably by reason of their difficulties might expect. To which Oglethorpe answered that he could not say anything that was angry or seemed unkind when he was going to leave them.

Oglethorpe ordered the people to meet him in the town house of Savannah, where he informed them that it was necessary for the welfare of the colony that he should go to England, that he would return to them in the month of June or July following and that, in his absence, he had directed an assistance, which would be a loan to those who were industrious in the cultivation of lands. But as Oglethorpe did not express what particular action should entitle each person to claim or to what value or in what manner such assistance was to be so claimed or granted, the execution thereof must in a great measure either be guided by my discretion, which would naturally raise an odium upon me for assigning a merit to each person's industry.

Several times I urged to Oglethorpe that the difficulties which seemed thus to threaten in his absence, from the state of the colony and such orders, were impossible for me to surmount. Oglethorpe, at the time of his departure from the colony, wrote sundry letters directed to the respective commanding officers in the southern division and elsewhere within the colony. He acquainted each of them that he had left me in the charge of the whole colony and directed each of them to apply to me for what each person might require for its use and safety.

Very few persons throughout the whole colony could be properly said to support themselves. If support or employ was not provided for the generality to subsist by, the remainder must want or desert. And as such a state of affairs in the colony was well known, my duty to Oglethorpe forbide me to imagine that he did not represent them in such a light before you, but I am led to believe by many of your orders that Your Honors were acquainted that very few of the inhabitants had attempted to cultivate their lands or raise food for their support and that many had met with ill success in the attempt.

31 May 1737. James Smith, one of the millwrights, complained that William Sterling had assaulted and abused him with a great stick without any provocation. I sent for Sterling to answer the complaint. It appeared that Sterling with others of his countrymen were walking up and down Bull Street, while Smith and others with him were sitting on a piece of timber by the water side, that Smith held a stick which he pointed towards Sterling, who came to him directly, asked him what he meant, held up his stick and threatened him, that Smith said he did not fear him for all he was a Scotchman, upon which Sterling beat him and bruised his shoulder. Smith said the pointing his stick was occasioned by his company then being in discourse about gunning and that he said, when he pointed the stick, if that was a gun he could shoot them two men. Sterling said that the night before Smith and others were together while he and some of the Scotch gentlemen were walking in the street, that Smith (as he believed by his voice) said if the Devil was to cast his net what a parcel of Scotchmen he would catch, that he apprehended the pointing the stick was another instance of reproach which he and his countrymen had frequently met with and that it was very hard that they could not walk up and down the streets without being reproached for their country. Both parties were very warm. The complainant, as he was a young lad, well behaved and very industrious, gave me reason to believe what he said was true. I therefore ordered Sterling to appear at the next Court, having first tried all means of reconciliation in vain.

In half an hour after this, one of the millwrights' laborers being drunk at the water side and seeing Mr. Cuthbert and Andrew Grant coming down Bull Street, he shook a hammer which he had in his hand and swore if he could have his will he would knock them Scotch sons of bitches' brains out. Edward Jenkins, overhearing these words, brought him before me, and he appearing to be very drunk, I sent him to the stocks. A great many of the Scotch gentlemen being at my house and appearing very warm, I took this opportunity to represent to them the imprudence of thinking any trifling reproach given to any one of them an injury to the whole body of Scotchmen. Their daily spending their time in walking the streets, drinking at public houses, ingrossing the conversation of all strangers and an imperious manner of behavior I fear has rendered them odious to too many.

9 June. Mr. Wesley intimated to me that I stood accused among the people of several acts of injustice and intending revenge to several people, which by his discourse he seemed to believe. Upon my promise of not mentioning it again to the parties, he told me that he had it from Mr. Bradley, who said had given him instances of short measure and short weights and that because Bradley had made a complaint of me to Mr. Oglethorpe when here I had hindered the building of his house. I told him that he knew very well Mr. Oglethorpe had entered into Bradley's complaints and that his determination was that Mr. Bradley should first make his complaint to me and if I did not redress him that he might make his complaint to the Trustees. I added that Mr. Bradley's large demands on the store without any evident cause had given me sufficient uneasiness, but I defied him to mention anything wherein I had not kept within the bounds of civility. If I was charged with behavior in a sour manner it might be a just charge, because I had had so many unreasonable demands that it was very difficult to distinguish whether I could be justified by the people's necessities or whether I should not stand charged by the Trustees for doing things without their orders. I think I might be allowed, when I know things were without order, to act cautiously and show an unwillingness in the execution. I added that I perceived by this that there were some people endeavoring to raise an ill opinion in him of me and I thought it was as much his business as mine to prevent, that for my part I had ever espoused his character and always discouraged those who lessened it.

11 June. John White, a laborer with the millwrights at Ebenezer who was apprehended last Monday on a violent suspicion of felony (goods being found on him), being brought before me, it appeared that he got in at the window of the hut of William Aglionby and intended to steal several things which he had bundled up in the absence of Aglionby. He had confessed that he had broke open a chest in said hut, which belonged to James Corneck, and took the things which he had bundled up, that he had a shirt on his back when he was taken which belonged also to said Corneck. He was therefore committed and the evidences bound over to prosecute him at next court.

15 June. Mr. Vanderplank complained that he met George Roan drunk in the streets, who had assaulted him and torn his clothes, that John Thomson had encouraged Roan by saying, Are you a freeholder? meaning (as Vanderplank supposed) that freeholders were to do as they pleased and were not to be apprehended. I committed Roan to jail and bound Thomson over to answer the complaint at next court.

17 June. John Desborough's wife complained that in a reckoning with Henry Lloyd, one of the victuallers, for carpenter's work done by her husband and sons, Lloyd had charged 'em 6/9 for 9½ pounds meat. I believed it to be extortion. Lloyd being brought before me, it appeared that Desborough had importuned Lloyd several times to let him have some back and some smoked beef, which he had bought for his own use and was unwilling to sell. As it did not appear that Lloyd made any common practice of selling provisions and that this was at the importunity of the complainant and that the provisions sold was an extravagant kind of food and not necessary, I discharged the warrant, recommending it to the plaintiffs to be more frugal of their money and at the same time cautioned Lloyd not to encourage the people to spend their time in his house in an idle manner.

23 June. Mr. Wesley having lately intimated that Mr. Brown of Highgate had complained that he had lately received short weight and short measure at the store, I therefore wrote to Mr. Brown to give me an account that I might rectify it, upon the receipt of which I examined into the particular charges. As to the soap, my servant at the store proved that he saw Mr. Brown's servant put some in his pocket. My servant also insisted that he gave him full weight. As to the vinegar, it appeared that the cask brought was filled, supposing it held four gallons but in reality it held 4-7½ wine measure, which is the measure that commodity is now bought and issued by. I could see no reason to think these complaints just, but I acquainted Mr. Brown that I was always ready to hear any complaints. I insisted that if he had any complaints of that kind to make they ought to be made first to me.

John Desborough complained that he received molasses at the store and there being some spilt by my servants out of his bag into a puddle of water he saw them take up water and dirt to fill it again. I examined into the matter and found that some of the molasses had been spilt but in a clean place and they did take up what they could of it and put it in the bag again, but when Desborough found fault with it they emptied the whole bag again and filled it with fresh molasses. My servants complained that, notwithstanding they had behaved in this manner to please him, both he and his wife had grossly abused them, called them thieves, cheats and rogues and included me with them. I reprimanded the servants for taking molasses from the ground, which must unavoidably have dirt in it. I acquainted Desborough that if he expected to have any goods from the store he must come for 'em in a quiet manner, as I would not encourage anyone in the store in any crime whatsoever I would never suffer them to be insulted in their duty.

17 July. I went up to Tomochichi's and took him with me to Mr. Matthews. Upon my arrival at Tomochichi's, I saw the man who had been shot. The bullet went in under his jaw near the ear and out at his mouth. Upon the inquiry I found that Tomochichi's Indians had frequently got liquor at Mr. Mackay's plantation, which lies on [the] Carolina side of the river. Daniel Mackay, who was lately a servant to Mr. Patrick Mackay, supplies them with liquor and frequently trades with them and particularly had invited Tomochichi and the Queen to trade and bring their people with them.

The present case was a Savannah and a Nauchee Indian had been at Mackay's and, being in liquor, were wrestling together at Tomochichi's. The Nauchee threw the Savannah down. A brother to the Savannah, seeing him fall, took a bottle of rum out of the Nauchee's hand and throwed it into the river. The Nauchee went away in a sullen humor, seeming to mutter. [He] returned again, took his gun and came near a hut, in which was a woman and a man and shot the man, who was one of the Creeks, with whom I cannot find he had any difference. Tomochichi first intended to have taken satisfaction of the rest of the Nauchees that were settled by him, but, finding the wounded man in a way to recover, he had shook hands and smoked with them.

20 July. Mr. Bradley having sent his servant to me to desire to know if I had any meat for his family, I acquainted him that at present there was little or no salt meat to be got but that I had bought some good dried fish, of which he might have any quantity. He answered that he nor any of his family never was used to any such food. He then added that he must kill a cow or calf to feed his family. I told him I desired whenever he killed any cattle he would let me know what it was he did kill and the weight, because it was necessary there should be an account made of it. I told him I understood by the Trustees' directions that they had limited the provisions for himself and family, that his pay for the cultivation of the land was to come out of the produce, that I was to deliver to him all things that should be necessary for such cultivation. I again urged that whenever he killed any cattle which was put in his care for the Trustees' use, as it was not his own property he ought to let me know, and that I should always think the less I had to do with him the better!

Although I might be well justified to be uneasy under the burden I had long struggled with, I was much more affected by the advices I received that the Spaniards had formed a design and might be daily expected to invade the colony. It is easy to imagine that all the sad state of affairs in the colony before mentioned must naturally appear with a calamitous aspect, the stores being near empty of all necessary support and means of defense and no hopes of any immediate supply. Therefore I was obliged to be at a farther extraordinary expense to supply your magazine whereby in case of attack the inhabitants might not want necessaries of life or ammunition, when it was very probable they must soon be obliged to leave their usual labor and spend their time in military exercises, to guard against a scarcity which very lately had like to have been fatal and would be also such to the expected forces.

Having in all cases executed the trust reposed in me with my endeavors for frugality and regard to the public safety and received repeated approbations as well by Your Honors' orders as by letters from Oglethorpe (wherein the strongest assurances were given that Your Honors would never blame me without first giving me opportunity to justify myself) and not being conscious of any just cause, I am surprised to find myself discharged from all offices, given up to the arbitrary opinion of those who succeed me in my employ and therefore have it in their power to raise merits to themselves by malicious representations of my conduct and proceeded against by them without cause in a manner contrary to all laws, customs and usages of the mother country and contrary to your orders!

Thomas Jones, whom Your Honors appointed to succeed me as keeper of your stores at Savannah, well knew that I had been examined by Oglethorpe, that Oglethorpe had published in the town house to a very great number of people that he knew of no frauds or other criminal matter which I had committed and desired that if such were known by other persons they should declare it. Jones also well knew that no such matter then appeared by any sufficient proof whatever, but, contrariwise, that Oglethorpe had often declared that, although the late expenses for the support of the colony had much surprised Your Honors, he plainly saw that until the military succour with himself arrived such expense was unavoidable.

Soon after Oglethorpe was gone to the southern parts of the colony, Jones gave out in speeches that I had imposed upon the inhabitants by issuing the stores at unreasonable prices and had took such advance to my own benefit, that I was a very great villain and deserved to be hanged, and, the better to support such wicked, false and malicious speeches and render them more fatal to me, Jones nurtured and countenanced any discontented person in any reproachful tale which any of them would relate, promising they should be protected and have satisfaction against me.

Wickedly and maliciously designing to destroy my good name and character as well in this colony as in other places, Jones invented and reported that I was incapable of rendering any just account of my trust, that Jones had prepared indictments against me which would lay me fast, and also artfully and wickedly prevailed with Thomas Christie, the recorder of Savannah, whereupon Christie issued a warrant against me, charging me with a design secretly to depart the colony. I was thereby arrested and obliged to find sureties and be bound in a very large penalty not to depart the colony without Your Honors' license or otherwise to go to jail.

Jones wrote a letter to Oglethorpe at St. Simon's and informed him that I was preparing to abscond and contracted with Captain Stewart, master of the ship *Charles*, for that purpose. In consequence of which information, Oglethorpe wrote to me and acquainted me that he had received such information from Jones and that, although he did not give credit to it, yet he was obliged to give such orders as would prevent the attempt and accordingly ordered a Constable with a sufficient number of assistants to go on board the ship, which then lay at Tybee, and continue on board there till the ship would sail over the bar. Oglethorpe being a short time after at Savannah, I demanded that Jones should give reasons for his information, to which demand Jones answered that it was not proper to name the persons who had given him such accounts. When I insisted that such excuse was not sufficient when injuries of that nature were committed, Jones pretended that my goods were removing by water and mentioned a particular time when in fact Jones well knew that my servants had brought some provisions and necessaries by water from my farm to Savannah for the use of part of my family as were obliged to be in town with me.

Jones gave out in speeches that I should very soon be confined in a more severe manner and should not be suffered to go any more to my farm and procured several actions to be served at my farm upon me at the suit of people to whom I was no ways indebted and thereby brought a prisoner to Savannah and also used his utmost endeavors to procure others by insinuating to everyone who he could find to have any demand on me that everything I had would soon be seized in Your Honors' name, whereby I was very much pressed for payment. Jones daily invents unreasonable and malicious suggestions against me and shows so many and unfair and ensnaring practices as plainly tend to prevent claimants of their past due, ruin the credit of the colony, keep me under terrors and incertainties. I am truly apprehensive that, should it please Almighty God to put a period to my life, I am in danger, after all my known fatigue and faithful service, to leave a widow, an orphan and the fruits of all my labor at the mercy of those who, while living, seeks and pursues my destruction!

[8]

I not only found abundance of lots untouched and many which had little done upon them but (which was yet worse) divers improvements that had been made now going to ruin again, the land overrun with rubbish and seeming to be wholly given up and abandoned.

WILLIAM STEPHENS, 1737

WHEN he was hired by the Trustees of Georgia in 1737, William Stephens (1672–1753) was sixty-five years old, a somewhat down-at-the-heels gentleman who had sold his family estate to pay debts and lost his job as a timber agent. The Trustees hired him to report to them on events and suggest improvements for Georgia. In 1741 he was appointed President of the northern half of the colony, and the following year his authority was extended throughout the province. He served as President and secretary until 1750. When he arrived in Savannah, Stephens found himself in the midst of a hornet's nest of what he called "clamorous malcontents." These extracts are drawn from his *Journal of the Proceedings in Georgia* (London, 1742), I, pp. 7–74.

Tuesday, November 1, 1737. About ten of the clock we arrived at Savannah. Mr. Causton showed me the house he had provided for me, and after dinner I got some goods ashore as well as people. In the evening, upon spending a leisure hour with Messrs. Causton, Christie and Anderson at a public house, Mr. Robert Williams came in to us and at first sight began to lay open his mind pretty freely concerning what difficulties the landowners lay under, as well with respect to the want of Negroes as the tenure of tail male, vehemently exclaiming it was his resolution, as it was also of many others, to leave the colony unless some remedy could be found before they were quite ruined. I endeavored to persuade him into better temper, told him that if he or any others thought themselves aggrieved in anything their wisest course would be to represent it in a decent manner to the Trustees.

Thursday, November 3. I had a long detail of the cause of discord between Mr. Causton and the Parson [John Wesley] ever since Mr. Williamson married Miss Hopkins, niece to Mr. Causton. It was carried now to that height as to engage great part of the town, which was so divided that the partisans on both sides did not stick to throw plenty of scandal against their adversaries.

Friday, November 4. Great part of my time taken up this day in listening to abundance of tales which were obtruded upon me, told in favor of one or the other as they liked or disliked.

Sunday, November 6. Went to church in the forenoon, but I was concerned to see so thin an audience, which proceeded from a grown aversion to the preacher since this public strife sprung up. Several of the Scotch gentlemen having hinted to me their desire of a conference, I sat with three or four of them over a cup of tea towards evening for an hour, when they told me of Mr. Wesley's informing them that Mr. Causton persuaded him to write to the Trustees and acquaint them that the Scotch here were universally a turbulent people who lived idle and continually fomented mischief. It seemed to me that Mr. Wesley had brought it forth now maliciously when he and Mr. Causton were fallen out in order to exasperate the Scotch against him.

Monday, November 7. Took my breakfast with Mr. Wesley and we had some talk about the differences betwixt him and Mr. Causton. The first rise of it was upon young Williamson's marrying Mr. Causton's niece, whom the parson had a liking to for himself and who, whilst she was unmarried, used constantly to receive the sacrament, which is here administered weekly to some few in private. But upon Miss Hopkins's entering into wedlock, she refused to go to him when sent for, probably by direction from her husband, for which reason (or some other unknown to me) Mr. Wesley refused her the sacrament at the next communion.

Tuesday, November 8. Mr. Robert Williams and Mr. Patrick McKay called on me this morning and renewed the discourse we had the first night I came conerning the difficulties they lay under in making further improvements on their lands, telling me they designed to draw up a short memorial of grievances.

In the afternoon I sat awhile with the Magistrates, who were met at Mr. Causton's, them telling me of Mr. Bradley's indecent behavior, his frequent killing of cattle. Before my coming, he had bid upon defiance of the court. On several occasions, Mr. Wesley and he and some others who were closely linked in opposing the Magistrates used to come into the court in a menacing manner, crying out "Liberty!", calling to the people to remember they were Englishmen, &c. Mr. Wesley was generally the principal speaker to harangue the people, though he had no sort of business there. They had been divers times apprehensive of being mobbed and turned off the bench. In this manner was the town divided. The Constables, Tythingmen, &c. were many of them so influenced and led away by these means that often they neglected the due execution of warrants. Tho' it was well known there were abundance of unlicensed tippling houses in all parts of the town where spirits were sold, the Magistrates never could procure one presentment against them, so little regard was paid to their authority. Mr. Christie said plainly he resolved to quit. After two or three hours conference on such topics we parted.

Wednesday, November 16. Mr. Bradley came and sat some time with me in the morning, entertaining me with a long narration of his grievances (almost endless to go through the particulars of). He was subjected to Mr. Causton, who, being jealous of him as of one capable of discerning his dark practices, had therefore set himself against him and not only refused in an arbitrary manner to deliver money and stores to him as he had a right from the Trust to demand but sought all ways possible to ruin him, whereof his late prosecution was a flagrant instance. Some other persons coming to speak with me put an end to our farther conference. I saw plainly that every hour of my time might be so employed if I showed too much inclination that way.

Thursday, November 17. In the evening Mr. Brownfield came and sat with me alone, informing me of most of the transactions here. He professed a neutrality as to all parties, condemning without distinction most of their proceedings. The parson, Mr. Causton, Bradley, &c. he equally censured for violence and passion, but I found him attached more particularly to Messrs. Williams, McKay and that knot who complained so loudly of the tenure of their land and the impossibility they lay under of improvements and found themselves every year falling more and more back, notwithstanding their utmost endeavors, thrift and industry.

Tuesday, November 22. This morning early I went to meet the Magistrates at Mr. Causton's, this being the day to which the court was adjourned. I found them in dispute about putting on their gowns, whether it would be proper at this time or better deferred till matters were more composed. Mr. Parker asked me how well his gown would fit such mean apparel as indeed he had on, and I found the poor man's low circumstances sat heavily on his thoughts. I was surprised a little at Mr. Christie, the Recorder, showing such an indifference to put on his gown. He had executed that office during so many years, for which he had no other recompence than to bear the brunt of all clamor and esteemed among the disaffected no other than Mr. Causton's tool. Mr. Causton replied that it was well known he himself was the butt which all the fury was shot at and that the Recorder had not so much reason to complain on that score. After much time spent in this conference, it was judged most advisable to adjourn the court.

Saturday, December 3. Mr. Wesley went off last night and with him Coates, a Constable, Gough, a Tythingman, and one Campbell, a barber. There scarce could be found men more obnoxious. Coates especially had been a long while one of the principal fomenters of mischief, always taking upon him in court to be an advocate and pleader for any delinquent, going from house to house with idle stories to fill people's heads with jealousies. Add to all this, he had never improved one foot of land since he came to the province or built anything more than a very mean hut.

Gough was also a very idle fellow, pert and impudent in his behavior, always of late kicking against the civil power and making it his business to enflame a sedition. He likewise had little to show of any improvement more than setting up the shell of a house which he never near finished. He went off in many people's debts, leaving a wife and child behind him, who scarcely grieve at his absence since he used to beat them more than feed them.

Campbell was an insignificant loose fellow, and all the visible motive at present to be found for his going off was to escape his creditors.

Tuesday, December 6. After dinner walked out to see what improvements of vines were made by one Mr. Lyon, a Portuguese Jew, which I had heard some talk of, and indeed nothing had given me so much pleasure since my arrival as what I found here, though it was yet only in miniature. For he had cultivated only for two or three years past about half a score of them, which he received from Portugal for an experiment, and by his skill and management in pruning, &c. they all bore this year very plentifully a most beautiful, large grape as big as a man's thumb and bunches exceeding big. From these he has raised more than a hundred, which he has planted all in his little garden behind his house at about four foot distance each in the manner and form of a vineyard. Next year he says he does not doubt raising a thousand more and the year following at least five thousand. From hence I could not but reflect on the small progress that has been made hitherto in propagating vines in the public garden, where it must be owing to the unskillfulness or negligence of those who had undertaken that charge.

Thursday, December 8. In the afternoon I had some conference with Mr. Causton, as it was necessary to break through this stubborn knot of ill-designing people and restore unity as far as possible. It was both our opinions that if the parson had taken a few more with him, provided their creditors did not suffer, the colony would be better without them. But there were yet some few among the discontented whom I could wish to see reconciled, men that made good improvements and such as had formerly been of a peaceable and quiet temper.

Sunday, December 11. Mr. Vanderplank died early this morning and was buried in a soldier-like manner in the evening, about forty men (the number of a ward) under arms attending him to the grave, firing three volleys and several minute guns from the fort discharged during the time of his interment. Now the town wholly destitute of a minister, Mr. Causton read the funeral service.

Tuesday, December 13. In my walk towards evening, upon hearing of some preparations made for a small collation at the old Indian town, which is about a furlong out of town, I went out of curiosity to see what passed. There I found a table spread with a cloth, &c., Mrs. Matthews (formerly Mrs. Musgrove) sitting at the end of it, with two young girls, her husband and Tomochichi near by. A young shoat just ready barbecued over a fire in the wood was set on the table. They asked us very kindly to sit down and take part with them. We who had no stomach to eat did not refuse taking two or three glasses of wine.

Thursday, December 15. The fellow whom I hired to attend my servants proved such a rascal in filling their heads with bad notions of the place and other discouragements that I thought proper to discharge him before he had done more mischief. And it was a sad case too well known that great numbers of newcomers were often so poisoned at first by the venom of ill-designing people to spoil any hopes of good from them.

Sunday, December 18. Nobody to officiate at church now.

Wednesday, December 21. This being Mr. Oglethorpe's birthday, which is celebrated here annually, the Magistrates, military officer and principal inhabitants met at the fort, where, some bottles of wine and some biscuit being prepared, about noon His Majesty's health and the Royal family's were drank under a discharge of thirteen guns, then the Honorable Trustees and next the Captain General of these provinces. In the evening a handsome cold entertainment was provided at a tavern by the subscription of upwards of thirty who (as many as could find them) brought partners to dance, which they did, and were merry.

Friday, December 30. Spent the whole afternoon among the neighboring lots, observing what improvements were made—or I might rather say what a visible neglect was to be observed almost everywhere. I not only found abundance of lots untouched and many which had little done upon them but (which was yet worse) divers improvements that had been made now going to ruin again, the land overrun with rubbish and seeming to be wholly given up and abandoned.

[9]

Was Georgia fine and flourishing, what should drive people away from it? The people who have left are not idle, drunken and indolent. They have found the impossibility of living in this place and withdrew to other colonies where they might enjoy their liberties and properties. The few that remain must quickly follow!

Colonists to the Trustees, 1739

Unhappy colonists in Georgia began sending petitions to the Trustees and Parliament in England, complaining about land laws, the prohibition against slavery and a dictatorship of petty officials. Contemporary copies of these documents are in the Egmont Papers at the University of Georgia.

A Petition to the Trustees

Savannah
December 9, 1738

May it please Your Honors: We whose names are underwritten, being all settlers, freeholders and inhabitants in the province of Georgia and being sensible of the great pains and care exerted by you in endeavoring to settle this colony since it has been under your protection and management, do unanimously join to lay before you, with the utmost regret the following particulars. But in the first place we must beg leave to observe that it has afforded us a great deal of concern and uneasiness that former representations made to you of the same nature have not been thought worthy of due consideration, nor even of an answer. We have most of us settled in this colony in pursuance of the description and recommendation given of it by you in Britain and, from the experience of residing here several years, do find that it is impossible the measures hitherto laid down and pursued for making it a colony can succeed. None of all those who have planted their land have been able to raise sufficient produce to maintain their families in bread-kind only, even though as much application and industry have been exerted to bring it about as could be done by men engaged in an affair on which they believed the welfare of themselves and posterity so much depended and which they imagined must require more than ordinary pains to make succeed. So that by the accumulated expenses every year of provisions, clothing and medicines &c. for themselves, families and servants, several have expended all their money, nay even run considerably in debt, and so been obliged to give off planting and making further improvements. And those who continue are daily exhausting more and more of their money and some daily increasing their debts without a possibility of being reimbursed according to the present constitution.

This being now the general state of the colony, it must be obvious that people can not subsist by their land according to the present Establishment, and this being a truth, resulting from trial, practice and experience, cannot be contradicted by any theoretical scheme or reasoning. The land then, according to the present constitution not being capable to maintain the settlers here, they must unavoidably have access to and depend upon trade. But to our woeful experience likewise the same causes that prevent the first obstruct the latter. For though the situation of this place is exceeding well adapted for trade and if it was encouraged might be much more improved by the inhabitants, yet the difficulties and restrictions which we hitherto have and at present do labor under debar us of that advantage. Timber is the only thing we have here which we might export, and, notwithstanding we are obliged to fell it in planting our land, yet we cannot manufacture it fit for a foreign market but at double the expense of other colonies. As for instance, [the people at] the River of May, which is but twenty miles from us, with allowance of Negroes, load vessels with that commodity at one-half of the price that we can do. And what should induce persons to bring ships here when they can be loaded with one-half of the expense so near us. Therefore the timber on the land is only a continual charge to the possessors of it, though of very great service in all the Northern colonies, where Negroes are allowed and consequently labor cheap. We do not in the least doubt that in time silk and wine may be produced here, especially the former. But since the cultivation of land with white servants only cannot raise provision for our families as before mentioned, therefore it is likewise impossible to carry on these manufactures according to the present constitution.

It is very well known that Carolina can raise everything that this colony can and they, having their labor so much cheaper, will always ruin our market unless we are in some measure on a footing with them. And as both the land is worn out in four or five years and then fit for nothing but pasture, we must be always at a great deal more expense than they in clearing new land for planting. The importation of the necessaries of life come to us at the most extravagant rate, merchants in general, especially of England, not being willing to supply the settlers with goods upon commission because no person here can make them any security of their lands or improvements as is very often practiced in other places to promote trade, when some of the employer's money is laid out in necessary buildings and improvements, fitting for the trade intended without which it cannot be carried on. The benefit of the importation, therefore, is all to transient persons, who do not lay out any money amongst us but on the contrary carry every penny out of the place and the chief reason for their enhancing the price is because they cannot get any goods here either on freight or purchase for another market. If the advantages accruing from importation centered in the inhabitants, the profit thereof would naturally circulate amongst us and be laid out in improvements in the colony.

Your Honors we imagine are not insensible of the numbers that have left this province, not being able to support themselves and families any longer. And those still remaining, who had money of their own and credit with their friends, have laid out most of the former in improvements and lost the latter for doing it on such precarious titles. And upon account of the present Establishment, not above two or three persons except those brought on charity and servants lent by you have come here for the space of two years past, either to settle land or encourage trade. Neither do we hear of any such likely to come until we are on better terms. It is true His Majesty has been graciously pleased to grant a regiment for the defense of this province and our neighboring colony, which indeed will very much assist us in defending ourselves against all enemies but otherwise does not in the least contribute to our support. For all that part of their pay which is expended here is laid out with transient people and our neighbors in Carolina who are capable to supply them with provisions and other necessaries at a moderate price which we, as before observed, are not at all capable to do upon the present Establishment.

This then being our present condition, it is obvious what the consequence must be. But we for our parts have entirely relied on and confided in your good intentions believing you would redress any grievances that should appear and now by our long experience from industry and continual application to improvement of land here do find it impossible to pursue it or even to subsist ourselves any longer, according to the present nature of the constitution and likewise believing you will agree to those measures that are found from experience capable to make this colony succeed and to promote which we have consumed our money, time and labor. We do from a sincere and true regard to the welfare and in duty both to you and ourselves, beg leave to lay before your immediate consideration the two following chief causes of these our present misfortunes and this deplorable state of the colony and which we are certain if granted would be an infallible remedy for both.

1st. The want of a true title or fee simple to our lands, which if granted would both occasion great numbers of new settlers to come amongst us and likewise encourage those who remain here cheerfully to proceed in making further improvements, as well to retrieve their sunk fortunes as to make provision for their posterity.

2d. The want of the use of Negroes with proper limitations, which if granted would both induce great numbers of white people to come here and also render us capable to subsist ourselves by raising provisions upon our lands, until we could make some produce fit for export and in some measure to balance our importation. We are very sensible of the inconveniences and mischiefs that have already and do daily arise from an unlimited use of Negroes, but we are as sensible that these may be prevented by a due limitation, such as so many to each white man or so many to such a quantity of land or in any other manner Your Honors shall think most proper.

By granting us, Gentlemen, these two particulars and such other privileges as His Majesty's most dutiful subjects in America enjoy, you will not only prevent our impending ruin but, we are fully satisfied, also will soon make this the most flourishing colony possessed by His Majesty in America. And your memories will be perpetuated to all future ages, our latest posterity sounding your praises as their first founders, patrons and guardians. But if by denying us those privileges, we ourselves and families are not only ruined, but even our posterity likewise, you will always be mentioned as the cause and authors of all their misfortunes and calamities which we hope will never happen.

From the Inhabitants of Savannah
to the Trustees

Savannah

November 22, 1740

May it please Your Honors: Some time in July last we received intelligence from our friends and relations in England that Your Honors, resolving to take the present state of this colony into serious consideration, had in order to be fully and truly informed of the grievances the people here labor under, sent instructions to your Secretary and the Magistrates here to acquaint the inhabitants that they should write their grievances and complaints and get the seal of this town affixed to them in order to have the same transmitted to the Honorable Board. But to our very good surprise, no mention of anything of that nature was made for four months after we received that advice, when suddenly and without any previous notice on Monday the tenth of November last, at a Court holden on account of the claims of land, Your Honors' Secretary Colonel Stephens did then and there read some paragraphs of a letter from the Honorable Board, as he said,

66

directing the people to set forth their miseries, hardships and difficulties to Your Honors. Then he told us that with great care and pains he had formed an answer to the paragraphs above mentioned and had drawn up the state and condition of the colony justly as he thought. A long paper was then read over to us setting forth the colony in the most advantageous light, enumerating the many useful, fine and curious productions of it, with sundry other matters and things, that we the old settlers here cannot join in. For we cannot call to remembrance ever to have seen a hedge in the country, far less pomegranates growing in them. As to the silk, the wine, the oil, the wheat &c., the small quantities of either of them that has been raised here in the space of eight years too plainly shows that the produce is not so extraordinary as your Secretary would make Your Honors believe. Notwithstanding, eighteen persons, some landholders, some not, swore to the truth of the above-mentioned paper and signed the same in public Court.

We, whose names are under written, who refused to put our hands to any such declaration, modestly told Your Honors' Secretary that we apprehended by the paragraphs he had read the meaning of the Honorable Board was that every person should write their own grievances. He told us no, unless we signed what he had prepared, our own writing would be of no effect, neither should we have the liberty of the seal. Therefore, as we cannot swear to the truth of many particulars in that paper and as we think it does not set forth any of our grievances in a proper manner, we, the poor remnant of the inhabitants of this place, earnestly beg leave once more to address Your Honors and lay before you our yet miserable and lamentable state and condition.

In our representation to Your Honors dated the 9th of December, 1738, we declared the impossibility of living in this country without free titles to our lands and the use of Negroes properly limited. But, to our very great sorrow, Your Honors denied us every article. Many hardships and difficulties have we suffered since that time, still expecting Your Honors would open your ears to our cries and give attention to our just and reasonable complaints. But our grievances still continuing and no redress in view, affliction is daily added to our afflictions and the grounds of our complaining is greatly enlarged. Our continuance here has increased our experience and convinced us more and more of the impossibility of living here in any shape, unless we have the liberty and freedom before mentioned. Could Your Honors see the fruitless industry that most people have used here? Could you see the many tracts of land that have been cleared here with the sweat of the brows of many a poor man, who never was bred to such labor? And all these abandoned, the owners either dead through want of due sustenance and their hard work in the scorching sun or else fled from their plantations at the approach of oppression and poverty. No other arguments would be necessary to convince the Honorable Board that the present establishment can never answer.

Could Your Honors only view this town of Savannah? Could you see the number of lots fenced and the many thousand huts that are built? We are sure you would not say we had been idle but rather industrious. And all those houses was once full of people. Now alas! they are almost desolate and forsaken. Could Your Honors see this with your own eyes? Surely, gentlemen of so benevolent and benign dispositions as you are would not withhold from a number of distressed people as we are what would make us easy, happy and contented. And, we are persuaded, had a true and genuine state of this colony ever been laid before Your Honors by the person or persons employed by you for that purpose, without all doubt our grievances had been removed long 'ere now. But we apprehend fair and specious accounts is all they send Your Honors. They represent the state of the colony quite different from what it really is. The province is shown as in a prosperous condition, when at the same time 'tis evident to every person in this place, to all our adjoining neighbors and even to those very persons who we believe write you these accounts that Georgia is going hourly to destruction.

We therefore entreat Your Honors to give ear to us this once, this last time we ever shall be able to address the Honorable Board unless our requests are complied with. Will Your Honors but credit us, while we write nothing but what is agreeable to reason? Will you believe us, while we write nothing but what is truth? Most of us have been in this colony for seven years past. We have tried all that in us lay to make the province flourish as well as our own families prosper, but to no purpose. We are just now as far from being able to support ourselves by our lands as we was the first year the colony was settled. Proofs of this are plenty. Too many instances, sad instances of fruitless and misspent time and labor, are to be seen throughout this province.

In the township of Savannah, upwards of eighty-three five-acre lots, some wholly, some in part, have been fenced and cultivated. But instead of supporting and maintaining the owners, they runned them in debt and ruined them. The forty-five-acre lots answered no better end, as plainly appears by the annexed affidavits. The people who hold 500-acre tracts are losers, according to the quantity of land cleared and planted by them.

In short, so far has planting been from supporting this colony that we may justly say it never maintained one single person in it. Had not Your Honors' public works employed many of the people, together with the scout boats, the Rangers and other things of that nature, the generality of the inhabitants must have starved. Can we bring any stronger proofs to Your Honors of the decay of the place than to inform you that it is deserted by its inhabitants and forsaken by its people? In the town of Savannah, at this present time, there's seventy-two empty houses and huts, there's not many more inhabited and these very poorly, some of them by Your Honors' Dutch servants. The five-acre lots are grown up with weeds. The forty-five-acre lots are in the same condition. The villages are forsaken. In Hampstead, there's only one family. In Highgate, two. Newington is abandoned. Abercorn has only three families. Tybee is without inhabitants; so is Skidaway; Ogeechee is in the same state. And most of the 500-acre tracts that once was settled are now lying waste and uncultivated. Certain it is that this town for near these twelve months past has been almost wholly supported by the money expended in building the Orphan House, Mr. Whitefield having daily employed at a medium for the above-mentioned space of time, sixty persons, some carpenters, bricklayers, sawyers, plasterers and common laborers, the wages of which people have amounted to near £1500 Sterling. This has kept the few people that remained together who otherwise would have been scattered abroad and none left here by this time but those who have salaries from Your Honors and the Dutch servants you maintain.

Was the province of Georgia so fine and flourishing, as some would make Your Honors believe, what should drive people away from it? Who would be such fools as to leave their houses and plantations in a prosperous and thriving colony and run away into other provinces, where they are strangers, unknown and unacquainted? No man of common sense can be supposed guilty of such folly. The people who have left this are not the idle, the drunken and the lazy and the indolent, as some have informed Your Honors, but many the most industrious. They have found by long experience the impossibility and improbability of living in this place, unless Your Honors approved of our representation; and, when your denial came, they withdrew to other colonies, where they might enjoy their liberties and have properties.

We, the few that remain, must quickly follow them who are gone if Your Honors does not think fit to grant the following (as we think) reasonable articles, which we humbly lay before the Honorable Board, viz.:

1st. A free and ample title to our lands, as the rest of His Majesty's colonies have.

2d. The use of Negroes properly limited.

3rdly. That any person having a right and title to land here shall have liberty to take the same up where he finds it most convenient (the land not being already taken up by another) different lands, suiting different capacities, trades and occupations.

4thly. That we be released from the excessive quitrent of twenty Shillings for the 100 acres of land, none of the neighboring colonies paying one-sixth part so much. And we must inform Your Honors that the qualities of land here is not so extraordinary as some may imagine, for from the best observations of people who have travelled over it from the seacoast five or six hundred miles back, nine-tenths of the country is pine barren, as it is called here, which within land is good for no purpose except for cattle to range on in the summer.

5th. That we may have the liberty of choosing our own Bailiffs yearly. And in case of danger, or any extraordinary affair that may happen whereby the welfare of the colony shall lie at stake, a number of men shall be appointed to assist the Magistrates, that it may not be left to the opinion of one or two men at most, as it is now done. One great misery that has always and does now attend this colony is the Storekeeper and Cashkeeper, at least the cashpayer, being a Magistrate, by which means such person has an opportunity of leading aside most of them who receive salaries from Your Honors and many other people of weak minds, and so is capable of the most illegal acts.

6th. That our Constables and Tythingmen may be under the command of Your Honors and the Magistrates only.

That Your Honors may grant our request and comply with our desires is our earnest and sincere wish. If so, Georgia will yet, we hope, flourish; the town of Savannah that is now deserted, be full of inhabitants; our villages that are now abandoned, quickly be stocked with people; and the whole country have cause to rejoice.

$\lceil 10 \rceil$

I had been so poisoned by the glaring colors in which Oglethorpe had displayed the prospects of Georgia that I was determined to go thither. I then considered myself as one setting out to begin the forming of a new world. Nor could any offer have diverted me from adding one to the number of the foolish Georgia emigrants.

Phillip Thicknesse

Young Phillip Thicknesse came to Georgia in 1736 and became a servant to Thomas Causton, the much-maligned storekeeper at Savannah. He told about his adventures and disappointments in Georgia in his *Memoirs and Anecdotes* (1788), from which this narrative has been adapted.

The truth was that I had been so poisoned by the glaring colors in which Oglethorpe had in his printed books displayed the prospects of his new colony of Georgia that I was determined to go thither and at length prevailed upon my mother to consent to it. This project filled me with infinite delight, for I then considered myself as one setting out to begin the forming of a new world. I felt a delight and a faith not to be removed, nor could at that time any offer, however advantageous in appearance, have diverted me from adding one to the number of the foolish Georgia emigrants.

Upon our arrival in Georgia, I was much surprised to find the town of Savannah, or rather the spot where the town now stands, situated upon a high bluff of barren land and directly opposite to a low swampy island, on the muddy shore of which I could count at least twenty alligators basking thereon! The bluff, upon which the town of Savannah is built, was called by the Indians Yamacraw and Tomo Chachi was King of Yamacraw. Mr. Causton, the chief Magistrate, to whom I had letters, received me civilly.

Tomo Chachi, the Creek Indian King, was not only a very humane man, but I may add he was a very well-bred man. For Mr. Oglethorpe, having signified to Tomo that he wished to build the first city of his colony upon the very spot where Tomo's palace then stood, he found it no difficult matter to prevail upon his majesty to remove his court three miles higher up on the banks of the same river. Nor did I discover any other traces of a cruel or savage disposition in King Tomo than thus moving to oblige Mr. Oglethorpe and stepping in between a criminal and the executioner, saying "Whip me, whip me!" when one of our people was under the lash for ill-treating an Indian woman.

Their rude dress, painted faces, sliced ears, nose bobs! and tattooed skins rendered their external appearance to us Britons singularly savage, but, by making frequent excursions to the court of new Yamacraw and picking up a little of their language, I soon became convinced that my person and property was as safe at the court of Yamacraw as at any court in Christendom, nor could I perceive that King Tomo, Senauke, his queen, or Toonahowi, their nephew and heir, were not as happy as the princes of the most polished courts in Europe. And yet they had not been long returned from visiting the court of Great Britain, where Sir Robert Walpole or the Duke of Newcastle, I forget which, made some difficulty of sitting down in their presence! The King's coach, with the lion and the unicorn supporters, did not incline them to forget their own supporters of bears and buffaloes. Nature, with which they had only been accustomed to converse, surpassed in their imagination all that art could produce!

The first visit I made the court of Yamacraw, their majesties were just returned in their canoes from an oystering party, and I had the honor of partaking with them a *répas* to which they sat down with as good an appetite as ever European princes did to a barrel of pyefleet. The Indians, who dwell within the reach of the salt water creeks, make fires at low water on the islands of oysters, which are then left high and dry, and roast the greatest part of an island at once. It is said, too, that the raccoons and possums visit those islands and slip a dead shell into a living oyster, in order to avail themselves of the next tide to eat what their forecast and sagacity had made thereby come-at-able prey.

Strange as it may appear to us rarified Britons, who have been accustomed from our infancy to admire paintings, buildings, jewels, &c., I am convinced that those Indians at that time were insensible to every kind of our works of art but such as struck their senses with the personal comforts the objects would produce and that King Tomo's blanket, which kept him warm, was in his opinion more valuable than the gold watch given him at St. James's. After cultivating a good acquaintance with those children of nature, I soon became satisfied, whether I met them alone or in company, that I was perfectly safe, and therefore I made frequent excursions into the woods, apprehensive enough of the danger of rattle snakes but without any from the straggling Indians!

In one of my woodland excursions and about four miles from Savannah, I found a fertile piece of ground upon the banks of a rapid creek, which at high water was isolated. This spot so delighted me that with Mr. Causton's permission I built a wooden house thereon and there I passed much of my time. My gun supplied me with squirrels, wild fowl, &c. and the town only with rice to boil by way of bread. The Indians sometimes visited my island for a day or two, and then I had plenty of venison, which they boil'd down and ate dipped in wild honey. This was a true Robinson Crusoe line of life, but it was such as even in those days suited my romantic turn. In this situation I wanted nothing but a female friend, and I had almost determined to take to wife one of Queen Senauke's maids of honor. I seriously paid my addresses to her, and she in return honored me with the appellation of "auche" (friend). She had receiv'd a pair of Indian boots, some paint, a looking glass, a comb, and a pair of scissors as tokens of my love, and one buffalo's skin had certainly held us had not an extraordinary incident arose, which determined me to return immediately to England.

Walking upon the margin of my creek and playing upon the flute, such was the effect of an affectionate and warm imagination that I had a transient but perfect sight of my mother as if she had actually been before me. Strongly possessed with the talk and idleries which children hear and many men cannot overcome, it's no wonder that a boy, as I then was, concluded it was my mother's departed shade! My squaw, my island, and my Robinson Crusoe plan instantly lost all their charms, and, though at that time I had an account of a very useful servant, bound to serve me four years, being on his passage to join me, I determined to leave.

I immediately set out for Savannah and, on my way thither, having my fowling piece reversed at my back, I was most substantially alarmed by a very uncommon rattling at my heels. At that time I had never seen a rattle snake alive, but I instantly suspected what it proved to be. My fright, however, was so great that I drop'd my gun and run hastily to some distance. And when I turned about, I saw the snake winding her tail foremost into a hole in the ground. And though I was exceedingly alarmed, I by degrees ventured to go back for my gun, at a little distance from which I perceived not only the snake which first alarmed me but two others, half of each of their bodies out of their holes. And the sun, which shone in between the trees, rendered their backs as beautiful as their tails were dreadful. I ventured to lay my gun upon the ground and, getting their heads upon a line, I shot them all three. The largest had seven rattles, and the other two had five each. It is said they are three years old before the first rattle appears and that they have an additional rattle every year, as long as they live.

The Indians wear shoes called moccasins. They are of one piece of deer skin gathered up and sewed like a purse at the top with a deer's sinew. They cover their legs and thighs with pieces of leather and leave broad flaps which play to and fro as they walk, at which the rattle snakes generally bite and thereby they avoid the danger. When the Indians are bitten, they tie a leather thong tight above the wound and their wives or children suck forth the poison but not always with success, the limb swells immediately and the patient dies in twenty-four hours.

Mr. John Wesley and I seldom met, but the day I had embarked with a view of returning to England, I was agreeably surprised to find him with me in a small sloop bound to Charles Town in South Carolina, in which I had engaged my passage. He was going to get prayer books printed and I to find a conveyance to England. Our sloop commander proved to be a perfect reprobate mariner and we, fresh water sailors, thought he carried too much sail. I urged him—for it blew hard—to show less canvas, and Mr. Wesley implored him *to swear not at all*! But our prayers prevailed not, more sail and more oaths seemed to be the consequence of our requests. By this time we were out of sight of land, the gale increased, and we run gunwhale under water. If there was no real danger, we apprehended much. I saw no possible chance of saving our lives had the sloop overset. Nothing but a float of alligators, ready to take us on shore, could have preserved us. We got, however, safe on shore at Charles Town the next morning, where Mr. Wesley and I parted in good fellowship.

The colony of Georgia was, at the time I returned to England, still under the management of certain trustees and as I was the first of the emigrants who had returned from thence I was sent for to attend those gentlemen at their office in Old Palace Yard. At that time, Mr. Oglethorpe was just nominated colonel of a regiment to be forthwith raised for the defence of the new colony. And as he had permission to recommend some of his friends to serve in it, he promised me a pair of colors, and I concluded the examination I was to undergo in Old Palace Yard would establish his friendship to me. [But] as I went thither [I] determined to answer openly and candidly to all the questions they put to me. So, when they showed me *upon paper*, forts raised where no ground had been broken and flags flying where no staffs had been erected, I plainly told them the truth. I assured those gentlemen that I had not seen worms sufficient to reel off a single skein of silk. I did not find myself higher in the favor of my colonel! Nay, on the contrary, I soon perceived, if I did not raise my own flag staff by some more friendly hands than his, I might probably be only commissioned to serve in one of those *paper forts* I had seen elevated in Old Palace Yard!

Alarms and Expeditions

ONE of the reasons for the misery of early Georgia was that Oglethorpe could not provide the colonists with both "guns and butter." He was too often treating with Indians in the forests or fighting the Spanish in Florida, while problems were neglected back in Savannah. Oglethorpe had returned to Georgia for the third time in September, 1738, with nearly seven hundred soldiers and a commission as General of the combined forces of Georgia and South Carolina. He discovered for himself the mismanagement of the colony and dismissed several officials, including the storekeeper Thomas Causton, the surveyor Noble Jones and the gardener Joseph Fitzwalter. He faced a mutiny of soldiers at Fort St. Andrew's on Cumberland Island, which he put down, though grazed by a bullet. [Document Eleven] In October, Spain and England declared war.

In the summer of 1739, Oglethorpe made a visit to the Indians who lived in western Georgia and attended a great assembly of Creeks at Coweta Town, near present-day Columbus. He wanted to warn the Indians not to provoke the Spanish to attack, but he also wanted to be sure the Indians would be willing to fight with the English when hostilities finally broke out. Oglethorpe was accompanied by his agent to the Creek Indians, the Scottish-born Patrick Mackay, and his agent for the Cherokees, Lieutenant Thomas Eyre. On their return journey, Oglethorpe heard alarming news. Slaves on plantations along the Stono River in South Carolina had rebelled. Oglethorpe was convinced that slaves in Georgia would become allies of the Spanish in Florida. He also learned that the anticipated war with Spain had begun.

In November, 1739, the Spaniards attacked Amelia Island and killed two Georgians. Oglethorpe collected 900 British troops and 1100 Indians for an attack on the Spanish in Florida. By the end of January, 1740, two small forts, Diego and Moosa, had capitulated, but the great citadel at St. Augustine withstood the Georgians' long siege, which was abandoned in July, 1740. Oglethorpe later claimed that support for the British from other colonies had been slow and inadequate, while the Spanish had been able to resupply their forces. [Document Twelve]

Oglethorpe returned from Florida depressed and sick with a lingering fever. Then, as the great Spanish armada had threatened the shores of England in 1588, so another Spanish armada bore down on nearly defenseless Georgia in 1742. Wracked by dissension and desertion and abandoned by Carolina, Georgia should have been an easy prey and a minor obstacle as the victorious Spanish forces swept on to their real objective, Carolina. As he reported to the Duke of Newcastle, Oglethorpe bravely checked the Spanish invaders at Bloody Marsh in July. This was a small battle in the annals of military conflicts, but it saved Georgia and was Oglethorpe's finest hour. [Document Thirteen]

In March, 1743, Oglethorpe led a second expedition against St. Augustine. The march was grueling, a deserter gave tactical information to the enemy, the Spaniards refused to engage Oglethorpe, the Georgians declared a hollow victory and returned home without dislodging the Spanish. The enthusiasm and naivety of a young soldier named Edward Kimber are evident in his colorful and atmospheric military journal. [Document Fourteen]

A tour of Georgia in 1745 by an anonymous "young gentleman" (could this have been Edward Kimber?) gives a rather dispiriting picture of the province, fatigued by military distractions and waiting for the end of the Trustees' rule, which was due to expire in a few years. We are indebted to him for a detailed description of Frederica soon after its brief period of glory as Oglethorpe's military headquarters. [Document Fifteen]

⌈ 11 ⌉

He fired, the bullet whizzed above my shoulder, and the powder singed my clothes. I closed in with my sword and, seizing his firelock with my left hand, tore it from him, saying, "Wretch, let go your arms, I will not kill you, I'll leave you to the hangman!"

JAMES OGLETHORPE, 1738

WHEN General Oglethorpe returned to Georgia in September, 1738, he found how badly managed the colony had been during his absence. In November he faced a mutiny of unpaid soldiers at Fort St. Andrew's on Cumberland Island. This brief account of the mutiny was sent by Oglethorpe to Harman Verlest, one of the Trustees' secretaries in London. A manuscript copy is in the Egmont Papers at the University of Georgia Library.

I send to you an account of the mutiny at Saint Andrew's. On the 1 November I went up to Saint Andrew's to review the two companies there encamped near the fort. I saw them under arms by daybreak, and after they were dismissed I went up to the fort to breakfast at the commanding officer's barrack. A great number of them without their arms came crowding into the fort and, in a very loud manner, demanded to speak to me. They grew very clamorous and would hardly bear to stay 'till I had done breakfast. As I came out, I immediately suspected from the behavior of the people that there was some bad design on foot and found myself at once in their hands, for they had numbers enough to secure the guard and fort. Upon which, I thought the best way would be to get the crowd out of the fort where all our ammunition and stores were. I walked therefore nimbly out of the gate, the crowd followed me. As soon as I was beyond the barriers I turned short and then began to ask what they were so clamorous for and at the same time whispered an order to the officer of the guard to secure the fort. They made several unreasonable demands. My first answers were very civil, but they grew more exorbitant. At last one said they would have beds in the camp and provisions gratis. I told him to go to his quarters. He said they were cold ones, that they would not be so answered but would have their provisions and cried out, "Now it's your time," one and all. On

77

which I seized him prisoner, and pulled him within the barriers. Another said, "You shall then take us all." Upon which I bade Captain Desbrisay seize him, which he accordingly did. We carried the two prisoners within the gate of the fort and called out to shut the barriers. The mutineers strove to crowd in. Captain [Hugh] Mackay and Mr. [Patrick] Mackay strove to stop them at the barriers, but one of the soldiers whose name was Ross seized Captain Mackay's sword which was broken in the struggle. Having delivered the prisoners to the guard, I went out of the gate to the barriers, and the mutineers, finding they could not force them, ran to the camp, crying out, one and all, "To arms!" I saw a Highlander holding down Ross, and called to him not to hurt him, on which he let him go, and Ross ran to the camp. I then considered whether it was best to stay in the fort and let the mutineers make themselves masters of the camp or go and hinder their assembling. I was sure that all those who came over with me were well affected and yet believed that if the mutineers were once masters of the camp, they might force them to join with them. I therefore thought it was better to take one bold step and go into the midst of the camp at once than suffer the innocent men and their families to fall into the hands of the mutineers.

Whilst I was thinking of this, Captain Desbrisay came up to me from the camp with an account that the mutineers were assembling and that several had their arms loaded before and the rest were loading. I sent to turn out the quarter guard, ordered the Highlanders and boat crews to come up with their arms and ran down with Captain Desbrisay into the camp, hoping that my presence might awe them and prevent mischief. I no sooner turned into one of the streets of the camp but I saw a great many men with their arms, and one just behind the corner of the hut about five yards from me presented his piece at me. I stept back and called to him, "Down with your arms." At which he cried, "No, by God, I'll down with you!" On which I rushed forward. He fired, the bullet whizzed above my shoulder, and the powder singed my clothes. At the same time I heard another shot fired, and the bullet whizzed by me and struck the mutineer. He strove to club his firelock, but, before he made sure of his blow, I closed in with him with my sword and, seizing his firelock with my left hand, tore it from him, saying, "Wretch, let go your arms, I will not kill you, I'll leave you to the hangman!" And did not touch him with my sword. At the same time another presented at me and missed fire. I ran and seized his piece, which he immediately let go, and ran away. I called to the rest who were gathering and, presenting that piece, told them I would shoot them that resisted and would pardon them if they would disperse, which they immediately did. Then turning 'round, I saw several of the officers coming down the street to me, and the mutineer who had fired at me on the ground and a Highlander going to

78

strike with his broadsword. I called to him to hold, which he accordingly did. Captain Desbrisay came up to me with a musket which he had taken away from one of the mutineers who had missed fire at him. Captain Mackay, who was slightly wounded in his hand, also came up with a musket in his hand, which he had fired at the mutineer who had fired at me about the same time. I then walked through all the camp and, calling out to the Sergeants, obliged all the men to keep their quarters and sent an officer down each street to go into their huts and examine their arms, who found twenty-five of them loaded with ball and most of them had been loaded before I reviewed them in the morning.

I went up and ordered the Quarter Guard and the Fort Guard, sending off all those men who were suspected and turned out those under arms whom I was most secure of. I then ordered all the other men to assemble without their arms and spoke to them. I saw amongst them the mutineer whom I had left prisoner in the fort, for the guard at the fort had let the two prisoners go and had told the officer that the men were in the right, for that they were not to starve. I ordered that ringleader to be seized and, having spoke to the soldiers, asked them if they had any grievances? They said they had none but that the King's pay was not sufficient to keep them without provisions and that they had had provisions at Gibraltar as well as pay and that Colonel Cochran had not paid them their sea pay during the time they were at sea. I then reprimanded them for their behavior that day and declared, upon their showing the utmost grief, a pardon for all except the five ringleaders that were prisoners. I that evening spoke one by one to every man in them two companies without any officer present to know if they had any grievances, but they all said, No, their officers treated them well and they had been constantly paid, except their sea pay, concerning which Colonel Cochran had an account to settle with them. I ordered that he should pay the sea pay to each Captain and settle the account, so that the men might be paid to the 13th of the month.

The Indians dance 'round a large fire by the beating of a small drum and six men singing. Their dress is very wild and frightful, their faces painted with several sorts of colors. They paint the hair and stick it full of feathers. They have balls and rattles about their waist.

PATRICK MACKAY, 1739

PATRICK MACKAY (1700–1777) sailed to Georgia with his wife, daughter and brothers Hugh and Charles in 1733, after his father's financial collapse. Oglethorpe appointed him agent to the Creek Indians. In the summer of 1739 Mackay accompanied Oglethorpe on a visit from Frederica to the Indians in western Georgia. In the autumn, he followed Oglethorpe to the gates of St. Augustine on the first of two expeditions against the Spanish in Florida. This unsigned manuscript, attributed to Mackay, is in the Stowe Manuscripts at the British Library and was published in Newton D. Mereness, ed., *Travels in the American Colonies* (New York, 1916), pp. 218–236.

His Excellency General Oglethorpe, making a tour into the Indian Nations to establish peace between them and the English, ordered me to attend him, it being about 400 miles through the woods. *July the 8th* we began our journey and went by water as far as Ebenezer. The General took horse and rode to the Uchee Town, he having sent the boat 'round there, where we arrived *July the 19th. July the 24th* the General set out with about twenty-five persons in company and some Indians, all well armed, it being very necessary so to be. For not long before a party of the Choctaw Indians came down to the General, who gave them presents, and they stayed among the English as friends but did not prove so, for in their return home they met two English and shot three of the others' fingers off. However, he made his escape to a town of the Lower Creeks, who, upon hearing his relation of what the Choctaws had done, immediately armed themselves and went in pursuit of the Choctaws, whom they [found] encamped 'round a fire. The Creeks immediately charged them, killed a great many and took the rest prisoners. The General had also at this time two of the Choctaw Indians with him, who had put themselves under his protection for fear of the people of the Creek Nation who would have killed them for the barbarity of their countrymen to the two English traders.

But now I return to our journey, which we continued, being supplied with venison by the Indian hunters and also wild honey, of which they took plenty. *July 27th* we arrived at Great Ogeechee River, which we swam our horses over, and the packhorseman got his things over in a leather canoe which they carry for that purpose, and at every river where they are to use it they stretch it with stakes made on purpose. *July the 28th*, the things being all got over the river, we set forward, the Indians killing plenty of deer and turkeys for our refreshment, also several buffaloes, of which there is great plenty, and they are very good eating. Though they are a very heavy beast, they will outrun a horse and quite tire him. *July 31st* we travelled over many hills, from which we had a very pleasant prospect of the valleys which abounded with fine green trees and abundance of grapes and other fruits but which were not ripe. From the top of one of these hills, we perceived a great smoke at a distance from us, which we imagined to be at the camp of a party of Spanish horse which were sent out on purpose to hinder us if possible from going to make this treaty of peace with the Indians and which has since been of so great service to us, the friendly Indians annoying the Spaniards very much.

We encamped at Oconee River, where we found a horse belonging to one of the Spaniards. We crossed the river and killed two buffaloes, of which there are abundance, we seeing several herds of sixty or upwards in a herd. We camped at Ocmulgee River where are three mounds raised by the Indians over three of their great kings who were killed in the wars. *August the 6th* we came to Dollus Rivulet where we encamped. In the night came to us Captain Wiggin, Mr. Guddell and two of the chief Indians. Before they came to us, they whooped, which our Indians answered. Then they came to our camp and saluted the General in a very friendly manner, which he returned. *August the 7th* we set forward and on our way we found several strings of cakes and bags of flour, &c. which the Indians had hung up in trees for our refreshment. *August the 8th* we encamped about two miles from the Indian town.

The Indians sent boys and girls out of their town with fowls, venison, pompions, potatoes, watermelons and sundry other things. About 10 o'clock we set forward for the Indian town and were met by the Indian king and some of their chiefs. The king had English colors in his hand. We saluted them, and they returned our salute and, then shaking hands with the General and company, the king very gracefully taking him by the arm led him towards the town. And when we came there, they brought us to logs which they had placed for that purpose covered with bear skins and desired us to sit down. Which when we had done, the head warriors of the Indians brought us black drink in conch shells which they presented to us and, as we were drinking, they kept whooping and hollering as a token of gladness in seeing us. This drink is made of a leaf called by the English cassina (and much resembles the leaf of Bohea tea). It is very plenty in this country. Afterwards we went to the king's house, or rather hut, where we dined.

At night we went to the square to see the Indians dance. They dance 'round a large fire by the beating of a small drum and six men singing. Their dress is very wild and frightful, their faces painted with several sorts of colors, their hair cut short (except three locks, one of which hangs over their forehead like a horse's foretop). They paint the short hair and stick it full of feathers. They have balls and rattles about their waist and several things in their hands. Their dancing is of divers gestures and turnings of their bodies in a great many frightful postures. The women are mostly naked to the waist, wearing only one short petticoat, which reaches from their waist a little below their knees. They are very nice in smoothing and putting up their hair. It is so very long, when untied, that it reaches to the calves of their legs.

Their houses or huts are built with stakes and plastered with clay mixed with moss, which makes them very warm and tight. They dress their meat in large pans made of earth and not much unlike our beehives in England. They do not make use of mills to grind their corn in but in lieu thereof use a mortar made out of the stock of a tree which they cut and burn hollow and then pound their their corn therein. And when it's pounded sufficiently they separate the husks from the meal by sifting it through a sieve made of reeds or canes. The chief business of the women is planting corn and other things and minding the business of the house. The men hunt and kill deer, turkeys, geese, buffaloes, tigers, bears, panthers, wolves and several other beasts whose skins they sell to the traders for powder, ball and what other necessaries they want.

August the 12th we set out from this town, which belonged to the Cowetas, to go to a town of the Cussetaws. As we drew near the town, the king came with English colors in his hand attended by his chief men. We saluted them, and they returned the salute. The king and his chief men conducted the General to their square, where he dined, and after dinner the General went to Captain Wiggins's house, where he lay that night. *August the 17th* the Indians went into the square to dance and some of the English danced with them, which pleased them very well. *August the 21st* His Excellency General Oglethorpe went to the square to give the Indians the presents he had caused to be brought for them and to establish that peace with them which has since been so beneficial to the English. He also settled the trade between the Indians and the traders. *August the 25th* the General set out from the Indian Nations on his way home.

September 12th the General arrived at Fort Augusta. The fort saluted the General with nine guns. The General stayed at the Captain of the fort's house. *September 6th* several of the Cherokee Indians came to the General, who received them with all tenderness. *September 8th* the General went to Carolina Fort, which saluted him with fifteen guns. At night came down the Cherokee Indians and saluted the fort, which returned them nine guns. *September 10th* the Cherokees came to settle a peace with the General. *September the 13th*, this day arrived advices to the General of a declaration of war with Spain. At noon the General gave the Cherokee Indians their presents. They took their leave of him and returned very well satisfied. *September 16th* the General set out from Fort Augusta and about seven or eight miles from thence we stopped at a fort belonging to Carolina, which saluted the General with fifteen guns. The General stayed and dined there. This fort is situate[d] on a hill and commands two rivers. Near the fort are about one hundred houses.

September 17th we set out from this fort and, as we were going down the river, we met a trading boat going to Fort Augusta. The people on board her told us the Negroes in Carolina had raised up in arms and killed about forty white people. We went to the Uchee Town and from thence to Fort Prince George, where we found thirty men come from Purysburg to strengthen the fort. *September 20th* a Negro came to the General and told him that what was said of the Negroes rising in Carolina was true and that they had marched to Stono Bridge, where they had murdered two storekeepers, cut their heads off and set them on the stairs, robbed the stores of what they wanted and went on killing what men, women and children they met, burning of houses and committing other outrages and that one hundred planters who had assembled themselves together pursued them and found them in an open field, where they were dancing, being most of them drunk with the liquors they found in the stores. As soon as they saw their masters, they all made off as fast as they could to a thicket of woods, excepting one Negro fellow who came up to his master. His master asked him if he wanted to kill him. The Negro answered he did, at the same time snapping a pistol at him but it missed fire and his master shot him through the head. About fifty of these villains attempted to go home but were taken by the planters who cut off their heads and set them up at every mile post they came to.

September 23rd the General set out for Savannah and arrived *the 24th*. *October 5th* Tomochichi Mico or King of Yamacraw died, greatly lamented by all his people. *October 6th* he was buried in the square facing the church at Savannah. *November 5th* the General set out for Frederica and arrived *the 8th*. Thus ended our profitable voyage to the Indian Nations, which has been attended with the success desired, the friendly Indians annoying the Spaniards very much.

After our arrival at Frederica on the *14th of November*, advices came to the

General that the Spaniards had been upon the Island of Amelia and had killed two of the Trustees' servants and cut off their heads but was so terrified for fear of the English coming upon them that they ran away, leaving a hatchet and knife behind them. *November 17th* His Excellency General Oglethorpe, being designed for the Island of Amelia, ordered me to attend him, which I accordingly did. We arrived at Amelia about 11 at night. Early next morning, the General gave orders to surround the island by water, and he himself would march through the body of the island with the men divided into small parties which he according did and continued so doing till night but could discover nothing but their tracks and one of their war sticks which they had dropped in haste. About 10 at night the General set out for Frederica and, having a fine gale of wind, arrived at 6 next morning *November 23rd*.

Helaspelle and Toonahowi, nephew to Tomochichi aforementioned, with several other Indians set out for St. Augustine, vowing to have revenge for the two men killed on Amelia. *November 27th* the Spaniards came a second time on the Island of Amelia and fired at the very sentinels. The friendly Indians were then there, but they were so numerous the Indians durst not attack them.

December the 3rd His Excellency General Oglethorpe set out for the Spanish lookout to observe the motions of the Spaniards and see what preparations they were making, taking a body of 200 men with him. But they discovered us before they could land and fled to Augustine, leaving us the house built for a lookout. We marched along the beach and came within twenty-five miles of the town of St. Augustine, where we discovered a party of Don Pedro's horse with some Indians and Negroes, but as soon as they saw us they made the utmost speed to the town of St. Augustine and our Indians pursued them till they came to Diego Fort. In the pursuit they killed one Negro as he was going into Diego Fort and brought his scalp to the General, who rewarded them very well. Afterwards we went to Frederica, where we remained till the *1st January* [when] the General set out with a body of 180 men.

We arrived at Talbot Island *January 3rd* and went from thence to Saint George's, from whence we saw a sloop off of the Spanish lookout on Saint Juan's Beach. The General endeavored to get to her in his cutter, but the wind blew so fresh it obliged us to return back. The General went to the Spanish lookout and set me and two more on shore there with orders to make a fire, that the sloop might see the mouth of the river. Soon after the General came and took us with him to Saint George's. *January 5th* the sloop came over Saint Juan's Bar and anchored in the river and the Captain came ashore and offered his service to the General to assist him taking the two forts up the river, which the General accepted of. *January the 6th* the sloop and boats came to sail, having a fair wind, and went up the River Saint Juan about 4 in the afternoon.

We landed on a point of land distant about five miles from the fort San Francisco de Pupo. The Indians went out on discovery but could see nobody, so we set forward again and came to an anchor close under a point of land near the two forts. Here we landed the Indians on the south side of the river to waylay the path to St. Augustine and to bring intelligence of what discoveries they should make. Here we lay all night. Early next morning the General went in his boat to see if he could meet with any of our Indians. He soon met with one of them who told him all was quiet and that we were not discovered and that his comrades had waylaid the path to St. Augustine. Hereupon the General returned to the sloop and boats and ordered them to weigh their anchors and stand for the forts, which they did, and on our way we met some of our Indians in a canoe who told us the Spaniards at Picolata Fort had discovered us and were fled and our Indians had set fire to their fort. The Spaniards at San Francisco de Pupo seeing some of our Indians took them for Spanish Indians and manned a launch in order to fetch them over and when they had got about halfway over the river they discovered our boats and returned for their fort in greater haste than they set out. The General ordered the men and cannon to be landed under shelter of a point of woods which was within a mile of the fort.

As soon as we had landed, we marched in the woods till we came within musket shot of the fort, where we raised a battery for our cannon, in the meantime keeping them employed with our small arms. The firing continued very hot on both sides till such time we had finished our battery from which we began to play upon the fort. The fire from the fort seeming to abate, the General sent a drum to summon them to surrender the fort to the English, which, if they did, they should have good quarters. Their answer was, "Take us if you can!" Whereupon our cannon began to play a second time upon the fort very briskly and every shot taking place soon obliged them to alter their tone and cry for quarters, which upon their surrendering up the fort was immediately granted. In this fort was one Sergeant and a command of ten men with one Indian, seven pieces of cannon, ammunition, provision and several other stores.

January the 8th the General gave orders for repairing this fort, raising parapets and pallisading it all 'round. We also mounted three more cannon besides the seven pieces which were in the fort before, also leaving a detachment of fifty men with ammunition and provision. *January 9th* the General ordered a detachment of thirty men of the regiment and a party of Indians to go on the other side of the river and see if they could discover any Spaniards. They accordingly went and discovered a party of Spanish horse being about twenty or thirty in number who as soon as they saw the English approach fled. Our Indians pursued but could not come up with any of them. *January 11th* the General set out for Saint Simon's Island and on his passage rec[eiv]ed advice that His Majesty's ship the *Flamborough* was arrived in Jekyll Sound and that seven more ships of war were on their passage to assist at the Siege of St. Augustine. *January the 17th* the General arrived at Saint Simon's and *the 19th* got to Frederica. *January the 28th* came a boat from San Francisco de Pupo with advice that a detachment of the regiment had taken three Spaniards with letters from Saint Mark's to St. Augustine.

May the 3rd the General set out for the siege of St. Augustine with a body of 600 men, also giving me orders to attend him. We [had] also 150 Indians of different Nations, the main body of them being to follow us as soon as possible with provisions and other stores. *May the 8th* at night we landed at the Spanish lookout on the Florida side of Saint Juan's River. Here we lay very quiet till about 4 o'clock the next morning. Then we sent out a party of about fifty Indians on the scout who returned at night with a Spanish Negro who they had taken prisoner. They also pursued six other Spaniards as far as the fort, from which the Spaniards fired several cannon shot at them but did no execution. This day arrived two sloops and four schooners from Charles Town with provisions and men for the siege. *May the 10th*, the men being landed, we proceeded in order to attack a fort about twenty-three miles distance from St. Augustine. *May the 11th* we came within shot of the Fort Diego which began to fire at us but did us no hurt. *May 12th* we attacked the fort with a very hot fire on the south side. They also continued a brisk fire of their cannon at us. About 12 o'clock we summoned the garrison to surrender the fort and they should have good quarters. To which they consented and delivered the fort up, in which we found thirteen pieces of cannon with small arms, ammunition and provisions, also a garrison of forty-eight men, likewise horses and abundance of cattle, which we drove up and killed for the use of the army. The Indians also took one of Don Pedro's horsemen who was going express to St. Augustine. The English and Indians so harrassed the Spaniards that they were afraid to appear without the walls of St. Augustine. *May the 13th* we marched to Saint Juan's River where we found Colonel Vanderdusen and part of the Carolina regiment, also Lieutenant Colonel Cook from Saint Simon's. *May the 18th* the General came from Diego. He had marched within two miles of St. Augustine, where were a party of Spaniards, being about 400 men and a troop of horse, drawn up in a line just before the town. But when they discovered the English they immediately fled into the town, leaving several horses which we took. *June the 5th* the General went with a body of 800 men along the sea beach to see if the Spaniards would venture out and hazard a battle. He marched as far as Moosa, a small fort about two and one-half mile distant from St. Augustine, and found it deserted by the Spaniards, who on their discovering our troops fled to St. Augustine. We displayed six stand of English colors on the ramparts to try if we could provoke the Spaniards to come out and give us battle, but all would not do, so we set fire to the fort and returned to Diego, struck the tents and put them on board the vessels in order to go to St. Augustine Bar.

June the 11th came up with the men of war who lay off the Bar of St. Augustine to assist at the siege. *June the 12th* the General landed on the island of Saint Eustasia over against the Castle of St. Augustine [and] the captains of the men of war landed 400 men at the same time, a party of our Indians came up with a party of Spanish horsemen and killed four. *June 13th* Captain Warren went on board a large schooner to go over Augustine Bar and ordered the *Falcon* sloop and another sloop to follow him. When they came to the bar, there was not water enough for the schooner to go over, so he was obliged to stay till next morning. But the *Falcon* sloop got in over the bar that night. The same day we took a fort near the castle and hoisted our colors there. *June 14th* the schooner got over the bar and anchored under the side of a hill within a mile of the castle, from whence they fired very smartly at us but none of their balls took place. The next day I went on shore on the Island of Saint Eustasia, where I was taken sick and continued so during the whole time of the siege afterwards, and, at the breaking up of the siege, was sent sick to Frederica. Thus far and to this time I was constantly with His Excellency General Oglethorpe, being in most or all the places of action till the day of my being taken sick.

$\begin{bmatrix} 13 \end{bmatrix}$

The Spaniards, after an obstinate engagement of four hours, passed all our batteries and got out of shot of them towards Frederica. I advanced with a party of Indian rangers and the Highland Company, resolved to engage them in the woods before they could get out and form in the open grounds.

JAMES OGLETHORPE, 1742

IN THE SUMMER of 1742 the Spanish in Florida massed an invasion of Georgia. Wracked by dissension and desertion, Georgia should have been an easy prey and a minor obstacle as the victorious Spanish forces swept on to their real objective, Carolina. But, as he reported to the Duke of Newcastle on July 30, 1742, Oglethorpe led his forces to victory, repulsing the enemy at Bloody Marsh. The source of this letter is Allen D. Candler, *Colonial Records of the State of Georgia, XXXVI*, typescript, 1937, pp. 31–43.

JAMES OGLETHORPE TO THE DUKE OF NEWCASTLE

Frederica

July 30, 1742

The Spanish invasion which has a long time threatened the colony of Carolina and all North America has at last fallen upon us and God hath been our deliverance. General Hozcasilas, Governour of the Havanna, ordered those troops who had been employed against General Wentworth to embark with artillery and everything necessary upon a secret expedition. They sailed with a great fleet. Amongst them were two half-galleys carrying 120 men each and an 18-pound gun. They drew but five feet water, which satisfied me they were for this place. By good great fortune one of the half-galleys was wrecked coming out. The fleet sailed for St. Augustine in Florida. Captain Hamer the latter end of May called here for intelligence. I acquainted him that the succors were expected and sent him a Spanish pilot to show him where to meet with them. He met with ten sail which had been divided from the fleet by storm but, having lost eighteen men in action against them, instead of coming here for the defense of this place, he stood again for Charles Town to repair. And I, having certain advices of the arrival of the Spanish fleet at Augustine, wrote to the commander of His Majesty's ships at Charles Town to come to our assistance.

I sent Lieutenant Maxwell who arrived there and delivered the letters the 12th of June and afterwards Lieutenant Mackay, who arrived and delivered letters on the 20th of June.

Lieutenant Colonel Cook, who was then at Charles Town and was Engineer, hastened to England and his son-in-law Ensign Eyre, Sub-Engineer, was also in Charles Town and did not arrive here 'till the action was over, so for want of help I myself was obliged to do the duty of Engineer.

The Havanna fleet, being joined by that of Florida, composed fifty-one sail with land men on board, a list of whom is annexed. They were separated and I received advice from Captain Dunbar, who lay at Fort William with the guard schooner of fourteen guns and ninety men, that a Spanish fleet of fourteen sail had attempted to come in there, but, being drove out by the cannon of the fort and schooner, they came in at Cumberland Sound. I sent over Captain Horton to land the Indians and troops on Cumberland. I followed myself and was attacked in the sound by fourteen sail but with two boats fought my way through. Lieutenant Tolson, who was to have supported me with the third and strongest boat, quitted me in the fight and run into a river where he hid himself 'till next day when he returned to Saint Simon's with an account that I was lost, but soon after found I was arrived there before him, for which misbehavior I put him in arrest and ordered him to be tried. The enemy in this action suffered so much that the day after they ran out to sea and returned for St. Augustine and did not join their great fleet 'till after their grenadiers were beat by land.

I drew the garrison from Saint Andrew's, reinforced Fort William and returned to Saint Simon's with the schooner.

Another Spanish fleet appeared the 28th off the bar. By God's blessing upon several measures taken I delayed their coming in 'till the 5th of July. I raised another troop of Rangers which with the other were of great service.

I took Captain Thomson's ship into the service for defense of the harbor. I embargoed all the vessels, taking their men for the service and gave large gifts and promises to the Indians, so that every day we increased in numbers. I gave large rewards to men who distinguished themselves upon any service, freed the servants, brought down the Highland Company and Company of Boatmen, fitted up as far as we had guns. All the vessels being thus prepared on the 5th of July, with a leading gale and spring tide, thirty-six sail of Spanish vessels run into the harbor in line of battle.

We cannonaded them very hotly from the shipping and batteries. They twice attempted to board Captain Thomson but were repulsed. They also attempted to board the schooner but were repulsed by Captain Dunbar with a detachment of the regiment on board.

I was with the Indian Rangers and batteries and sometimes on board the ship and left Major Heron with the regiment.

It being impossible for me to do my duty as General and be constantly with the regiment, therefore it was absolutely necessary for His Majesty's service to have a Lieutenant Colonel present, which I was fully convinced of by this day's experience. I therefore appointed Major Heron to be Lieutenant Colonel and hope that Your Grace will move His Majesty to be pleased to approve the same.

The Spaniards after an obstinate engagement of four hours in which they lost abundance of men passed all our batteries and shipping and got out of shot of them towards Frederica. Our guard sloop was disabled and sunk, one of our batteries blown up and also some of our men on board Captain Thomson, upon which I called a council of war at the head of the regiment, where it was unanimously resolved to march to Frederica to get there before the enemy and defend that place, to destroy all the provisions, vessels, artillery &c. at Saint Simon's that they might not fall into the enemy's hands.

This was accordingly executed, having first drawn all the men on shore which before had defended the shipping. I myself stayed 'till the last, and, the wind coming fortunately about, I got Captain Thomson's ship, our guard schooner and our prize sloop to sea and sent them to Charles Town. This I did in the face and spite of thirty-six sail of the enemy. As for the rest of the vessels, I could not save them, therefore was obliged to destroy them.

I must recommend to His Majesty the merchants who are sufferers thereby, since their loss was in great measure the preserving the province. We arrived at Frederica and the enemy landed at Saint Simon's.

On the 7th a party of theirs marched towards the town. Our Rangers discovered them and brought an account of their march, on which I advanced with a party of Indian Rangers and the Highland Company, ordering the regiment to follow, being resolved to engage them in the defiles of the woods before they could get out and form in the open grounds. I charged them at the head of our Indians, Highland men and Rangers, and God was pleased to give us such success that we entirely routed the first party, took one Captain prisoner and killed another and pursued them two miles to an open meadow or savannah, upon the edge of which I posted three platoons of the regiment and the company of Highland foot so as to be covered by the woods from the enemy, who were obliged to pass through the meadow under our fire. This disposition was very fortunate. Captain Antonio Barba and two other Captains with 100 grenadiers and 200 foot, besides Indians and Negroes, advanced from the Spanish camp into the savannah with huzzahs and fired with great spirit but, not seeing our men by reason of the woods, none of their shot took place but ours did.

Some platoons of ours in the heat of the fight, the air being darkened with the smoke and a shower of rain falling, retired in disorder.

I, hearing the firing, rode towards it and at near two miles from the place of action met a great many men in disorder who told me that ours were routed and Lieutenant Sutherland killed. I ordered them to halt and march back against the enemy, which orders Captain Demere and Ensign Gibbon obeyed, but another officer did not but made the best of his way to town. As I heard the fire continue, I concluded our men could not be quite beaten and that my immediate assistance might preserve them, therefore spurred on and arrived just as the fire was done. I found the Spaniards entirely routed by one platoon of the regiment under command of Lieutenant Sutherland and the Highland Company under the command of Lieutenant Charles Mackay.

An officer whom the prisoners said was Captain Don Antonio Barba was taken prisoner but desperately wounded. Two others were prisoners and a great many dead upon the spot. Lieutenant Sutherland, Lieutenant Charles Mackay and Sergeant Stuart having distinguished themselves upon this occasion, I appointed Lieutenant Sutherland Brigade Major and Sergeant Stuart Second Ensign.

Captain Demere and Ensign Gibbon being arrived with the men they had rallied, Lieutenant Cadogan with an advanced party of the regiment, and soon after the whole regiment, Indians and Rangers, I marched down to a causeway over a marsh very near the Spanish camp, over which all were obliged to pass and thereby stopped those who had been dispersed in the fight in the savannah from getting to the Spanish camp. Having passed the night there, the Indian scouts in the morning advanced to the Spanish camp and discovered they were all retired into the ruins of the fort and were making entrenchments under shelter of the cannon of the ships. That they guessed them to be above 4000 men. I thought it imprudent to attack them defended by cannon with so small a number, but marched back to Frederica to refresh the soldiers and sent out parties of Indians and Rangers to harass the enemy. I also ordered into arrest the officers who commanded the platoons that retired.

I appointed a general staff: Lieutenant Hugh Mackay and Lieutenant Maxwell, aides de camp, and Lieutenant Sutherland, Brigade Major. On the 11th of July the great galley and two little ones came up the river towards the town. We fired at them with the few guns we had so warmly that they retired, and I followed them with our boats 'till they got under the cannon of their ships which lay in the sound.

Having intelligence from the Spanish camp that they had lost four captains and upwards of 200 men in the last action, besides a great many killed in the sea fight and several killed in the night by the Indians even within or near the camp and that they had held a council of war in which there were great divisions, insomuch that the forces of Cuba separated from those of Augustine and the Italick Regiment of Dragoons separated from them both at a distance from the rest near the woods and that there was a general terror amongst them. Upon which I was resolved to beat up their quarters in the night and, marching down with the largest body of men I could make, I halted within a mile and a half of their camp to form, intending to leave the troops there 'till I had well reconnoitered the enemy's disposition.

A Frenchman who without my knowledge was come down amongst the volunteers, fired his gun and deserted, our Indians in vain pursued and could not take him. Upon this concluding we were discovered. I divided the drums in different parts and beat the grenadiers' march for about half an hour, then ceased and we marched back with silence.

The next day I prevailed with a prisoner and gave him a sum of money to carry a letter privately and deliver it to that Frenchman who had deserted. This letter was wrote in French as if from a friend of his, telling him he had received the money, that he should strive to make the Spaniards believe the English were weak, that he should undertake to pilot up their boats and galleys and then bring them under the woods where he knew the hidden batteries were, that if he could bring that about he should have double the reward he had already received, that the French deserters should have all that had been promised to them. The Spanish prisoner got into their camp and was immediately carried before their General Don Manuel de Montiano. He was asked how he escaped and whether he had any letters but, denying his having any, was strictly searched and the letter found and he upon being pardoned confessed that he had received money to deliver it to the Frenchman for the letter was not directed. The Frenchman denied his knowing anything of the contents of the letter or having received any money or correspondence with me, notwithstanding which a council of war was held and they deemed the Frenchman to be a double spy. But General Montiano would not suffer him to be executed, having been employed by him. However they embarked all their troops and halted under Jekyll. They also confined all the French on board and embarked with such precipitation that they left behind them cannon &c. and those dead of their wounds unburied. The Cuba squadron stood out to sea to number of 20 sail. General Montiano with the Augustine squadron returned to Cumberland Sound having burnt Captain Horton's houses &c. on Jekyll. I with our boats followed him. I discovered a great many sail under Fort Saint Andrew's, of which eight appeared plain; but being too strong for me to attack I sent the scout boats back.

I went with my own cutter and landed a man on Cumberland, who carried a letter from me to Lieutenant Stuart at Fort William with orders to defend himself to the last extremity.

Having discovered our boats and believing we had landed Indians in the night, they set sail with great haste insomuch that, not having time to embark, they killed forty horses which they had taken there and burnt the houses. The galleys and small craft to the number of fifteen went through the inland water passage. They attempted to land near Fort William but were repulsed by the Rangers. They then attacked it with cannon and small arms from the water for three hours, but the place was so bravely defended by Lieutenant Alexander Stuart that they were repulsed and ran out to sea where twelve other sail of Spanish vessels had lain at anchor without the bar during the attack without stirring. But the galleys being chased out, they hoisted all the sails they could and stood to the southward. I followed them with the boats to Fort William and from thence sent out the Rangers and some boats who followed them to Saint John's, but they went off rowing and sailing to St. Augustine.

After the news of their defeat in the grenadier savannah arrived at Charles Town, the men of war and a number of Carolina people, raised in a hurry, set out and came off this bar, after the Spaniards had been chased quite out of this colony, where they dismissed the Carolina vessels and Captain Hardy promised in his letters to cruise off St. Augustine.

We have returned thanks to God for our deliverance, have set all the hands I possibly could to work upon the fortifications and have sent to the Northward to raise men ready to form another battalion against His Majesty's orders shall arrive for that purpose. I have retained Thomson's ship, have sent for cannon, shot &c., for provisions and all kinds of stores, since I expect the enemy who, though greatly terrified, lost but few men in comparison of their great numbers, as soon as they have recovered their fright, will attack us with more caution and better discipline.

I hope His Majesty will approve the measures I have taken and I must entreat Your Grace to lay my humble request before His Majesty that he would be graciously pleased to order troops, artillery and other necessaries sufficient for the defense of this frontier and the neighboring provinces or give such directions as His Majesty shall think proper and I do not doubt but with a moderate support not only to be able to defend these provinces but also to dislodge the enemy from St. Augustine if I have but the same numbers they had in this expedition.

⌈ 14 ⌉

The Cowhati Indians return'd, bringing with them five scalps, one hand which was cut off with the glove on, several arms, clothes and two or three spades. We heard them long before they came in sight by the melancholy notes of their warlike death-houp.

EDWARD KIMBER, 1743

EDWARD KIMBER, who was a volunteer in Oglethorpe's fruitless second expedition against the Spaniards in March, 1743, wrote his account under the pseudonym of G. L. Campbell. This narrative has been extracted from his *Relation of a Late Expedition to the Gates of St. Augustine on Florida* (London, 1744).

General Oglethorpe, after the brave defeat of the formidable invasion of Georgia by the Spaniards in July, 1742, receiv'd repeated advices of their preparations for another and more powerful attempt on that colony. To divert the hopes of the Spaniards to make a conquest, to show them that he was as undaunted at the head of his handful of men as they could be with their thousands, to pen them up within the walls of their castle was His Excellency's laudable design in undertaking the incursion of March, 1743, which with unheard-of boldness he penetrated fifty miles into the enemy's country, encamp'd under the very walls of the castle of Augustine without their daring to show themselves.

On *Saturday, February 26, 1743*, the detachment of the regiment appear'd under arms at Frederica. Their arms and ammunition were examined, and everyone receiv'd his complement of cartages and was order'd to provide himself with a haversack and water bottle for the march. Afterwards they march'd out of the town, and each platoon fir'd at a mark before His Excellency for the prize of a hat and matchet to the man who made the best shot at an hundred yards distance. He afterwards gave beer to the soldiers and order'd the whole to be ready to proceed by nine the next morning.

Sunday, February 27. The whole detachment, rangers, &c. embark'd on board the guard schooner and the two hir'd schooners at ten in the morning. At two, weigh'd and fell down below the point-guard, saluting the town with twenty-one guns.

Tuesday, March 8. This morning the wind blowing very hard, we hous'd our guns and lash'd our two nine-pounders to the mast, putting our swivels into the hold. We got down our fore-topsail, cross-jack and crotchet-yards and made everything ready lest we should be blown out to sea. Soldiers of this regiment are as good sailors as there are to be met with. Join'd to the qualities of the good soldier and able sailor, they are also expert fishers and most excellent huntsmen, characters of great importance and absolutely necessary in this country.

On *Wednesday, March 9*, at two in the afternoon, we landed at St. Mathia's on Florida and, after being review'd and after the General's making a speech, His Excellency order'd some barrels of beer to be given to the soldiers. We took up our quarters in a sand hill overgrown with palmettos in a savannah. At one end of this savannah, the General fix'd his headquarters, his tent by day being a kind of alcove that some shrubs had form'd on each side and his retreat by night a palmetto hut, his servants building themselves shades of boughs, &c. on each side of him. The men built themselves small huts, divided themselves into separate messes and with the utmost decorum enter'd into all the economy of families. Every officer had a hut. Their provisions consisted of rice, beef, flour and molasses, which were deliver'd for two or three days at a time from on board the store-schooner.

Friday, March 11. The drums beat to arms at nine and we remain'd in that posture till twelve at noon, expecting immediately to march but had then orders to retire to our huts. The General's policy was very observable in the frequent alarms his people receive and the frequent motions he obliges them to make, knowing very well that the rust of inactivity and idleness too soon corrupts the minds and enervates the body of the soldier. To this are perhaps owing the many different fatigues his regiment goes thro' in Georgia which he is always promoting, as clearing roads, draining swamps, marshes, &c.

At four o'clock, the Cowhati Indians who went to Augustine return'd, bringing with them five scalps, one hand which was cut off with the glove on, several arms, clothes and two or three spades, which they had the boldness to bring away after having attack'd a boat with upwards of forty men in it under the very walls of the castle, killing about twenty of them and oversetting the rest. We heard them long before they came in sight by the melancholy notes of their warlike death-houp.

As to their figure, 'tis generally of the largest size, well proportion'd and robust. Their color is a swarthy, copper hue, their hair generally black and shaven or pluck'd off by the roots all 'round their foreheads and temples. They paint their faces and bodies with black, red or other colors in a truly diabolic manner.

Their dress is a skin of blanket tied or loosely cast over their shoulders, a shirt which they never wash and which is consequently greasy and black to the last degree, a flap before and behind to cover their privities hanging by a girdle, boots about their legs and what they call morgissons or pumps of deer or buffalo skin upon their feet. Their arms and ammunition, a common trading gun, a pouch with shot and powder, a tomahawk by their side, a scalping knife, pistol, &c. They hunt for their provision and, when boiled or barbecu'd, tear it to pieces promiscuously with their fists and devour it with remarkable greediness.

Imagine to yourself a body of sixty or seventy of these creatures marching in rank and file, with the mournful howls and cries and every now and then popping their pieces off. His Excellency was seated to receive them on a buffalo's skin surrounded by his officers. He shook them by hand, welcom'd them home in the Indian tongue and thank'd them for the service they had done. The war captains, or old men, had three hogs, fish, oysters, bread, beer and divers other refreshments given them. They retir'd and made themselves drunk that evening.

Monday, March 14. At three in the afternoon, the "general" was beat thro' the camp, half an hour after the "assembly," and immediately the "troop," when the whole prepared to march. At four, we reach'd a place on the beach where a boat had landed some barrels of beer, which was distributed at a pint a man. Such an unexpected bounty from the General wonderfully elated the soldiers. We march'd briskly along St. Juan's beach till the cover of night. The fiery heat of the sun almost scorch'd and blinded us. The water we brought in our canteens and bottles was boiling hot, and our arms burnt us when we touch'd the steel.

Tuesday, March 15. After an hour's march arriving to the road that leads to Diego, we struck into it from the beach. Here it must be noted that every person carried his own provision in his knapsack or haversack on his back, officers and gentlemen not excepted, of which we had for seven days at the allowance of a pound of biscuit and ten ounces of cheese per man. Our men found out the contrivance of putting orange peel into their bottles, which temper'd the water's heat and, by its generous bitter, imparted a noble warmth to the stomach.

Wednesday, March 16. We continued our march, diversify'd with the sight of a million of parakeets and other birds. Marching thro' the woods is rather more incommodious than the beach on account of so many stumps and palmetto roots, which bruise our feet and often occasion us to tumble down. About eight o'clock we arriv'd about one mile from the ruins of the Mousa and three from St. Augustine. A double guard being mounted and sentries placed, we laid down on our arms to take some little repose. When we dug wells, no water could be had that was drinkable. Necessity obliging, we strain'd it from the mud thro' our teeth and handkerchiefs. Here we could plainly hear the tatoo beat in the castle of St. Augustine.

Thursday, March 17. Halting at daybreak, we form'd in a small marsh on both sides enclos'd with thick woods. Amongst them the General ordered a vacancy to be cut, to conceal his men from view. Here he was resolv'd to wait for the enemy if they should have the courage to venture from their walls. We were almost devour'd with vermin and distracted for want of water, which we could not find. His Excellency and six or seven horsemen, in order to decoy them out, rode as far as the out-sentries of the Spaniards, who retir'd without firing into the castle, pursu'd by him to the very walls. Finding nothing could provoke them to appear, he returned, proposing to lie in the same posture for two or three days. However, this design was balk'd by the desertion of one Eels, a fellow who was discontented and knew our number, disposition and everything which could induce them to sally upon us. He was pursued but hid himself in the woods, from whence he afterwards went to the enemy.

Finding our situation would be too dangerous, His Excellency order'd the whole to march. When our Indians discovered a cool spring, the very mention of which occasion'd several of our men to desert their arms and run toward it, for which two of them were tied neck and heels as an example to the rest. Then setting forward, we arriv'd at night to the wood near Diego, after so prodigiously fatiguing a march of more than twenty miles. Numbers dropp'd down thro' the excessive, torturing heat.

Friday, March 18. The men's feet are very much blister'd and even our old marchers jaded to death.

Sunday, March 20. An Indian conjurer prophesies the Spaniards will be down upon us this night, and therefore, to humor those people's superstition, a double watch is kept and another advanc'd guard mounted.

⌈ 15 ⌋

Frederica is divided into streets distinguished by the names of the captains of the regiment, along whose sides are planted orange trees. Some houses are built entirely of brick, some of brick and wood, some few of tabby-work, but most of the meaner sort of wood only.

A YOUNG GENTLEMAN, 1745

AN ANONYMOUS "young gentleman" published his account of travels along the Georgia coast in *The London Magazine* in 1745–46. The author was probably Edward Kimber, who wrote the preceding account of the second attack on St. Augustine, and these descriptions may be based on Kimber's experiences in 1743, for the author begins by saying he came to Georgia on a ship carrying Virginia recruits to help Georgia, perhaps in preparation for Oglethorpe's second assault.

We embarked on a sloop bound for Frederica in Georgia. Our provisions were too small. Add to this a vessel that could hardly keep above water, she was so foul and rotten, and no hands that could be of service but the master, a Negro fellow and a boy. Our lading consisted of all the scum of Virginia, who had been recruited for the service of Georgia and who were ready at every turn to mutiny, whilst they belched out the most shocking oaths. They would not be persuaded even to go upon deck for the discharge of nature, but, performing all those offices below, we began to fear a plague as well as drowning. We cast anchor in St. Simon's harbor and, immediately debarking, set out for Frederica.

Frederica, on the Island of St. Simon, the chief town in the southernmost part of the colony of Georgia, stands on an eminence upon a branch of the famous River Alatamaha, which washes the west side of this agreeable little island and, after several windings, disembogues itself into the sea at Jekyll Sound. It forms a kind of a bay before the town and is navigable for vessels of the largest burden, which may lie along the wharf in a secure and safe harbor and may upon occasion haul up to careen and refit, the bottom being a soft oozy clay intermixed with small sand and shells.

The town is defended by a pretty strong fort of tabby (a mixture of lime, made of oyster shells, with sand, small shells, &c. which, when hardened, is as firm as stone), which has several eighteen-pounders mounted on a ravelin in its front and commands the river both upwards and downwards and is surrounded by a quadrangular rampart with four bastions of earth, well stockaded and turfed, and a palisadoed ditch, which include also the King's storehouses (in which are kept the arsenal, the court of justice and chapel), two large and spacious buildings of brick and timber. On the rampart are mounted a considerable quantity of ordnance of several sizes.

The town is surrounded by a rampart, with flankers, of the same thickness with that 'round the fort, in form of a pentagon, and a dry ditch. And since the famous attempt of the Spaniards in July, 1742, at the northeast and southeast angles are erected two strong covered pentagonal bastions capable of containing 100 men each, to scour the flanks with small arms, and defended by a number of cannon. At their tops are lookouts, which command the view of the country and the river for many miles. The roofs are shingled out of wood, but so contrived as to be easily cleared away if incommodious in the defence of the towers.

The whole circumference of the town is about a mile and a half, including within the fortifications the camp for General Oglethorpe's regiment at the north side of the town, the parades on the west and a small wood to the south, which is left for conveniency of fuel and pasture and is an excellent blind to the enemy in case of an attack. In it is a small magazine of powder. The town has two gates called the Land-port and the Water-port, next to the latter of which is the guard house and underneath it the prison for malefactors, which is an handsome building of brick. At the north end are the barracks, which is an extremely well contrived building in the form of a square of tabby-work, in which at present are kept the hospital and Spanish prisoners of war.

The town is situated on a large Indian field. To the east it has a very extensive savannah, wherein is the burial place, through which is cut a road to the other side of the island, which is bounded by woods, save here and there some opening glades into the neighboring savannahs and marshes, which much elucidate the pleasure of looking. Down this road are several very commodious plantations, particularly the very agreeable one of Captain Demery and that of Mr. Hawkins. Preeminently appears Mr. Oglethorpe's settlement, which, at distance, looks like a neat country village, where the consequences of all the various industries of an European farm are seen. The master of it has shown what application and unabated diligence may effect in this country. At the extremity of the road is a small village called the German Village, inhabited by several families of Salzburgers who plant and fish for their subsistence. On the river side one has the prospect of a large circuit of marshes, terminated by the woods on the continent, in form like an amphitheater and interspersed with the mean-ders of abundance of creeks formed from the aforesaid river. At a distance may be seen the white post at Bachelor's Redoubt, also on the main, where is kept a good look-out of rangers.

To the north are marshes and a small wood, at the western extremity of which are the plantations of the late Captain Desbrisay and some others of less note, together with a look-out, wherein a Corporal's guard is stationed and relieved weekly, called Pike's, on the bank of the river, from whence they can see ves-sels a great way to the northward. On the south is a wood, which is, however, so far cleared as to discover the approach of an enemy at a great distance. With-out it, to the eastward, is the plantation of Captain Dunbar and, to the west-ward, a Corporal's look-out.

The town is divided into several spacious streets, along whose sides are plant-ed orange trees, which in some time will have a very pretty effect on the view and will render the town pleasingly shady. (The inhabitants begin to plant this charming fruit very much and 'tis to be hoped will banish their numerous peach trees to their country settlements, which are nurseries of mosquitoes and other vermin.) Some houses are built entirely of brick, some of brick and wood, some few of tabby-work, but most of the meaner sort of wood only. The camp is also divided into several streets, distinguished by the names of the captains of the several companies of the regiment, and the huts are built generally of clap-boards and palmettoes and are each of them capable to contain a family or half a dozen single men. Here these brave fellows live with the most laudable econ-omy, and, though most of them when off duty practice some trade or employ-ment, they make as fine an appearance upon the parade as any regiment in the King's service, and their exact discipline does a great deal of honor to their officers.

They have a market every day. The inhabitants of the town may be divided into officers, merchants, storekeepers, artisans and people in the provincial ser-vice. And there are often also many sojourners from the neighboring settlements and from New York, Philadelphia and Carolina on account of trade. The civil government does not seem yet to be quite rightly settled by the Trustees but is at present administered by three Magistrates or justices, assisted by a recorder, constables and tythingmen. The military is regulated as in all garrison towns in the British dominions. In short, the whole town and country adjacent are quite rurally charming, and the improvements everywhere around are foot-steps of the great skill and industry imaginable, considering its late settlement and the rubs it has so often met with.

At the south point of this Island of St. Simon's are the ruins of the town of St. Simon's, destroyed by the Spaniards at their invasion. By the remaining vestiges, it must have been a very uniform place, and the situation is quite charming, though it now makes one melancholy to see such a desolation in so new a country. The only building they left standing was an house which they had consecrated for a chapel. The fort has some remains still and seems to have been no extraordinary affair, though no place was ever better defended, and the enemies seem, by their works and entrenchments, to have thought themselves sure of keeping the town but found themselves woefully mistaken.

Down the beach to the westward is a look-out of tabby-work, which is a very good mark for standing over the bar into the harbor, and on the opposite point of Jekyll Island is a very remarkable hammock of trees, much taken notice of by seamen on the same account. Somewhat lower and more northerly is the plantation called Gascoign's, which underwent the same fate with St. Simon's. An officer's command is stationed at south point, who disposes his sentries so as to discover vessels some leagues at sea, and upon any such discovery an alarm gun is fired and an horseman sent up with notice to the headquarters, which is nine miles from this place. If they appear to make for the harbor, a perpendicular mounted gun is fired as a signal, which, by the ascent of the smoke, is a direction to a ship a long way in the offing and is a most lucky contrivance. The road from hence to Frederica is cut through the woods and through the marshes raised upon a causeway. To make a good horseman in America is no easy matter without considerable practice, and accidents often happen to the best of us by the intricacies of the tracts and paths. The horses are the most hardy beasts imaginable, and, though they can't all size with European horses, they make it out in service.

Nature, in all its gay varieties, seemed to open her charms to delight our senses in our little inland voyage from St. Simon's Island to the chief town of the north part of the colony. My mind will ever retain the diversity of scenes that presented to our admiring eyes in this passage, and, now I endeavor to commit some faint sketches of them to paper. Rivers and creeks glide with a peaceful and, as it were, contented current into wide arms and breaks of the sea, foaming and lashing the shores with repeated fury. The marshes and savannahs extended along their borders, disposed with so seeming a regularity as to make the whole prospect look like one continued canal, the effect of the most studious contrivance, whilst at a distant view you take in a large tract of hoary woods, interspersed with verdant spots that bear the semblance of the most refreshing meadows.

Rustic grottos, rugged caverns, mossy caves and cooling cells seem to border their sides. Here the lofty oak with all his kindred tribe (as the live oak, water oak, swamp oak, marsh oak, holly oak, &c.), clad in robes of antique moss, seems by its venerable appearance to be the real monarch of the woods; the cedar, sweet as the cedar of Lebanon; the towering evergreen pine; the fragrant hickory; the mournful cypress; and, here and there, the triumphant laurel are seen in full luster and preside over an infinity of lesser products. The savory sassafras shrub perfumes the air, the prickly-pear shrub offers his tempting fruit to the hand, but wisely tells you, by the points that guard it, not to indulge to excess; the delicious mulberry, the swelling peach, the olive, the pomegranate, the walnut, all combine to furnish out the paradisical banquet.

Across the glade trips the timorous deer, the nimble squirrel skips from tree to tree, and at their roots scour through the brakes the wonderful 'possum, the squeaking raccoon and millions of the changeable lizard. (The 'possum is a creature sized like an hare and very remarkable for its false belly, in which, at a time of danger, her young ones creep, and so she carries them off with her. It eats like a pig and is very nourishing. The raccoon is delicate eating, somewhat tasted like lamb. Its pizzle is very commonly used as a tobacco stopper. Squirrels are also most delicious food.) Now harmony breathes forth her choicest airs, and music fills the vocal groves. The silver-breasted mock bird diversifies her note, now briskly chirps like the soaring lark, now melts in the softer strain of saddening Philomel. The magnificent red bird joins in the chorus, which seems now and then interrupted by the turtle's melancholy wailing.

Adown the stream the view is still more enchanting by the sporting of the finny race. The shining mullet, the noble bass, the warrior stingray with his redoubted tail, the drum, the nimble catfish alternately shoot their heads above the waves, in which large banks of oysters appear like frightful rocks. Here the dreadful alligator sports himself in the canes, and there the heavy porpoise rolls in sluggish wantonness.

Now night succeeds the day, which seems just to have withdrawn its beams to give place to new scenes of wonder. What clear and serene skies! how bespangled with those glittering sparks, those worlds unknown! (You perceive here also thousands of minute stars attracting your eyes and floating before you. These are the fireflies, which look like so many glow-worms. They are a very small insect with some luminous qualities or particles that I never could well examine, but surprise a stranger much.) But hark, what a confused multitude of sounds from yonder marshes! All the tumult and cries of a great city are imitated by the bull frogs, lizards, grasshoppers, marsh frogs, &c., &c., &c. Another way the hissing of serpents! Here the rustling of the deer amongst the leaves in yonder wood and now and then the prowling wolf, with the discontented bear, more disturb the stillness of the night and make the air tremble with their superior voices. What glaring eyes are those in the neighboring thicket that beam fire upon us? We present our pieces. We fire, and the whole country echoes back the groans.

This voyage took us up six days on account of the halts we made and our waiting for tides, and the winds not much favoring us, though the distance is only about 100 miles. Our vessel was an open, fixed-oared boat, in which we stowed both baggage and provisions and slept and watched by turns. The sand-fly is so minute an insect as scarce to be perceivable with the naked eye, only appearing like the sporting particles of dust that float in the sunshine. It even intrudes itself into the mouth as you breathe and insinuates into all the small apertures of your garments, nor can you any way fend yourself entirely from them. Mosquitoes are long sharp flies, whose venom, I believe, according to their bulk, is as baleful as that of a rattlesnake. I have felt them and heard their cursed humming too often for it ever to be obliterated from my memory. Raising a thick smother of smoke is the best means to drive them from an house or apartment, and with us smoking tobacco is generally the subterfuge. There are abundance of other torments in these climates, as cock-roaches, wood-ticks, &c., &c. And this colony is either not so enervated as their neighbors or else are poor enough to scorn umbrellas and mosquito nets as Jamaican and Carolinian effeminicies!

Our first stage we made New Inverness, or the Darien, on the continent near twenty miles from Frederica, which is a settlement of Highlanders living and dressing in their own country fashion very happily and contentedly. There is an Independent Company of foot of them, consisting of seventy men who have been of good service. The town is regularly laid out and built of wood mostly, divided into streets and squares. Before the town is the parade and a fort not yet finished. It is situated upon a very high bluff or point of land from whence with a few cannon they can scour the river. Otherways it is surrounded by pine barrens and woods, and there is a route by land to Savannah and Fort Argyle. The company and troops, armed in the Highland manner, make an extreme good appearance under arms.

The whole settlement may be said to be a brave and industrious people but were more numerous, planted more and raised more cattle before the invasion, with which they drove a good trade to the southward. But things seem daily mending with them. They are forced to keep a very good guard in this place, it lies so open to the insults of the French and Spanish Indians who once or twice have shown stragglers some very bloody tricks. They have here all sorts of garden stuff and game in abundance in the woods and marshes, as ducks, wild geese and turkies, partridges, curlews, rabbits, and the rivers abound with fish. We stayed here two days and in a day and an half arrived at St. Catherine's, which is an island reserved to the Indians by treaty.

We found about eight or ten families upon it, who had several plantations of corn. It seems to be a most fruitful soil and to have larger tracts of open land than any I have observed and to abound in all kinds of game, on which the good Indians regaled us, and for greens boiled us the tops of china-briars, which eat almost as well as asparagus. When we departed, they gave us a young bear which they had just killed, which proved fine eating.

We arrived in somewhat more than two days at the Narrows, where there is a kind of manchecolas fort for their defence garrisoned from Wormsloe, where we soon arrived. It is the settlement of Mr. Jones, ten miles southeast of Savannah, and we could not help observing as we passed several very pretty plantations. Wormsloe is one of the most agreeable spots I ever saw, and the improvements of that ingenious man are very extraordinary. He commands a company of marines who are quartered in huts near his house, which is also a tolerable defensible place with small arms. From this house there is a vista of near three miles cut through the woods to Mr. Whitefield's orphan house, which has a very fine effect on the sight.

The route from Wormsloe to Mr. Whitefield's orphan house is extremely agreeable, mostly through pine groves. It gave me much satisfaction to have an opportunity to see this orphan house, as the design had made such a noise in Europe. It is a square building of very large dimensions, the foundation of which is of brick with chimneys of the same, the rest of the superstructure of wood, the whole laid out in a neat and elegant manner. A kind of piazza-work surrounds it, which is a very pleasing retreat in the summer. The hall and all the apartments are very commodious and prettily furnished. The garden, which is a very extensive one and well kept up, is one of the best I ever saw in America, and you may discover in it plants and fruits of almost every clime and kind. The out-houses are convenient, and the plantation will soon surpass almost anything in the country.

We were received by the superintendent, Mr. Barber, a Dissenting minister, in a genteel and friendly manner. They were at dinner when we arrived, the whole family at one table, and sure never was a more orderly, pretty sight. If I recollect right, besides Mr. Barber, the schoolmaster and some women, there were near forty young persons of both sexes, dressed very neatly and decently. After dinner they retired, the boys to school and the girls to their spinning and knitting. I was told their vacant hours were employed in the garden and plantation work. Whatever opinion I may have of the absurdity of some of their religious notions, tenets and practices, yet so far as they conduce to inculcate sobriety, industry and frugality they deserve encouragement. 'Tis near eight miles from this house to Savannah, the road cut through the woods.

Savannah is situated on a navigable river which goes by the name of the town, and vessels of considerable burden may lie close to the shore, which is between forty and fifty feet above the water's edge. One main street runs through the whole town from the landing place. It has very near 350 houses, huts and warehouses in it, beside the public buildings, which are the storehouse of the Trustees, an handsome courthouse, a jail, a guard house and a public wharf, projected out many feet into the river. The streets are wide and commodious and intersect each other mostly at right angles. The whole town is laid out very commodiously, and there are several large squares. Many of the houses are very large and handsome, built generally of wood but some foundations are bricked. They have plenty of water and very good, and the soil is dry and sandy.

The houses are built some distance from each other to allow more air and garden room and prevent the communication in case of any accident by fire. The town is divided into wards and tythings, which have their several constables and tythingmen. The magistrates are three bailiffs and a recorder, who have power to judge in capital crimes as well as affairs of *meum* and *tuum*. They have a public garden in a very thriving way, which is a kind of nursery for the use of the inhabitants. The land, a considerable space 'round the town, is well cleared, and the passages lie open, a handsome roadway running above a mile from it and making the prospect very lightsome. The air is pure and serene and perhaps never was a better situation or a more healthful place.

A cursed spirit of dissension amongst themselves has rendered this sweet place so much less flourishing than it was at the beginning of the settlement. The inhabitants may be divided into magistrates, planters, merchants and storekeepers, artisans and servants, besides sojourners from the northward and southward. There are many pretty plantations in the country about Savannah, belonging to the inhabitants of that town, particularly Colonel Stephens's, Mr. Causton's, &c. A light house is erected on Tybee Island, which is a very good sea mark and the only one south of Carolina, though for the use of the harbor there is very little occasion for it at present, there being very little business stirring.

We set out in a few days in one of Captain Jones's scout boats, manned by a party of his marine company, and had a very pleasant passage to the Island of Port Royal in South Carolina.

The Royal Province

JUDGING by his correspondence, John Reynolds was a man overwhelmed by the enormity of the task at hand. He must have regretted Lord Hardwicke's intercession on his behalf which secured for him the governorship of Georgia. Reynolds was not impressed with Savannah, where the houses were "very small and mostly very old," the prison had no locks and the council house collapsed at his first meeting. In fact, everything in the infant colony seemed on the point of collapse, including the lighthouse at Tybee and the forts at Frederica and Augusta. [Document Sixteen] Nothing worked out right for him. A minority faction led by Edmund Gray boycotted the first General Assembly; his council turned on him, and the French and Indian War threatened the existence of the colony. Reynolds asked the surveyor John Gerar William DeBrahm to draw up a plan of fortifications, but nothing was implemented.

Joseph Ottolenghe, an Italian who moved to England and a Jew who converted to Christianity, was sent to Georgia in 1751 to promote the cultivation of silk and preach religion to the slaves. The earliest Georgians had been denied the use of slaves, though Oglethorpe made the mistake of displaying the importance of their labor by hiring skilled black carpenters from South Carolina to help build Savannah. The Georgians began to brood about how successful they might be with the help of such workers, and slavery was finally permitted in 1750. When Ottolenghe arrived in 1751 there were, according to DeBrahm, "scarce three Dozen of African servants" in Georgia, but Ottolenghe was afflicted by the brutal treatment given them and the greed of the planters. [Document Seventeen] Twenty years later there would be 13,000 slaves in Georgia.

The second Royal governor, Henry Ellis, was a confident leader. Though eleven of the nineteen members of the Commons House of Assembly had been given political appointments by his predecessor, Ellis won them over by appealing to their patriotism. He organized the province into five parishes and coached the Assembly in its constitutional responsibilities. Shrewdly, he enlisted the Indian traders in gaining the allegiance of the Creek Indians. Although his bills authorizing the issuance of paper money and offering debtors asylum from creditors for a seven-year period were later disallowed by the Board of Trade, both policies were in effect long enough to set Georgia on a sound economic course. His health broken by fevers, Ellis left Georgia after only a brief tenure as governor. [Document Eighteen]

The third Royal governor, James Wright, administered Georgia to the general satisfaction of his superiors in England as well as the people of his province for fourteen years. Wright's reputation was tarnished by the events of the American Revolution. In fact, two revolutions occurred during his years of service and he played major roles in both. By concluding the Treaty of 1763 at the Augusta Indian Conference, Wright promoted a social revolution. Land-hungry settlers flocked into the cession between the Savannah and Ogeechee rivers, and traders who did business with the Indians had to make way for greedy newcomers who had no intention of doing so. Captain Gavin Cochrane, who toured Georgia and South Carolina in 1766, reported on the vicious "crackers" of the frontier. [Document Nineteen]

⌐ 16 ⌐

The town of Savannah contains about 150 houses, all wooden ones, very small and mostly very old. The biggest, used for the meeting of the President and Assistants, fell down whilst we were all there.

JOHN REYNOLDS, 1754

JOHN REYNOLDS (c. 1713–1788) was a naval officer for twenty years before he was appointed the first Royal governor of Georgia. He was greeted with enthusiasm upon his arrival in October of 1754 but, after three years of service and political disputes with the provincial assembly, he was much detested. After his return to England, Reynolds resumed his naval career. This selection of Reynolds's letters to the Board of Trade are taken from Allen D. Candler, *Colonial Records of the State of Georgia, XXVII*, typescript, 1937, pp. 69–72, 151–152, 237–243, 259–263.

Savannah

December 5, 1754

I humbly beg leave to acquaint Your Lordships of my arrival here on the 29th of October and that the people appeared extremely well pleased on that occasion. As I have not yet had time to visit [the] other part of the country, I must defer giving Your Lordships an account of it 'till I have properly informed myself.

The town of Savannah is well situated and contains about 150 houses, all wooden ones, very small and mostly very old. The biggest was used for the meeting of the President and Assistants and wherein I sat in Council for a few days, but one end fell down whilst we were all there and obliged us to move to a kind of shed behind the courthouse, which being quite unfit, I have given orders with the advice of the Council to fit up the shell of a house, which was lately built for laying up the silk but was never made use of, being very ill calculated for that purpose, but it will make a tolerable good house for the Council and Assembly to meet and for a few offices besides. The prison, being only a small old wooden house without the least security, I have also ordered to be mended and some locks and bolts to be put on for the present.

I have, with the advice of the Council, published a proclamation for continuing all officers till farther order and issued writs for electing representatives to serve in General Assembly to meet here on the 7th of January, and the erecting of courts of justice and judicature according to His Majesty's instructions is now under our consideration.

There has been a few of the settlement Indians down already upon hearing of the arrival of a Governor, and I heartily wish the intended presents from England were arrived, for I am informed that numbers of them may be expected on that occasion as soon as their hunting season is over, who will take it very ill to be dismissed without presents. It appears to me also of the greatest importance to His Majesty's service to have some troops in this defenceless and remote province, which, as Your Lordship knows, is the south frontier of His Majesty's dominions in North America and so near the Spanish town of Augustine that the Negroes frequently desert thither from hence and even from Carolina, and the Spaniards very much encourage them to do so, as I am informed. And to the southward of the northern boundary of this province lies the Indian Nations of the Chicksaws, Creeks, Yuchis, Chactaws and four-fifths of the Cherokees, who should be awed by our strength as well as courted by our presents.

And particularly now as several letters from Mr. McGillivray and others, Indian traders of reputation at Augusta, have been received here by Patrick Graham, Esquire, since my arrival, giving accounts of the artifices of the French Governor at Mobile, who had invited thither all the chiefs of the Upper Creek Nation and being returned they say they had a grand conference with that Governor, who was at great pains to persuade them that the English were their utter enemies, showed them a fictitious letter wrote with red ink and a fictitious Captain who it was said was the bearer of it. This letter contained a proposal from the English Governors to the French to join together in order to destroy the Indians. At the same time he strongly recommended to them to put themselves under the protection of the French, being the only friends they could safely confide in, for the English wanted nothing but the Indians' lands and at last will make slaves of them; that it was high time for the Indians to begin upon the English, and they (the French) were ready to support and assist them, &c. Mr. McGillivray observes that however silly and shallow these arguments may appear to us, yet they may have a great effect to our prejudice upon the minds of the Indians and especially on such of them as are in the French interest already, of whom there are but too many in the Creek Nation.

Georgia
May 1, 1755

I am just returned from the southern frontiers of this province, which is the Island St. Simon's, whereon stands the town of Frederica, which was formerly fortified and in the late war garrisoned with a regiment of His Majesty's troops. It is now in ruins, the fortifications entirely decayed, and the houses falling down. There still remains twenty pieces of cannon, some of them eighteen-pounders, but all spoilt for want of care. The rest of the guns were removed to Savannah after the regiment was broke and are also ruined by lying many years in the sand without vents or tampions. Frederica is the best situation of any for a garrison to cover and protect the province from invasion by sea but is not at all proper for a capital; for, though it is not above seven miles from the mainland in a direct line, yet it is at least twenty miles to go through the rivers and creeks, which in a serpentine course divide the vast body of morass that lies between Frederica and the main. The whole country is extremely well watered with rivers navigable for very large boats, but all the inlets upon this coast, as well as Carolina, are bar'd.

Upon the bar of St. Simon's, which is the inlet to Frederica, there is three fathom at low-water, as there is also on the bar of Ossabaw and on the bar of Tybee, which last is the inlet to Savannah River. These are the best inlets in the province, and Ossabaw is the best of them. It is the inlet to the River Ogeechee, a fine fresh water river which runs from the Nation of the Upper Creek Indians and falls into the sea between the islands of Ossabaw and Wassaw. It is navigable for ships of 500 tons up to a bluff upon the main, fourteen miles from the sea, where a town has been laid out and called Hardwicke. It has a charming situation, the winding of the river making it a peninsula, and it is the only fit place for the capital. There is many objections to this town of Savannah's being so, besides its being situated at the extremity of the province, the shoalness of the river and the great height of the land, which is very inconvenient in the loading and unloading of the ships.

Many lots have already been granted in Hardwicke, but only one house is yet built there. And, as the province is unable to be at the expense of erecting the necessary public buildings and the annual sum of £500 allowed for erecting and repairing public works, entertaining Indians and other incidental expenses being insufficient for all those purposes, I am in hopes Your Lordships will think proper to get a sufficient sum allowed for erecting a courthouse, an assembly house, a church and a prison at Hardwicke, which will be such an encouragement to private people to build there as will soon make it fit for the seat of government to the universal benefit of the province.

Georgia

May 31, 1755

There are but very few settlers arrived here, the reason of which I apprehend to be the appearance there is of war and the defenseless state of this frontier province, which has neither cannon, small arms, ammunition, fortifications nor sufficient troops, and peoples' lives and fortunes consequently in the utmost danger. And this is what I have had the honor to acquaint Your Lordships with by several letters and memorials of mine, as well as the representations of the general assembly.

A party of the Cherokee Indians with their chiefs are arrived in this town, and more of them are hourly expected, as well as parties of the Creeks, Chickasaws, Yuchis and Choctaws, it being customary upon the arrival of a new Governor for the neighboring Indians to come to him to renew the peace. And they always expect to receive presents, but particularly upon that occasion. I have already had the honor to acquaint Your Lordships in former letters of the great and absolute occasion there is for Indian presents. These people appear to be extremely dissatisfied at hearing that there is none for them, and, if the presents do not arrive soon, I don't know what may be the consequence.

The opportunities here of sending or receiving intelligence from England happen so very seldom that I am obliged to send His Majesty's scout boat with these to Charles Town, to be sent home in the first ship. And I rather send her that the coxswain may make strict inquiry at Charles Town if any public letters for me are sent that way from England, for the Carolinians are so jealous of this province that they are apt to stifle the letters that are directed hither. His Majesty's proclamation lay three months in a merchant's warehouse there before they sent it here, and, as I have not yet received any commands from Your Lordships, I suspect that they may have fallen into such hands.

Georgia
January 5, 1756

I have consulted with Mr. DeBrahm, one of the surveyors (who is a very able engineer and who is now fortifying Charles Town) about what will be necessary to be done to put this colony into a proper state of defense and making an estimate of the expense as far as it can be done in this part of the world. And I have transmitted to Your Lordships a representation and estimate thereof accordingly, wherein Your Lordships will be pleased to observe that the number of artillery represented are only what are necessary for present use, but it will be proper to have a greater number in order to have a ready store to supply the wants from a nearer place than England. Likewise the number of Negroes augmented will shorten the time of their employ and a master gunner should be allowed at each fort to take charge of, and be accountable for, the ordnance stores. I need not mention the necessity of a good engineer to superintend the whole, and I beg leave to recommend Mr. William DeBrahm, who is a German gentleman of great honor and ingenuity.

Mr. Pownal informs me by letter of the 19th of September that Your Lordships would have me transmit to you an account of the present actual state of defense of this colony in relation to the ordnance and stores of war, to forts and fortifications and to the number of inhabitants, with the true state of all places already fortified or which I judge necessary to be fortified with my opinion in what manner His Majesty may further contribute to the security and defence thereof, how many men are able to bear arms and how the militia are armed, mustered and trained. The real state of defense of this colony is such that it may be laid before Your Lordships in very few words.

At Augusta, which is 150 miles northwest from Savannah, there is now remaining a wooden fort of 120-foot square, but it is so rotten that great part of it is propped up to prevent its falling. It has eight small iron guns, which are honeycombed, the carriage rotten, and there is no ordnance stores. This is the only fortification in the province. For Frederica, which lies 100 miles southwest from Savannah and in the late war was well fortified, is now totally dismantled, and nothing remains there but twenty old cannon without carriages or any ordnance stores. At Savannah here are eleven old cannon, three- and four-pounders, without any carriages or any ordnance stores, except twenty-seven old swivel guns and sixty-one old muskets, most of them with broken stocks and many without locks. This is the true state of the forts, fortifications and ordnance stores in this province.

According to the best account I can get, the number of white people in this colony, including men, women and children, are 4500. The number of Negroes are 1855. Of the white, 756 are able to bear arms, of which number the militia now consists, but they are very badly armed, many being unable to purchase arms according to the militia act. They are divided into eight companies, which are trained and mustered by their respective officers six times a year, but most of them are very remotely situated from each other, it being 200 miles from Augusta to Frederica.

In regard to my opinion how His Majesty may farther contribute to the security and defense of this colony, I refer Your Lordships to the representation before mentioned in case of a war. But if a peace should be established, even then I think there ought to be two companies of foot and two troops of rangers and that Frederica should be fortified and likewise that a fort should be built upon the forks of the Oconee and Altamaha river, because the French at Albamous and Mobile will always be tampering with the Indians, as the Spaniards at St. Augustine always are. And annual presents for the Indians should never be omitted. These things are absolutely necessary for His Majesty's service to secure this province, which, Your Lordships will please to remember, is one of the frontiers of North America. And in my opinion, if it was well peopled, it would soon become one of the best colonies, if not the very best, in His Majesty's dominions. But it cannot be expected that any substantial people will settle here unless some way could be found to invite them. And I think if the town of Hardwicke was made a free port for seven years it would invite many substantial traders to settle there and consequently would be the most effectual means of peopling the province and with that sort of people, too, who would make it flourish most.

The sum of £500 a year, allowed for erecting and repairing public works, entertaining Indians and other contingencies, is very insufficient. Many things that are absolutely necessary to be done cannot be undertaken for want of money, particularly the building of a jail, repairing the lighthouse, the courthouse and the church, mounting the few guns we have, clearing the river of wrecks and old trees that interrupt the navigation of it, &c. And as I apprehend that I am confined to that sum I shall not presume to draw for any more without farther orders.

I sent the Indian presents to Augusta to be distributed and appointed all the Indian chiefs to meet me there in the first week of December. I went thither accordingly, but, the Indians neglecting the time of appointment, I stayed there ten days and then returned to Savannah, leaving Mr. William Little, Commissioner and Agent for Indian Affairs, to deliver my speeches and the presents to them, which he did to above 300 Indians who arrived there a week after I came away, and peace and friendship were renewed between us.

Whilst I was absent from thence at Augusta, and what indeed was one reason of my returning hither so soon, two transports arrived here from Nova Scotia with 400 French Papists and letters to me from Lieutenant Governor Lawrence, acquainting me that for the better security of that province and in consequence of a resolution of his in council he had sent those people to Georgia and he did not doubt of my concurrence. The season of the year would not admit of their going back again, and therefore I was obliged to receive them. And, their provisions being all expended and the poor wretches ready to perish, I was obliged to order them to be supplied immediately, which, with the hire of some boats, to distribute them about the province, has occasioned an expense of near £80.

I beg leave to acquaint Your Lordships that it is absolutely necessary that a Chief Justice should be sent hither from England, there being nobody in the colony capable of presiding in the Courts of Judicature wherein great irregularities are committed for want of somebody properly qualified to direct the form of their proceedings.

Georgia
March 29, 1756

The distribution of the Indian presents at Augusta in December made it necessary to prorogue the Assembly, which was to have met on the 7th of January, to the 2nd of February. And two of the representatives, during the recess between March and January having been appointed members of the Council and a third, who had not qualified, having acquainted me by letter that he would not

114

serve, I ordered a writ to issue for the election of three members to complete the number which His Majesty has been pleased to direct that the said Assembly shall consist of. And accordingly three members were returned, against either of whom no objection appeared. But yet none of them were admitted to sit, and twelve members only, of which there was a great majority of very troublesome people, would have proceeded upon business without admitting them. I gave the House time enough by short adjournments to recollect that they were wrong and in a message explained to them how they were so.

But nothing would do, for they expect to have the same privileges as the House of Commons of Great Britain and in some respects more. They ordered a message I sent for their last adjournment to be upon the table after it had been read to them, confined the speaker in his chair and forced him to sign a paper (against which proceeding I transmit Your Lordships a copy of his protest), some private members seized upon the minutes, made such alterations as they pleased and refused to deliver them to my written order. Whereupon I found it necessary to dissolve the said Assembly. And the circumstances of this colony are such at present that it is my opinion no Assembly can be had that will raise any money for the support of government or even for holding the Courts of Oyer and Terminer unless the Governor was to admit of their exorbitant claims, now perhaps even then, for the most considerable people here are very indifferent about the administration of justice, having nothing to lose of their own, for they are deeply in debt in the neighboring province or otherways, and their creditors, in order to have a chance to be paid, have suffered them to bring their mortgaged Negroes hither, where they turn to much better account than in Carolina, whilst they pay neither taxes, parish rates, quitrents, customs nor anything else. However, I proposed the calling another Assembly immediately to the Council, but they voted against it.

I shall take this opportunity to acquaint Your Lordships that a great majority of the Council have all along appeared to be extremely greedy of power and would fain have all things determined by vote. Some have declared in Council that all the letters I write to Your Lordships ought to be approved of by the Board, one motive whereof I apprehend to be that if they could prevail with me to allow of this extraordinary claim there would be no danger of any inquiry into the disposal of all the public money which has passed through the hands of some of them and for which there remains nothing visible but a poor wooden church, a wooden courthouse and a lighthouse, all ready to tumble down, a small wooden house here called the filature and another at Ebenezer, a wooden Council house, which was only a mere shell without a chimney when I arrived and has cost near £300 since to make it useful.

⌐ 17 ⌐

The Negroes . . . loaded with a cruel slavery, ignorant of our language and manners, nurs'd in extravagant idolatry, loaded with hard labor and worse usages, ill fed, ill clothed, barbarously treated, insomuch that a dog and an horse are treated like humane creatures!

JOSEPH OTTOLENGHE, 1758

JOSEPH OTTOLENGHE (c. 1711–c. 1775), an Italian who became an Englishman and a Jew who converted to Christianity, was sent to Georgia in 1751 to promote the cultivation of silk and preach religion to the slaves. The earliest Georgians had been denied the use of slaves and brooded on how prosperous they might become with slave labor. Slavery was not legalized until 1750, and when Ottolenghe arrived there were, according to the engineer William De-Brahm, "scarce three Dozen of African servants" in Georgia. But Ottolenghe was afflicted by the brutal treatment given to them, and by 1771 there would be 13,000 slaves in Georgia. These extracts from Ottolenghe's letters are here published with the permission of the Archives of the United Society for the Propagation of the Gospel, London, from Bray/N. America/1 f11, using transcriptions generously provided by John C. Van Horne, American Philosophical Society at Philadelphia, with further generous assistance by Catherine Wakeling, Archivist of USPG.

JOSEPH OTTOLENGHE TO REV. SAMUEL SMITH

[Savannah, December 4, 1751]
Revd. Sir: In my last sent you by *The Charming Martha* I took the liberty to acquaint you with my safe arrival to Georgia. I shall now proceed and lay before you the method which I have taken to discharge that awful office which God was pleased to call me to, and the Honorable Associates to place me in. As soon as the fatigue of the voyage permitted it, I desired the Revd. Mr. Zouberbuyler that he would be so good to give the people notice in the church that I would instruct their Negroes three days in the week, viz. Sundays, Tuesdays and Thursdays, which he accordingly did. And that I might make it easy to the masters of these unhappy creatures I have appointed the time of their coming to me to be at night when their daily labor is done.

116

When we meet, I make them go to prayers with me, having composed for that purpose a few prayers suitable (I hope) to the occasion. I instruct them to read, that they may be able in time to comfort themselves in reading the Book of God. After this is done, I make them repeat the Lord's Prayer and the Belief and a short portion of the catechism, explaining to them in as easy and familiar a manner as I can the meaning of what they repeat, and before I part with them I make a discourse to them on the Being of a God or the life and death of our adorable Redeemer or upon some of the precepts of the Holy Gospel, generally introducing some event or story, taken out of the Bible, suitable to the discourse in hand. And in order to get their love, I use them with all the kindness and endearing words that [I] am capable of, which makes them willing to come to me and ready to follow my advice.

JOSEPH OTTOLENGHE TO REV. JOHN WARING

[Savannah, November 19, 1753]

Sir: I shall proceed with your commands in giving you an account of my proceedings with the Negroes. I never upon any account whatever, sickness excepted, omitted the discharging of my duty towards these unhappy souls committed to my charge. And tho' during the time of making the silk I have been employed by the public to direct that business, yet at night (which is the time which I'm obliged to fix for the instruction of the Negroes because then they have finish'd their daily task and some masters will suffer them to come to me) how much fatigu'd soever I find myself, I never neglect my duty.

I bless my God that I have all the success with these poor creatures that their circumstances and station in life can well admit of. I have a good many that can say the catechism perfectly well, and, as I take all the care imaginable to explain to them in as familiar a manner as I can adapt to their low capacity, I find upon examining them, which I do once a week, that by the blessing of God they daily improve in the knowledge of our holy religion. It is true that their number is not so great as I could wish by reason of their penurious masters, who think that they should be great losers should they permit their slaves to learn what they must do to be saved. Others again, especially those who resort to us from the West Indies, will upon no account whatever suffer their slaves to be instructed in the Christian religion, alleging that 'tis a just observation (of the Devil's framing I suppose) that a slave is ten times worse when a Christian than in his state of paganism. Should these poor souls come to behold the beauty of the Christian religion and observe that tho' their masters called themselves Christians and yet are a scandal not only to human nature but to our Holy Profession, they would despise such wretched masters!

117

I bless God that I have at times more than my present little house will contain, and as I ever treat them with familiarity and kind words (the only place perhaps where they are civilly used) they endeavor to find all the time which they can spare to be with me. As the first thing we do is to pray to God for His protection and blessing on our undertaking, few of them can but repeat them by heart. Their behavior is devout and at church demean themselves as becomes Christians. As I generally sing a psalm with them such as are us'd at church, several of them who have really good voices having learn'd the words and tune at school join the congregation at church. I gradually teach them prayers fitting their conditions and capacities.

I'm now building an house, driven to it by necessity, for that in which I live in is so small. Another motive that forc'd me to build is the scarcity of houses, especially since that so many people resort among us that has made houses both scarce and very dear, and as everybody is endeavoring to make the best of their old houses I found that my landlord intended to raise and repair his in order to make better rent of it. So that had I not taken the step which I took I might in a little time have found myself without an hole to put my head in. 'Tis true that I have brought myself even by building a little house of four small rooms only into debt, but 'twas not my choice but necessity.

JOSEPH OTTOLENGHE TO REV. JOHN WARING

[Savannah, November 18, 1754]
Revd. Sir: The colony hitherto has been unsettled and the people in it no way fix'd in their determination to settle in town or country, but since the news of the government's being settl'd and a Governor arrived, many families are withdrawn into the country to their plantations and many of those Negroes who had begun to make a tolerable proficiency are gone with them. But I bless God that there are many in town who have not bended their hearts to gain only but think it highly necessary to have their slaves instructed and [are] careful of sending of them, insomuch that at times a large room that I have for that purpose is as full as it can hold, tho' I must own that it is not the third part of the Negroes that are about us.

JOSEPH OTTOLENGHE TO REV. JOHN WARING

[Savannah, July 12, 1758]
Revd. Sir: I was extremely touch'd to find myself under so high a displeasure of

the Associates. I solemnly declare that not a year has pass'd since my coming into this province without writing to you or to the worthy and Revd. Mr. Smith. If my letters have miscarried since the breaking out of the [French and Indian] War, I'm not to be charged and punish'd for neglect. Five or six months' experience in these parts of the world would soon convince you that it is not so easy as imagined to write for England. Opportunities [to send letters] from hence are scarce, and those few during these unhappy times very precarious. Our Governor can tell [you] that even duplicates and triplicates are not always means sufficient for correspondence.

As for my not giving an account of the Negroes that comes to me for instruction, their numbers cannot be fixed because sometimes I have had fifty and more at once and perhaps in a month or two after it not half that number and at others not ten and so on more or less alternately. As they have no will of their own, their motions are guided by the despotic will of their owners and have no other leisure but what is allow'd them. 'Tis true that the public has of late demanded a good deal of their time in building of forts throughout the province and cutting of roads and consequently during that time few have resorted to me.

I have built a large room with a large chimney for the use of these poor souls, the latter extremely necessary for them who are of a chill constitution, ill fed and worse clothed, that many are not fit to be seen by a modest eye. I have laid myself under the expense of candles by teaching them by night, to cut off their pharaohs' excuse that they cannot send their Negroes by day because of their labor.

But then 'twill be ask'd what fruits have these methods produc'd with respect to the Negroes? To this I answer, as much as I could reasonably expect from a set of people naturally stupid, loaded with a cruel slavery, ignorant of our language and manners, no idea of our holy religion, nurs'd in extravagant idolatry, loaded with hard labor and worse usages, ill fed, ill clothed, cruelly corrected and barbarously treated, insomuch that a dog and an horse are treated like humane creatures when compared with the usages that these poor unhappy wretches are dealt with who first have been robb'd of dear liberty, their native country, beriev'd of their friends, parents, relations, wives and children and at once reduc'd to a most deplorable and cruel slavery! How often the present humane Governor and I have commiserate[d on] their hard and forlorn fate and propose to find out some relief for them. But who must give the consent to such regulations? Why the legislative body compos'd mostly of owners of Negroes, who would as soon consent to it as an assembly of lawyers would pass a bill to curtail their fees or reduce their practices to an honest and Christian standard!

On the fourth instant the whole silk house between 4 and 6 o'clock in the morning was entirely consumed by fire. There is also consum'd a large quantity of silk balls for as this year has produc'd the largest quantity of cocoons that Georgia ever saw so the loss of them must be great. 'Tis true that the silk reel'd and the seed for next year is preserv'd because at my house, but still the loss is great. There was no possibility of quenching the fire by reason of a powder magazine that lay just by and the people expecting every moment that 'twould blow up. And had that been the case the council house, the assembly chamber, the Secretary's and Surveyor General's offices, where all the writings of the colony are, must have been consumed, together with greater part of the town. The buildings of this town as well as the magazine are of timber, full of resin. Had there been the least breath of air that morning no human means could have sav'd the town.

JOSEPH OTTOLENGHE TO REV. JOHN WARING

[Savannah, October 4, 1759]

Revd. Sir: 'Tis now above a year since I had the pleasure to write an answer to one of yours. Expressions perhaps dropt from my pen that might have given offence, as I then labor'd under great afflictions, the filature just burnt to the ground, my wife languishing on a bed of sickness, myself far from being well and under the displeasure of both of the Honorable Society and the Associates. While under such a pressure of mind I might have then wrote what I should not have done in a more calm season.

Upon the whole, considering the many impediments that the instruction of Negroes is clog'd with, arising both from the unhappy circumstances of the Negroes and the ill disposition of their owners towards their being instructed, many of them nevertheless can repeat the church catechism by heart and give answer to such questions as their low understanding will permit of. Several of them can read tolerably well, and very few of them that cannot repeat the Lord's Prayer, Creed and Ten Commandments and such prayers as are fitting for their wretched conditions and judgements. Possessors of slaves purchase them for hard labor, out of which an annual profit is propos'd, to obtain which a daily task is allotted them and severely exacted from them. And as the Mahometans look upon their women to have souls of an inferior nature to those of men, so our Americans look upon their slaves to have no souls at all, and a favorite dog or horse meet with more humane treatments than they. As for the Negroes of these parts they are mostly Africans born and are as ignorant of our language as we are of theirs, and consequently no impression can be made on them until they are capable of understanding. It requires length of time, great patience and much industry before they can have a sensible idea of our language. Stupidity, the concomitant of a hardfelt everlasting slavery, the little time allow'd them for instruction and the few or no opportunities to converse with such as might produce an improvement in their learning, together with other causes of the like nature, are great impediments in their way of instruction. I do not know a greater piece of charity or a better offering fit for heaven than the bringing of these poor creatures from darkness and the shadow of death to the light and knowledge of the Gospel of our Redeemer. 'Twould not undo the heavy afflictive burden of slavery nor break asunder the cruel yoke of oppression, yet 'twould make the thorny path of bondage become somewhat smoother and some degrees sweeten the bitter cup of servitude so as to afford them strength to run with patience the race that is set before them.

[18]

I found the people here dissatisfied and discontent, inflamed with resentment and liberal in invectives. The present assembly was formed by dint of threatenings used, promises made, offices created, new commissions granted, old ones altered.

HENRY ELLIS, 1757

THE SECOND Royal governor, Henry Ellis (1721–1806), an Irish-born world traveller, reached Georgia in February, 1757, and soon won the goodwill of most Georgians by his tact, honesty and effective policy toward the Indians. But tiring of the heat in Savannah, which he claimed was the hottest in the world, he asked to be relieved of his duties in 1760. Governor Ellis's letters to the Board of Trade were taken from Allen D. Candler, *Colonial Records of the State of Georgia, XVIII*, typescript, 1937, pp. 4–15, 18–31, 114–117.

March 11, 1757

I embrace this early opportunity of transmitting to Your Lordships the truest idea I can form of the situation of things here upon the best but still imperfect information I have had time to acquire.

I arrived at Charles Town the 28th of January, where I was received with the greatest marks of respect by the principal inhabitants who think themselves closely connected and deeply concerned in the fate of Georgia. The friendly and confidential reception I met with from Governor [William Henry] Lyttleton [of South Carolina] was no less agreeable as the advantage I reaped from his advice and information. It afforded me an opportunity of settling a plan of good correspondence with him, of removing some provincial prejudices and of concocting such designs as seemed best calculated to unite and reconcile as much as possible the variety of little views and interests that subsist here and are apt to influence and interfere with the public measures.

On my arrival here Mr. Reynolds resigned his commission and instructions into my hands, conformable to Your Lordships' commands, whereupon I immediately qualified and took upon me the administration of government. The first instance of which I showed in rejecting Mr. Reid and Mr. Patrick Mackay, two councillors lately admitted by Mr. Reynolds in the room of two others that absented themselves but were not suspended and who returned to their seats on this change. But I did this with such apparent justice and impartiality that no umbrage was taken even by these gentlemen.

I found the people here exceedingly dissatisfied with each other and an almost universal discontent arising from the late proceedings and persons in power. Few approached me that were not inflamed with resentment and liberal in invectives urging that I should take some immediate and very violent steps, such as a total change of public officers and the dissolution of the Assembly and notwithstanding their prepossessions offered some very cogent reasons for this procedure. Sensible of my own inexperience and of the violence of such councils, fearful of being misled and aiming rather at healing the wounds and extinguishing the flame of party than stirring it anew, I forebore making any material alteration until I should be qualified to act from observation and experience, in order that the changes I shall then make may rather be attributed to my own judgement than to the advice of designing and interested people. This suspense will give time for men's passions to subside and for truth to appear through the cloud of party prejudice that at present obscures it.

I believe it may be advanced as a fact that the present assembly was formed by dint of very irregular and improper means. Threatenings were used, promises made, offices created, new commissions granted, old ones altered to facilitate the bringing in of such men as were to be the implicit tools of Mr. Little who, it was preconcerted, should be their Speaker. These machinations succeeded, men at their devotion were chosen, flexible, weak and ignorant, ready to join in anything they were put upon, however destructive to the true intent of their constituents. Not dishonest in their private characters, but easy, credulous and equally disposed to good or evil. And it is to be wished that those who had acquired such a degree of influence had employed it to other purposes than those of a private and sinister nature. As the former Assembly was treated with remarkable haughtiness, a conduct quite the reverse has been shown to this for very obvious reasons.

Those in power were early apprized of Your Lordships' intention to inquire into their conduct, hence there was a necessity of some steps towards their justification. Such is the address to His Majesty in favor of Mr. Reynolds's administration, not to mention a variety of other designs that the activity and opposition of the contrary party rendered abortive. For carrying these was not sufficient to have a majority in the Assembly who had but little credit. It was necessary the Governor and his minister should flatter the people even to the detriment of the province. Hence that remarkable speech at the opening the Assembly, declaring that the former taxes were sufficient and that no more would be asked, notwithstanding the sum arising from them the last year was one-third short of the service for which it was intended. It produced but £200 and the service required £300. The deficiency was taken from the contingent money which was to be reimbursed out of that to be raised the present year, although they were sensible it would be inadequate to the ordinary expenses of government exclusive of such a debt.

Other concessions were made such as the Assembly's recommending persons for the commissions of the peace at the request of the Governor. The Council, too, were desired to recommend officers for the new raised troops, precedents equally unjustifiable and impolitic but which were to serve two purposes, to cajole the people and to embarrass a future Governor. From these considerations joined to an information I received that the Assembly intended to address me at the instance of Mr. Little, their Speaker, in such a manner as would lay me under difficulties in case I found a dissolution requisite, which I had strong reason to believe would be the case from the dislike of the people they were preparing to testify by addresses from the different districts—and finding a recess would be agreeable at this season of the year after so long a sitting, I thought it prudent to adjourn them for a month and do intend to adjourn them further as I find it expedient. It behoves me to be very circumspect in what steps I take otherwise I shall soon find myself intangled in some very untoward transactions that neither quadrate with my own views nor those of Government. Everything is precarious in such a situation.

Whilst I am mentioning the inconveniences that abound here I think I ought not to omit the following very material one, namely that many lots of the best land in the province lie vacant in consequence of claims that are said to exist and were derived from a verbal cession of Mr. Oglethorpe. The claimants themselves have not attempted to establish their pretensions nor complied with any one condition in the Royal instruction. They do not reside here nor is it well known where they are but it is probable they are lying at lurch until contiguous lands [are] improved and the value of those they claim raised thereby. By this means the settling of the province is retarded and a considerable part of the quitrents lost. I therefore humbly beg leave to propose to Your Lordships whether it would not be proper to summon these people in the *London Gazette*, in that of South Carolina and by advertisements here to put in their claims and prove their rights within a given time to prevent the lands being forfeited and regranted. I presume nothing can be more equitable, and certainly nothing more immediately necessary. Therefore I shall impatiently expect Your Lordships' opinion of and instructions concerning it. For by the steps I intend taking, which upon a future occasion I shall communicate to Your Lordships, I make no doubt but we shall soon have a great influx of inhabitants.

The alarms to the northward and other circumstances seem to favor such an expectation. Upon this occasion I cannot help expressing my surprise that the Acadians which were sent here were not better disposed of than to be suffered to leave the province. Out of near four hundred that arrived, only about one hundred remain, some of which are dispersed among the plantations, and others have built themselves huts near this town and are very useful to the colony, as they employ themselves in making oars, hand spikes and other implements for sea craft that are immediately brought up and sent to the islands, where they meet with a good market.

I am informed by Mr. Reynolds that Your Lordships have had transmitted to you an account of a encounter that happened on the River Ogeechee between some of our settlers and a party of the Creek Indians, wherein two of the latter were killed. This untoward accident had near involved the province in a cruel war with them. All the Creek Nations were alarmed and on our side a general consternation prevailed. With advice of the Council, Mr. Reynolds resolved to raise some troops for the defense of the province. In consequence of which officers were commissioned and one troop of Rangers begun to be lured but was not quite completed when a conference with the Indians produced a temporary pacification. To this succeeded fresh causes of alarm, for from several quarters advices were received of a design meditated by the French against these provinces. This produced an address from the General Assembly, entreating the Governor to provide for their defense, which is said to have occasioned orders to be issued to build another scout boat and raising two more troops of Rangers.

But no part of this was actually put into execution at the time it was known here that I had landed at Charles Town. Then everything was precipitated. Officers were named and every other step taken that could deprive me of the means of obliging any person in the execution of this measure should it take place. Things were in this situation when I arrived at Savannah, and I was reduced to the dilemma either of cancelling this proceeding, commenced upon very substantial and pressing considerations, or risking the continuation of it upon my own credit, notwithstanding an instruction that directs us to undertake no military operations without the concurrence of the Commander-in-Chief.

But the reflecting that this was an exigence wherein that could not be obtained and that disbanding the men already raised might be attended with bad consequences, as well as being very unpopular since the people here would have concluded that they were to be abandoned to the mercy of their invaders, I judged it most eligible to let things remain as they were until His Majesty's pleasure or the opinion of Lord Loudoun [Commander-in-Chief of British forces in America, 1756–57] upon this affair should be known. I was induced the more to this by a letter I had from His Lordship, wherein he acknowledges the acceptance of some bills drawn on him by Mr. Reynolds for the raising and support of these troops without blaming or approving the measure itself by desiring that no more should be drawn upon him till the purposes for which they are drawn be signified, whence I would infer that His Lordship has not been so fully informed upon this subject as he had a right to expect.

Before I received the honor of his letter I had wrote His Lordship one notifying [him of] my arrival and containing the best account I was able to give of the state of this province, together with the particulars relative to these troops and begged a positive and precise instruction concerning them. But as the men already raised, being about forty, must be subsisted, the Captain takes this upon himself, depending upon the honor of the government for his reimbursement, requiring only certificates of me of the service. My Lords, whatever motives of a foreign power might induce Mr. Reynolds to raise this force, there are other very weighty considerations that prove the necessity of it at this juncture when danger threatens us from every quarter. The sources of all our embroils with the Indians are the irregularities committed by the Indian traders and the out-settlers. And how can we prevent these disorders without some coercive means of bringing offenders to justice? The laws at present are insufficient for this purpose and will be so without a military force whilst we are so thinly peopled and whilst so many find their account in disobeying them. To this weakness and insecurity may in a great measure be imputed the little progress this colony has made, notwithstanding the great and frequent helps it has had from England. For in a country that is exposed to every kind of outrage and injustice within and from without to every sort of depredation and attack, how can we expect that people will trust themselves of their property? Incessantly uneasy, incessantly in alarm, no person that has anything to lose or is exempt from the terrors of a jail will come among us. Besides, the Indians, excited by the French, allured by the prospect of advantage and having no reason to dread our resentment from a knowledge of our debility, will practice every species of enormity whilst it can be done with impunity.

The sum of all this will prove to Your Lordship beyond dispute how indispensable necessary it is to have some kind of military force in this province, not only to preserve its inward tranquility, but to defend itself and the other provinces to which it must be considered as a barrier against such powerful neighbors as the French, Spaniards and two of the most formidable of the Indian Nations. At present we enjoy a sort of calm. We hear of no settled plan among the Indians to attack us, although we are convinced they are not entirely satisfied with us. For some time past it is said they have been ill supplied by the French and this may be one of the causes why the late quarrel was so easily accommodated and that they remain quiet. When I came here I found Acouthla, one of the chiefs of the Lower Creek Nation, with several of his people who had been many days in town without being taken any notice of by Mr. Reynolds. I thought this was a time that could not justify such a neglect. They were in great want of provisions, which induced me to order them an immediate supply, which was received with very singular marks of satisfaction.

I then appointed a day to have a conference with them before the Council and upon that occasion urged every thing I was capable of to fix them in our interest and excite them to annoy our enemies and what I said made such an impression that Acouthla told me he had 100 warriors at our service, that he had given proof of his love to the English in the late war and that he was glad of this occasion to renew them, for which purpose he requested a Captain's commission. I readily gave him one, together with a drum, flag, gun, hatchet and a few other presents to himself and his followers and acquainted them that we would give twenty shillings for every scalp of our enemies and forty shillings for every prisoner. I did this with the advice of the Council, whom I convinced of the expediency of it. All this was highly pleasing to the Indians and as they set out immediately for their own country I sent by them a salutation to the chiefs of the Creek Nation and signified my intention of seeing them so soon as some presents which I expected from England should arrive.

Thoroughly convinced of the importance of standing well with these people, I shall exert every means and employ every art that contribute to that end. It were greatly to be wished that those little forts which were intended to secure our frontier, such as Augusta upon this river and Argyle upon the Ogeechee, as well as the fortifications on the islands towards the Spaniards, were put into a defensible condition. At present they are quite in ruins and are rather marks of our weakness than power. Was it practicable to raise a fund for this purpose here I would very gladly attempt it, nor should I despair of effecting it, but the poverty of this province makes it impossible. Nevertheless, poor as we are, we are not without hands, and I will endeavor to direct them to the execution of a plan that I have formed of raising a little fort here out of the wretched materials we have but which may enable us to make a short stand and be some cover against any sudden attack by sea or incursion of the Indians. For at this place, where we are most liable to be hurt by the enemy, no one work has been constructed towards its defense, save a little platform on which are four small guns improperly called a battery, as its situation is such that it neither covers the town nor could obstruct any armed vessels coming up the river should such an attempt be made. Yet however useless this is, it has been sufficiently expensive.

The representation of the defenseless state of this province that has been transmitted to Your Lordships by Mr. Reynolds is true as far as I can judge, and the plan proposed by Mr. DeBrahm of fortifying the province is judiciously concerted but so expensive that I despair of seeing it suddenly carried into execution. All therefore we can reasonably expect is what is absolutely and immediately necessary, such as the reparation of Fort[s] Augusta, Argyle and Frederica, with two or three troops of irregulars which I hope Your Lordships will see the necessity of and I doubt not will use your instances to obtain.

As soon as that spirit of contention has subsided which has long disturbed the minds of the people here and that I have taken the necessary precautions against any exigence that may happen in my absence, I intend making a tour of the province. I have a double view in this journey—one to inspect those places that are judged most proper to be fortified, the other to examine a spot that is esteemed a very proper situation for the capital. The former is very material for the safety of the province, and the latter no less concerns its interior prosperity. The spot I mean is Hardwicke, in regard to which different interests operate and consequently produce different opinions, though all agree in condemning our present situation, which indeed is a healthy one and that is all that can be said for it.

Being upon the extremity, it is exceedingly ill supplied and very inconvenient for trade and for the communication of the inhabitants that are widely dispersed over the province. Besides the lands contiguous to it are barren and the river shallow and intricate. These natural disadvantages, joined to the uncertainty of continuing here, have for some years past deterred anyone from building new or repairing old houses. Its proximity to Charles Town has prevented it from having any commerce of its own, for from thence the people here are usually supplied. Hence it is that there has been so little encouragement for merchants to come here. The few that are settled among us, having but a small vent for their goods, are obliged to sell at a huge advance, to the great detriment of the poorer sort of inhabitants. Hence it is that Carolina drains us of all the little specie that comes here, and the real value of the province is concealed by its commodities being sent thither to discharge our debts.

This province has been misrepresented. It is evidently capable of great improvement. It abounds with the finest rivers imaginable. The lands in general are good and have already afforded specimens—and those very large ones—of the best indigo made in North America. The raising of silk seems to be no longer a matter of curiosity. It employs many poor people and is approaching towards a staple. Had there been a sufficient quantity of seed this year a great deal of silk would have been produced, as numbers seem to engage in it eagerly from an experience of its benefit.

I have visited the filature here and found it much out of repair and standing in need of several material alterations, such as moving the pans and sinking a well.

Mr. Ottolenghe seems very capable and is zealous and active in his department. It is a pleasure to do business with such men. He convinced me how much these alterations were wanting and undertakes the inspection and management of the masons who are already begun to work. Mr. Bolzius, the minister of Ebenezer, is very solicitious that the filature there should be employed, as he thinks it would conduce to extend a knowledge of the art at present too much confined. Mr. Ottolenghe admits this but insists that it is too soon to employ two filatures before there is a sufficient quantity of cocoons to supply one.

My Lords, I was just going to put a period to this long letter when I was interrupted by a visit from Mr. Little, who, among other things, had the insolence to insinuate to me that if I had any design of dissolving the Assembly the consequences I might expect from such a step would be defeated inasmuch as he had taken measures to have the same men rechosen. I do not think myself at liberty to act as a private man nor to gratify my indignation at the expense of the public tranquility, otherwise we should try titles. I am in hopes I shall be able to effect my designs by gentler methods. 'Tis yet a moot point with me whether in a political light the members of this Assembly ought not to be considered as delinquents, for I do not find that they have committed any constitutional offense. All that can be apprehended from them is an opposition to my measures in order to justify the conduct of their friends lately in power and to whom they certainly owe some regard, since eleven of the nineteen members have been distinguished by such places of honor and trusts as this government affords. However 'tis possible they may be more tractable than is imagined, especially as whatever I shall propose will be most apparently for their own good. But if they should be obstinate or fractiously inclined, I think a way has to be found of getting rid of them without appearing to act from resentment.

In the instructions it is recommended to divide as soon as possible into counties this province and to make a distribution of the representatives conformable to that division. This is a regulation that will at all times be popular and is now earnestly wished for and of which as may avail ourselves in case of need, for whenever it takes place a dissolution will naturally follow. Although the King's instructions recommend this measure, they do not point out by what method it is to be done, whether at the will of the Governor solely or with the advice of Council. I should be glad Your Lordships would explain this in the first letter you honor me with. And, as I flatter myself I have proved clearly the necessity of removing the seat of government to a better situation, I am in great hopes Your Lordships will enable me to do this as soon as possible, since it can be done with much less inconvenience or injury to any person at present than some time hence when greater improvements are made here. The only obstruction to our immediate removal is want of money for the construction of the public buildings. £2000, I apprehend, would be sufficient, as a church, courthouse and jail are the only ones wanting. These that we have here are so ruinous as to be in a manner past repair, so that this expense must take place either here or there forthwith.

And, My Lords, is it not possible that a fund for this purpose might be found out of the savings of the silk money? Our church is so decayed that were the props which surround it knocked away it must inevitably tumble to the ground at once, and the public prison is shocking to humanity. It is scarce fifteen feet square and filled with felons, debtors, &c. promiscuously, and, being quite exposed to the scorching suns of this climate and often much crowded, the filth and vermin that these occasion is intolerable.

Savannah

May 5, 1757

In my last I acquainted Your Lordships that I intended visiting the southern parts of this province, which I have since done, and was not a little gratified by the state of things there.

I examined very minutely the principal rivers and found that called Great Ogeechee to have advantages much superior to any of the others. Its entrance is so deep as conveniently to admit of fifty-gun ships and would be a very proper station for our men of war intended to intercept the French vessels returning from the Mississippi. The spot that is thought proper to build the capital upon is about twelve miles up and very well adapted, as Your Lordships will see by the carte I transmit herewith. It is of a proper heighth, dry and consequently healthy, an excellent soil for gardens and the lands contiguous are rich and well settled. Its situation is very capable of being fortified, the harbor is excellent and the ships by a circumstance peculiar may be preserved from the worm as on one side of the peninsula the water is fresh and free from those destructive reptiles.

There are many other convenient rivers or inlets such as Midway, Newport, Sappelo and St. Simon's that must in time greatly facilitate the commerce and navigation of this province.

The lands towards the southern frontier are abundantly more fertile than those near Savannah. Many good settlements are already made there by people of a very sober and industrious turn that came from Carolina but, being greatly in debt, are not yet in a capacity of contributing much to the support of the colony, though in such a likely way of extricating themselves from these difficulties as can hardly fail unless some public calamity prevents it.

In my journey I met with many parties of Indians that were hunting, with whom I had much conversation. They seemed well disposed towards us, though they are apt to commit little disorders, such as killing of cattle and frightening the inhabitants, which it is next to impossible to prevent so long as there appears no power amongst us capable of restraining them, and they claim the lands that are above the flowing of the tides, which if they cannot be induced to relinquish must greatly straiten us that way. I think it would be possible to bring this about if we were authorized to undertake it, had a sufficient quantity of presents and watched a proper season. And until it is effected it is much to be feared that our back settlers will always be harassed by them.

Whilst I was in those parts I accidentally saw that odd character Gray, who occasioned so much disturbance here at Mr. Reynolds's arrival and whose settlement since on the south of the Altamaha excited some fears that he would embroil us with the Spaniards. Your Lordships have heard that the Governor of St. Augustine had sent a party of horse to threaten him with ill treatment if he continued there, which so terrified him that he removed to Cumberland's Island, whence after a short stay he returned and has since entered into a connection with one Alexander, a very bold sensible fellow who has long dwelt and acquired a great influence among the Lower Creek Indians that reside towards the Bay of Apalachee. By Gray's management this fellow has prevailed upon some of the chiefs of these people to go to Augustine and threaten the Spaniards with a war, if for the future they presume to molest or disturb those settlers. Intimidated by these menaces and alarmed by some of the Indian irregularities, the Governor has sent to invite Gray and Alexander to settle upon the River St. John's and establish an Indian trade under his protection, promising to furnish them amply with proper goods from New York.

This proposition Gray took an opportunity of communicating to me and of showing me letters relative thereto from one Fish who resides at that fortress and is agent to a company at New York that supplies the garrison with provisions. He had conceived an opinion that this permission would tend to preserve our claim to the lands on this side of that river provided he traded there with my license. But to me it seemed a dangerous experiment, as it would afford an opportunity to the Spaniards of practicing on these savages, of removing their old prejudices and fixing a good correspondence with them, and from their natural fickleness, of bringing them even to change sides, an event that could not fail of pernicious consequences.

Under these apprehensions, joined to my fear that Gray might turn traitor, I have urged every sort of argument to dissuade him from this design and as his activity will prompt him to some other enterprise, I have proposed to him to fix upon the River St. Mary's opposite to Fort William and assured him of all manner of countenance so long as he behaves well. To this he has agreed and I have granted him a license to trade with the Indians who inhabit thereabouts which must be very advantageous to him, as that place is nearer the center of the Creek Country than even Augusta, and he now seems inclined to quit the character of legislator, which he has long assumed, for that of a merchant. He is a shrewd, sensible fellow and affects an austerity of manners by which he has acquired a considerable influence among the people of this colony and made some impression upon the Indians and if he can be managed may prove an useful instrument in many respects. I cannot but admire the address of the Spanish Governor. He seems to be a man of excellent understanding and to pursue a plan of sound policy. He has taken infinite pains to gain the friendship of the Indians by a conduct full of uprightness and generosity. But their aversions are not easily conquered; he has had recourse to every justifiable art but hitherto unprofitably.

Had this taken effect it would have been a master stroke, as indeed is another that he is actually putting into execution. I mean that of drawing and settling about Augustine, in hopes they will cover him from the Indians, many of our back-settlers who fly for crimes and from the disturbances to the northward. But I do not despair of counteracting him by means of Gray and his partner, who frequently go thither and are well received by the Governor from a knowledge of their consequence. This is one of the uses I intend to make of them. Another will be to furnish us with early intelligence, which they may easily do as they will be a kind of advanced party, not to say barrier against the Spaniards and their Indian allies of Florida.

There has been another extraordinary fellow with me lately, one Moore, a man of distinguished valor who asks a commission to go up, no purchase or pay, with about fifty resolute fellows, good marksmen, his colleagues, to join the Chickasaws against the French. His intention is to intercept their boats, in which when the floods have subsided about the latter end of July, they carry goods from their settlements on the Bay of Mexico to supply that chain of forts that extends behind our colonies. My own opinion is that his scheme can have no bad consequences. Nevertheless I suspect encouraging him until I have consulted Governor Lyttleton.

My Lords, I have been fully employed of late in examining the interior state of this province in regard to its revenue and debts, its militia, its laws, &c. and on a careful survey have found everything in great disorder. Your Lordships are already acquainted with what passed here in 1755 when the conduct of Mr. Little created such general disgust that the Assembly attempted to inquire into it but were prevented by their dissolution at the beginning of the session, whereby no taxes were imposed for that year, while the expenses of the government were going on and, when the next Assembly met, it was found impossible from the poverty of the people to provide for more than one year's expenses at once.

By this means the province was burdened with a heavy debt which occasioned great embarrassment. This Mr. Little took advantage of by instigating the Assembly to usurp the power of auditing the accounts and issuing the public money, a measure that at one stroke put our Assembly on the footing of that of Carolina and subverted that check which ought to subsist for curbing the proceedings of that body. Not satisfied with this usurpation, he betrayed extreme partiality in the execution of it. He allowed of (for this Assembly was led by him) the accounts of his creatures only, which he contrived to pay out of the contingent money granted by Parliament and rejected and tore [up] those of his opponents, though examined and passed by the Governor in Council. By these and other unjustifiable steps he increased his interest with the Assembly and procured the address and representation of the state of the province, which he has carried with him for his master's and his own vindication. I need not anticipate Your Lordship's reflections upon these proceedings, which were surely unauthorized by the Royal instruction, incompatible with our constitution and pregnant with numerous and great inconveniences as we daily experience. However, I believe I shall be able to extricate the government from these difficulties and even prevent the like hereafter.

The Assembly have not met since my arrival but have been adjourned and prorogued from time to time that I might have leisure to settle my plan conformable to the disposition of the people which I have taken great pains to get acquainted with. I have now determined to call them together the 16th of June for a short sitting, as it will be a busy time of the year. I propose the passing of three acts only, the heads of which are already prepared, that is to say, one for the execution of my scheme to pay off the provincial debt, another for employing the hands intended for opening the roads to the construction of some places of defense, and a third for affording an asylum for seven years against their creditors to all persons in distressed circumstances, save such as come from that part of Carolina only that lies to the northward of us. This exception is requisite to prevent the ill uses that might be made by the people residing there who would have it in their power to contract debts one day and elude the laws and their creditors the next by flying into Georgia. It will also prevent any provincial altercation and hinder the people of that colony from making an opposition to this bill, as it will show a disposition to be just to them, while we are endeavoring to serve ourselves and manifest an equal regard to debtor and creditor. But the main object of this act is the speedy peopling of the colony by drawing a number of insolvents from the neutral islands of Santa Croix and Eustatia, where they have fled for shelter, and those also in the northern provinces who are in like circumstances—and not to weaken our neighbors, who in effect would be gaining nothing, as it would divide the power without agumenting it.

We already begin to apprehend that we shall have more people than we can furnish with good lands, for the Indians, imagining that all above the flowing of the tides are theirs, consider any settlement thereupon without their leave as a trespass, which they have a right to punish by plundering, so that we are considerably confined westward, since the tides do not flow above thirty miles up where the lands are more fruitful and tempt people to plans without liberty. These savages would have had no idea of fixing our limits that way had it not been put into their heads by Bosomworth who laid claim to those lands that lie behind us, and, I am assured, encouraged them to destroy the cattle they found there. He is a most mischievous, crafty and obstinate fellow, and his practices have so much intimidated people here that, although at the late courts he was afraid to try his title from the measures I took to render abortive the ill designs that had been concerted before my arrival, it is doubtful with me whether our people would have dared to decide against him, through fear of the troubles he might create by means of the Indians, with whom he keeps up an influence by insinuating that he is the guardian of their interests, which however without more substantial means would avail little. But he frequently makes them presents and treats them kindly at his house where he encourages them to come.

From the little countenance he has had from me and what has reached his ears that I have said concerning the precariousness of his title and the improbability of his ever reaping any advantage from it, it is likely if a compromise was thought necessary we should find him sufficiently tractable. And, My Lords, it were earnestly to be wished that some expedient might be fallen upon to put an end to this thorny affair, either by way of equivalent, by confirming to him a part of what he claims, or by any other method that Your Lordships' wisdom may suggest, as this colony in my opinion can never be exempt from apprehensions while it subsists. In my tour southwards I took a view of the islands Ossabaw, St. Catherine's and Sappelo, which indeed are very fine and worth contending for as they are said to contain near 40,000 of the best land in the province, which unfortunately must be waste till this contest be ended.

Whilst I am so anxious about extending our frontier, I am not less attentive in distributing to the best advantage the lands we have already. The monopolizing large tracts has been the common misfortune of these provinces. The people here are aiming at the same thing. Many purchase considerable quantities and then apply to me in Council for their family right, as they call it. As some of the Councillors themselves have a passion for this practice, I find it difficult to restrain it, so that I humbly conceive that if Your Lordships were pleased to give me a positive instruction to grant no lands to any person possessing above a certain quantity, say 1000, 2000 or 3000 acres, whether obtained by grant or purchase, it would give no material umbrage and could not fail of the best effects, by multiplying the plantations and consequently affording maintenance to a greater number of people.

I must now beg leave to remind Your Lordships of it by a particular instance that affects the people of this town very severely as well as others. Among the many visionary ideas that Mr. Oglethorpe entertained this was not the least absurd. He imagined that people here might subsist and even become affluent upon such small parcels of land as the little farms in England, which is absolutely impossible. The lands themselves are different as well as the nature of the culture, the produce and the climate. But riveted to this chimera, he established many little townships and minced all the lands 'round them into whimsical figures of five and forty-five acres, which he put people in possession of by a written order directed to the Constable.

A proclamation was published by Mr. Reynolds at his arrival, enjoining claimants to confirm their titles by new grants from the Crown, which induced many people to do so. But numbers have omitted it. Hence it follows that for five miles 'round, being the extent of this township, it is checkered with lots that have and have not apparent owners. The lots themselves are too small for a plantation and cannot be enlarged by obtaining a grant or even purchase of those adjoining till their property be ascertained, so that this tract which ought to supply the town with necessaries lies uncultivated and must continue so until Your Lordships find out a remedy. Since my arrival here some people of property have come in, and many more are expected from a belief that measures different from those hitherto pursued will take place.

Abundance of grants have lately been taken out and probably will continue to be applied for so that good lands and convenient situations must soon become scarce, which makes me more earnest to have it in my power to grant such as are vacant. I mean those said to belong to absentees which are now useless and even detrimental to the province, as they separate the inhabitants and consequently weaken them, as well as increase their labor upon the public roads, &c., an evil that ought to be attended to, whilst the people are so poor and so involved with their neighbors of Carolina that their utmost industry affords them but a scanty subsistence and a small surplus that goes thither to pay their debts. If we can forbear burdening them with public services and taxes, a little time will free them from their incumbrances and accelerate the prosperity of the province. This consideration makes me cautious of attempting many things highly necessary but which cannot be done without money. The public buildings are in a ruinous condition.

The lighthouse at the entrance of this river, an edifice raised at a vast expense and become extremely necessary for the commerce of these two provinces, is upon the point of tumbling down. Many fruitless remonstrances were made upon this subject to the late Governor. It was intended that the pilot residing there should have a house built at the public charge, without which it was scarce possible for him to continue. This has been resolved upon in Council but,

135

like many other useful things, neglected. These remonstrances were renewed to me and the facts sufficiently supported to convince me that there was an immediate necessity to take measures in consequence of them. I therefore advertised my intention of repairing the lighthouse and building a dwelling house for the pilot and desired those that were willing to undertake them to send in their proposals sealed to me in Council. At the same time I signified that those whose proposals were most reasonable should be preferred.

This had a good effect in convincing the public that I will not proceed on partial and jobbing principles. And the work will be done cheap. I cannot without indignation and surprise reflect upon the conduct of my predecessor in telling the Assembly in his speech at their last meeting that the taxes would be sufficient for the public service when at the same time if he knew anything he could not be ignorant that the public were indebted double the annual revenue or how he could think of leaving this province to me in such embarrassed circumstances after having practiced every kind of art to prevent my having any influence that might be directed towards its relief.

For every public office that either existed or were likely to be established were filled with his creatures, even when he knew of my arrival in America. Yet I am in hopes that if this was intended to answer any sinister purpose it will be defeated and that I shall be able to furnish the people here with better reasons for assisting me than those of a private, partial or mercenary nature. I have just been regimenting the militia, which before consisted of independent companies without connection, without subordination and without discipline. This step has afforded me an opportunity of gratifying some worthy men who are vain of military titles, of putting the militia in a condition of being useful and I may add of establishing a right that Mr. Reynolds intended giving up to the Assembly, that of appointing the officers. I have made a few alterations in the public offices by bringing in a pretty good man as deputy clerk of the Council, and a very good one, Mr. Thomas Burrington, to act as clerk of the Assembly in the room of wretched tools. Mr. John Graham, who is known to some of Your Lordships, I have named to the place of clerk of the accounts and Indian Commissary in the room of Mr. Little.

Scarce a week passes but we are visited by gangs of Indians led here by an expectation of receiving presents in consequence of the change of government. We treat them in the best manner we are able, furnishing them with provisions, some promises, a few presents and a great many fair words, and upon the whole have so managed that none have left us discontented. I hope the presents from England will soon arrive, for though it is possible to retain these people in good humor for some little time by such methods yet they cannot be practiced long with success.

November 25, 1757

I did myself the honor to write to Your Lordships on the 22nd October. A material transaction has since happened which I shall now relate. In my former letters I mentioned that I had sent an agent to the Creek country to invite the chiefs to Savannah to receive His Majesty's presents and to renew our friendships and alliance with them. At the same time I acquainted Your Lordships that I had lately had a meeting with Governor Lyttleton at Port Royal when it was agreed that these Indians should first go to Charles Town, where His Excellency had received intelligence they were preengaged to go by Mr. Pepper, his agent, who had been dispatched for that purpose to the Creek Nation from an apprehension that our interest was declining fast there. But Mr. Lyttleton was misinformed. His envoy, though sent up at great expense and esteemed well qualified, did not succeed in his commission, for the headmen could not be prevailed upon to return with him, although our agent was instructed not to attempt bringing them here until they had been at Charles Town, unless it appeared they had no immediate intention of going there. Mr. Pepper's miscarriage proceeded, I believe, from his being invested with and exciting a power that gave offence to the traders in the Nation, who, to lessen his consequence and gratify their resentment, counteracting his measures, though at the risk of their own safety.

To prevent any obstruction of this sort and even avail myself of these people's influence I wrote a particular and complaisant letter to each, requesting their assistance at this juncture in behalf of their country.

The consequence was that they, all to show their importance, exerted themselves to oblige me. The principal Indians of twenty-one towns to the number of 150 were induced to accept my invitation, set out accordingly with my agent and arrived at this place the 29th October. A treaty was concluded, confirming all our former ones, and by a new article therein it was declared that the Indians never sold nor alienated the lands and islands in dispute to Mrs. Bosomworth or to any other private person whatever but that they now gave the said lands and islands to me in trust as representative of His Majesty. Your Lordships will readily see the importance of this concession, which paves the way for obtaining an entire grant of these lands, greatly invalidates the Bosomworths' presentations and leaves them in a manner at the mercy of the Crown. The Indians of their own accord made this proposal in Council, to which however they were induced by the impressions that I had been making on them for several days before the talk, during which time I constantly entertained select parties of the leading men at my own house.

It will perhaps seem strange to Your Lordships that during the whole negotiation I never instigated the Indians to make war upon our enemies. But I hope to demonstrate that in this I acted prudently. 'Tis certain that the French by

137

means of the Albama Fort, whence the Indians are daily supplied with presents, have acquired a numerous party among those savages, wherefore if we should endeavor to make a breach between them it could only cause a civil war in the Nation, which would immediately destroy our Indian trade and considering our defenceless state might greatly endanger the safety of this province. Hence 'tis my firm opinion that it would be rash to attempt causing the Indians to break through their neutrality and that all I ought to endeavor is the maintaining our interest with them and this will be a great deal in our circumstances. The French, who are also sensible of their weakness on the Mississippi, observe the same conduct, but they disguise their real motive under the mask of friendship and regard for the Indians, boasting in all public talks of their disinterestedness and moderation.

The Indians stayed with us near three weeks and the charge of maintaining and accommodating such a number has been very considerable, I think about £270 exclusive of the agent's expense and wages, which amount to £790 more, and yet I can truly say there was not sixpence spent unnecessarily. I gave them about ⅜th of the presents, which I distributed with my own hands, knowing that would make them go much further and be better received. Besides, they had their guns, saddles and other utensils repaired, a job as chargeable as buying new ones, but this being customary in Carolina they expect it here, and I thought that at such a time nothing in reason should be denied them, lest a refusal in one instance should destroy the merit of all we had been doing. On the whole I am convinced there never was in this country so large a number of principal Indians that departed better satisfied with their treatment and if I know anything of their disposition I may safely affirm that they will not easily be gained from us unless there be some neglect or mismanagement on our part.

At the same time I must take the liberty to observe that in order to avoid such a misfortune the Governors of these provinces or whoever has the charge of Indian affairs should be effectually supported. I have ordered Mr. Graham, the Clerk of the Accounts, to transmit to Mr. Martyn an exact account along with the vouchers of the particular charges attending this transaction. I have likewise wrote to Mr. Martyn myself and given him my opinion at large of the properest assortment of goods for Indian presents hereafter and, as no relaxation or neglect must be suffered in this critical time, I hope Your Lordships will employ our good offices to obtain an immediate supply for what remains of the last must soon be exhausted.

$\begin{bmatrix} 19 \end{bmatrix}$

Crackers are a lawless set of rascals on the frontiers. They steal horses. Some stay in the Indian country and are perpetually endeavoring to stir up a war. They delight in cruelty, even to one another.

CAPTAIN GAVIN COCHRANE, 1766

AFTER he returned to London, Captain Gavin Cochrane reported to the Board of Trade on what he had seen of the Georgia frontier while commanding soldiers there. These extracts are taken from Cochrane's letters, June 10, 1766–November 14, 1766, in the Dartmouth Papers, Staffordshire Public Record Office.

My Lord: It was from an inclination to entertain Your Lordship a little at a leisure hour, and perhaps inform you of things you would be glad to know, that I used the freedom to propose writing to you what came under my knowledge during my having the honor to command the Royal Americans in South Carolina and Georgia.

The town of Savannah stands on a high sandy bluff from which is a steep descent to the river. Vessels of three or four hundred tons anchor here. The streets are a hot sand, the houses not numerous, and at a distance from each other; but the people in general are of some consequence and very hospitable. A capital situated in a corner on the frontiers seems not very well calculated for rendering the province populous. The town lots are small, which is something extraordinary.

From Savannah I was to go to Augusta where there is a good fort garrisoned by the Royal Americans. I was told that the country nigh the river was well inhabited, and at the same time advised not to go that way, as I would in all probability have my horse stolen; but that I should get a guide and go through the woods. After I passed the small town of Ebenezer, which is twenty-five miles from Savannah, I left the neighborhood of the river and saw very few houses, and most of those few but just put up. I rode the whole way through a pine barren and have rode twenty miles without seeing a house or a drop of water.

Augusta is a small town of straggling houses, with some considerable Indian

139

traders in it, the country about it indifferently well peopled. They have lately built a neat little church there and have an organ. The river runs just by the town and gives them the benefit of water carriage from the town of Savannah. The fort is not on the now frontiers but in the town on the river; the church is a mile and half beyond it, and the frontiers about twenty miles beyond that. As the fort was to be rebuilt I gave it as my opinion that it should be placed nigher the frontiers, but reasons were given to the contrary. The practice of horse stealing is very common here, which is very scandalous, owing to a lawless set of rascals who often come here. They are nicknamed Crackers and bring peltry to sell.

I visited Fort Prince George in the Cherokee country. The Indian trade carried on by the people of South Carolina is with the Cherokees; that carried on by the people of Georgia is with the Creeks. Between the mountains and the river are very rich plains on both sides, but not very broad. Fort Prince George stands on a little rising in the plain. On the opposite side stood old Theawee, which is now deserted, and the new town of that name is built about a mile and a half above the fort. I went to see it. The houses have a very neat look; are of a tolerable size, and are plaistered inside and out with a clay found here as white as common lime plaister. And over this the principal houses have the outside of their walls painted in different colors in chequer[board pattern]. Their dishes, &c. are made of this clay and look clean. The houses are not placed regular, but on little risings, and in the middle on the plains is the town house for councils and for dances. This is a large round house with the roof reaching almost to the ground, small holes to let in a little light, the fireplace in the center, but no chimney or hole to let out the smoke.

In my return from Fort Prince George, I came just time enough to prevent mischiefs happening between the inhabitants of the neighborhood and some Cherokees who were hunting. The people wanted to pick a quarrel and revenge themselves on the Indians for what they had suffered during the war. But, My Lord, our own bad people are not less dangerous or less industrious to create us trouble than those of the French were. Our people in general are but too apt to occasion discontent amongst the Indians by grossly imposing on them. The Cherokees complained that some families had settled on their hunting grounds and had planted corn. Repeated complaints came from the Cherokees that white people came into their hunting grounds. They brought three of those lawless people called Crackers, who behaved with the greatest insolence.

But a greater enemy than even the Crackers was the great quantity of rum that the traders, or people employed by them, carried into the Indian country. The better sort of Indians are sensible of the bad effects of rum. When they are in liquor then every thing they ever looked upon as bad usage comes fresh in their minds, and they don't care what they do.

I should explain to Your Lordship what is meant by Crackers, a name they have got from being great boasters. They are a lawless set of rascals on the frontiers of Virginia, Maryland, the Carolinas and Georgia who often change their places of abode. They steal horses in the southern provinces and sell them in the Northern; and those from the northern provinces they sell in the southern. They get merchants by degrees to trust them with more and more goods to trade with the Indians and at first make returns till they have established some credit, then leave those that trusted them in the lurch, return no more but go to some other place to follow the same practice. Some of them stay in the Indian country and are perpetually endeavoring to stir up a war. They delight in cruelty, which they often practice even to one another. In August last one of these rascals, one Proctor, was catched by the officer commanding at Fort Augusta and sent down to the Governor of Georgia. He had committed the most unheard of barbarities in the Cherokee War and had been lurking in Indian country ever since.

It was the 18th of July when I took a boat at Savannah to go to Frederica. The weather was extremely hot. We had not been two hours on board when one of the rowers by a *coup de soleil* lost his senses, insisted on jumping overboard and died soon after his being put on shore. When we had got five miles down the river from the town of Savannah, we turned into Augustine Creek, having the continent on our right and a string of islands on our left, which are so little separated from each other that the sea there has the appearance of a very narrow river and bears the name of a creek, a name given in America to rivers of a lesser size. The greatest opening to the sea is between the islands of Sapelo and St. Catherine, where it is nine miles broad. There is another of two miles broad. These islands between the Savannah River and the Island of St. Simon or Frederica are, I believe, all of them private property. They are very thinly inhabited. I could scarce see any houses on them, tho' they appeared to be good land.

The islands are in general very narrow. The Island of St. Catherine is twenty miles long and the property of Mr. Bosomworth, a clergyman who got that island and the Island of Sapelo and Blackbeard's Island with his wife, who was a Creek Indian and of great power in that Nation. Blackbeard's Island and Sapelo are now the property of a Mr. McKay, I think they call him. Sapelo is also twenty miles long. On Sapelo Island, as I was told, there is only an overseer, for that and Blackbeard's Island, and no inhabitants on St. Catherine's but Mr. Bosomworth and his family.

The town of Sunbury lies on this inland passage. I think it is reckoned about forty miles from the town of Savannah by land, by water it is much farther. Here I saw several ships. In this town are eighty houses and a few traders. The sixth day of my voyage I got to the Island of St. Simon or Frederica. The name of this island was changed from St. Simon's to Frederica by General Oglethorpe, who kept his regiment there. And during that time it was in a kind of flourishing condition, as appears by the ruins of the town of Frederica. Part of it was burnt by accidental fire. Other houses, tho' now in a wretched condition, appear to have been once very good. The island is twenty miles long, some parts two miles broad but the greatest part of it is but one mile broad. There are scarce any inhabitants on it but at Frederica, where there are about thirteen families of no great account living in the ruinous houses. The only person of note on the island is Capt. Demery who had been in the army, who has a house and very fine gardens about a mile from town.

There is a very small settlement on the Altamaha called the Darien Settlement. A good many grants of lands have been given on this river, but they are not yet settled. Fort Barrington is on this river, with a small garrison of rangers. The islands of Sapelo and St. Catherine's are, I believe, of much the same breadth as Frederica. A most beneficial trade with lumber might be carried on from them, as they are well wooded. The proprietor of Sapelo Island breeds mules and sends them to the West Indies.

On my return to Savannah, I came about fourteen miles by land that I might have a better view of that part of the country. I saw a good many gentlemen's plantations and good Indian corn growing, tho' the soil was sandy. I went and saw Bethesda, Mr. Whitefield's hospital, which was very neat and plain. There were few boys and girls there.

Revolution

AFTER the death of Henry Ellis's patron, Lord Egremont, George Grenville assumed the responsibility for addressing American problems. The national debt had doubled as a result of the recent war and Grenville saw no alternative to raising taxes. He pushed a cider tax through a reluctant Parliament, the most intrusive ever in England. Grenville believed that Americans, the beneficiaries of French removal, should share the financial burden. He placed great hopes in the Stamp Act of 1765 which required stamped paper to be used in all legal transactions, bills of lading and printed documents.

Grenville could not have anticipated the violence of the American reaction. The tax fell most heavily on merchants and lawyers. These generally conservative people encouraged popular leaders to organize demonstrations against the tax. The demonstrations, coupled with a ban on trade with Britain, had the desired effect. Goaded by the caustic oratory of William Pitt, Parliament repealed the Stamp Act in 1766. The new minister of the Exchequer, Charles Townshend, reasoned that if the Americans objected to internal taxes such as the Stamp tax, they might accept external taxes. Therefore in 1767 he persuaded Parliament to place taxes on American imports such as paper, glass, lead and tea. The revenue would defray the cost of governing the colonies.

The Townshend Duties brought forth the radicals in greater numbers than before. They organized committees in all major towns and enforced another ban on British trade. Again it worked. A new minister, Lord North, repealed all the taxes in 1770 except the one on tea. For a time radical agitation subsided except around Boston where Samuel

Adams skillfully orchestrated demonstrations in front of the state house that resulted in the so-called Boston Massacre. Lord North inadvertently played into the hands of militants by his attempt to rescue the nearly bankrupt East India Company. The tea was taxed twice, once in England and a second time in America. Americans preferred to buy cheaper tea from competitors of the East India Company. Americans accused Lord North's ministry of a sneak attempt to raise revenue under the guise of regulating trade. The most violent protest occurred in Sam Adams' Boston. As every American schoolboy knows, Bostonians dressed like Indians threw the tea overboard as the unprotesting crew watched.

Lord North pushed a series of punitive acts through a willing Parliament, closing the port of Boston, suspending government in Massachusetts and increasing the number of troops in that province. By an unfortunate coincidence, the long-delayed Quebec Act became law at the same time. That legislation permitted Canadians to retain their religious practices and their customary civil law. It extended the boundaries of Quebec to the Ohio and Mississippi rivers. Virginia, Massachusetts, Connecticut and New York all had land claims in the region and all found common cause in protesting the Quebec Act. Patrick Henry's "Virginia Resolves" denounced the recent acts and Virginia invited all the colonies to meet in Philadelphia in a Continental Congress.

Georgia did not attend. In the year of the Tea Party, Georgians applauded Governor Wright's skillful management of the Treaty of Augusta. Governor Wright could honestly advertise the new territory as far from the tumults of Boston. In 1774, the year of the First Continental Congress, Georgians were too frightened by Creek Indian war parties to worry about esoteric matters like the price of tea.

The First Continental Congress called upon the American provinces to unite in an "Association" to ban trade with England, and its members agreed to meet again in 1775 if England had not responded by then. Before the year elapsed, the war erupted at Lexington and Concord. When the Second Continental Congress convened in May, the

Massachusetts and Connecticut militia crowded around Boston in an unmilitary siege of the British troops there. The Continental Congress appointed George Washington to the command at Boston and renewed the Association. Local committees composed of the most radical elements of the population enforced the ban on trade with England. The Battle of Bunker Hill fought on Breed's Hill outside Boston in June, 1775, greatly encouraged the wavering. British regulars advanced in orderly lines which, however impressive to the sight, left them exposed to the deadly fire of the entrenched Americans. By July, 1776, radicals controlled the Congress and declared American independence. Georgians George Walton and Button Gwinnett joined Lyman Hall just in time to affix their signatures to the great document. That most radical of historic pronouncements proclaimed that the new nation committed itself to the proposition that all men were created equal and that government depended upon consent of the governed. A civil war had to be fought in America before these radical ideas were incorporated into law. Over two hundred years later, the Declaration still challenges Americans to live up to its ideals.

As the conservatives shrank away from the dangerous and unpredictable break with the mother country, the radicals wrote democratic state constitutions and drafted the Articles of Confederation which left political power where they thought it belonged, at the local level. Georgia's constitution, adopted in 1777, ranked with Pennsylvania's as the most democratic of all. Conservative Savannahians like John Wereat complained that the wrong sort had got into power.

Despite the grumblings of people like Wereat in Georgia and John Adams of Massachusetts (who complained about the "damned set of rascals" in Congress), the radical set managed to secure a treaty with France and to struggle through the war to a successful conclusion with almost no money. France actively entered the war after the continentals under Horatio Gates and Benedict Arnold stopped "Gentleman Johnny" Burgoyne at Saratoga on October 17, 1777. Instead of attempting a juncture with Burgoyne, General Sir William Howe left New York and went south to Philadelphia. George Washington, who had won a morale-boosting engagement at Trenton, New Jersey on Christmas night, 1776, could not prevent the British from taking Philadelphia. He and his troops could only endure bravely at Valley Forge.

After taking Philadelphia, General Howe seemed to lose interest in the war and was replaced by Sir Henry Clinton. Coached by the war minister Lord George Germain, Clinton decided to adopt the strategy so urgently promoted by the southern Royal governors. As a result, Lieutenant Archibald Campbell led an invasion of Georgia in late December, 1778. After overwhelming General Robert Howe's little army in Savannah, Campbell moved rapidly to Augusta, but the expected Indians failed to arrive on time. After two weeks in Augusta where heretofore secret loyalists had a brief holiday, Campbell withdrew as far as Briar Creek. The patriots won a tidy victory at Kettle Creek, but lost at Briar Creek. Thereafter the British retained possession of lower Georgia.

A French army under Count Henri d'Estaing, joined by General Benjamin Lincoln's continentals with Georgia and South Carolina militia, failed in an attempt to dislodge the British from Savannah in October, 1779. The successful defense of Savannah prompted General Clinton to send more troops South. Charleston fell on May 12, 1780, and resistance collapsed all over Georgia and South Carolina. Only a few hardy souls who sought protection among the "over the mountain" men in North Carolina kept the flickering flame of independence alive.

Congress dispatched the hero of Saratoga, Horatio Gates, to salvage the southern provinces. Gates proved marvelously inept. He lost his army to Lord Cornwallis at Camden on August 16, 1780. However, on October 7, 1780, North Carolina mountain men defeated Major Patrick Ferguson's loyalists at King's Mountain on their own initiative; Gates heard about it later. The southern department badly needed a new leader. Nathanael Greene had been itching to give up the unglamorous and all but impossible job of Quartermaster General and readily accepted Washington's invitation to replace Gates and take charge of the southern campaign. In January, Greene sent his best man, Daniel Morgan, toward Georgia. At Cowpens, Morgan defeated the dashing British cavalryman Banastre Tarleton. Then Greene pulled his scattered forces together and stood toe to toe with Cornwallis at Guilford Courthouse. Cornwallis marched his battered army northward into Virginia. Instead of following him, Greene turned his attention to the isolated British garrisons in Carolina and Georgia and reduced them one by one.

Short on supplies, Cornwallis waited on the Yorktown peninsula for naval support. George Washington, grown weary of watching Henry Clinton's immobile forces at New York, made the bold decision to trap Cornwallis. He persuaded French Admiral DeGrasse to blockade Chesapeake Bay while his continentals and the French army under Count de Rochambeau hurried south to pen up Cornwallis by land. DeGrasse managed to hold off the British fleet long enough for the allied forces to get into place. Cornwallis had no choice but to surrender. On October 19, 1781, seven thousand British troops stacked their arms while their band played "The World turn'd Upside Down." King George wept at the news and allowed his favorite minister, Lord North, to resign. The new minister, Lord Shelburne, sent his delegates to Paris to begin peace negotiations with Benjamin Franklin, John Adams and John Jay. By the Treaty of Paris, Britain recognized the independence of the thirteen colonies and placed their borders on the Mississippi River. The Rev. Thomas Taylor of Savannah spoke for all Loyalists, "Indeed we may truly say, 'The Glory is departed.' I could weep to think of our situation."

$\begin{bmatrix} 20 \end{bmatrix}$

*It is really a wretched state to be left in, government totally annihilated
and assumed by congresses, councils and committees and gross insults
committed and not the least means of protection or even personal safety,
and these almost daily occurrences are* too much*!*

JAMES WRIGHT, 1775

GEORGIA POLITICS swung wildly from conservative to radical during the two years 1774 to
1776. Governor James Wright's popularity plummeted. The Stamp Act of 1765 created a crisis
that threatened his leadership, but he weathered the storm and later most Georgians approved of
his conduct. Wright was convinced that Georgia would have remained quiet if the radicals in
South Carolina had ceased their instigations. The transplanted Carolinians who formed the Midway community in Georgia's St. John's Parish were the eager allies of militants in Carolina.
Low-country radicals regarded Savannah as a conservative bastion dominated by the governor
and, in collusion with backcountry allies, they planned to displace the coalition of merchants and
planters who controlled the General Assembly.

However, the radical faction made slow progress because of an unusual series of events which
had nothing to do with the troubling issues of the times. Governor Wright's Treaty of Augusta
in 1763 opened a strip of settlement between the Savannah and Ogeechee rivers and above
Augusta up to the Little River. Within ten years most desirable land was taken and the Assembly
pressed the government to obtain another cession from the Indians. Wright's successful management of the Second Treaty of Augusta in 1773 met with general approbation. During the
following year, Indian alarms caused the frontier people to proclaim their loyalty to the King
when the merchants in Savannah protested the ministry's punishment of Massachusetts in retaliation for the Boston Tea Party. Wright's interdiction of the Indian trade placed him on the
side of the settlers. If the governor had chosen to extract an additional cession of land as a condition of peace, the course of Georgia history might well have been different. Backcountry people complained bitterly that Wright was unduly influenced by the traders when he decided
against another cession and merely resumed normal trade. By December, 1774, Wright had lost
most of his support in the backcountry and the radical movement was gathering momentum.
Some of the following documents have been abridged, and the wording of Haddon Smith's
deposition has been altered to eliminate legalisms.

James Wright to Lord Dartmouth

Savannah in Georgia
August 24, 1774

My Lord: I acquainted Your Lordship that I should give you a full account of the conduct and proceedings of the Liberty People here as soon as I knew for certain what they did or meant to do. Everything, My Lord, was done that could be thought of to frustrate their attempt, but this did not totally prevent it. They have been strongly invited by the Carolina Sons of Liberty, who have been suffered to do whatever they pleased without the least mark of disapprobation or attempt to check them that I have heard of, and now again, My Lord, as in the time of the Stamp Act, I am to be reflected upon and abused for opposing the licentiousness of the people. And it's thrown out, "Why should our Governor do so-and-so when the people in Carolina have gone greater lengths than we have and the Governor has not taken any notice of it?" At such times as these, if a man has resolution and integrity enough to stand forth and attempt to do his duty, it's like being set up as a mark to be shot at and raising the resentment of great numbers against him.

I have been informed of another summons and meeting to be in St. John's Parish on the 30th instant and, My Lord, as long as these kind of summonses and meetings are suffered, a private man to take upon him to summon a whole province to consult upon and redress public grievances, I apprehend there will be nothing but cabals and combinations, and the peace of the province and minds of the people continually heated, disturbed and distracted and the proclamation I issued against them is termed arbitrary and oppressive and an attempt to debar them of their natural and lawful rights and privileges! In short, My Lord, if these calls and meetings are considered as illegal and improper it will require the interposition of higher authority to remedy the evil, for the executive powers of Government in the colonies are too weak to rectify such abuses, and prosecutions would only be laughed at and no grand jury would find a bill of indictment and the persons ordering and carrying them on probably insulted and abused.

Permit me, My Lord, to say how things appear to me. I conceive that the licentious spirit in America has received such countenance and encouragement from many persons, speeches and declarations at the time of the Stamp Act and ever since in Great Britain and has now gone to so great a length and is at such a height that neither coercive or lenient measures will settle matters and restore any tolerable degree of cordiality and harmony with the mother country, and, in short, things and circumstances in America have increased so fast and at this time so amazingly exceeded what at the first settling and planting the colonies

149

could possibly have been supposed or expected and America is now become, or indisputably 'ere long will be, such a vast, powerful and opulent country or dominion that I humbly conceive, in order to restore and establish real and substantial harmony, affection and confidence and that Great Britain may receive that benefit and advantage which she has a right to expect from the colonies, it may be found advisable to settle the line with respect to taxation, &c. by some new mode or constitution and without which my real and candid opinion is that, however matters may be got over at present and whatever appearance there may be of amity and union, the flame will only be smothered for a time and break out again at some future day with more violence.

Letters from Sir James Wright (Savannah, 1873), pp. 180–181

In January, 1775, Georgia's first Provincial Congress met in response to a notice in the *Georgia Gazette*, but only five parishes sent delegates. Even those who assembled could not agree on a course of action. Merchants opposed the banning of English imports, to the disgust of the most zealous activists. The Provincial Congress elected Noble Jones, Archibald Bulloch and John Houstoun as representatives to the Second Continental Congress. The three men decided not to go to Philadelphia because Georgia was so badly divided. They explained the province's situation in a letter to the Continental Congress: "The importers were mostly against any interruption, and the consumers very much divided . . . but more who called themselves neutrals than either." However, news of conflict at Lexington and Concord galvanized the radical movement. Delegates were again called to Savannah and Governor Wright reported what transpired.

James Wright to Lord Dartmouth

June 17, 1775

My Lord: It gives me much concern to acquaint Your Lordship that on Thursday, the 13th instant, the Liberty Folks here assembled in the town of Savannah and put up a Liberty Tree and a flag and in the evening paraded about the town, I am informed, to the number of three hundred, some say four hundred. The Liberty Tree and flag were kept up from Tuesday morning till now and is still flying in contempt and defiance of the Court and of all law and Government and which here as well as elsewhere seems now nearly at an end. And it has been debated whether or not to stop the courts and shut up the port. But this, I am assured, is laid aside for the present. But they have entered into an Association, and whatever is agreed upon by the Continental Congress will undoubtedly be adopted and carried into execution here and will meet with little or no opposition, for those who disapprove of these things and wish well to government say, "Why should they expose their lives and properties to the resentment of the people when no support or protection is given them by Government?" And therefore they find it most prudent to waive opposition and remain quiet.

There is soon to be meetings in every part of the province and at Savannah on the 22nd instant in order to choose delegates to meet in Provincial Congress at Savannah on the 4th of July, at which meeting I suppose they will entirely approve of whatever may be determined upon by the Continental Congress. They presume that there is no power to prevent them and proclamations &c. are only laughed at. Your Lordship cannot possibly conceive the dangerous consequences of suffering the Governor's letters to be made public, and it is just hanging them out and exposing them to the resentment of an enraged people who are ready to tear any man to pieces who writes anything contrary to their opinions or in opposition to their measures or schemes.

I have laid a state of the proceedings of all the Liberty People before His Majesty's Council and desired their opinions and advice what was proper to be done, whether any legal steps or whether by proclamation to take notice of their conduct and point out the illegality and dangerous consequences of such proceedings. All that were present were unanimous in opinion that no legal steps should be taken, because, as things are circumstanced, no prosecutions would prove effectual and it would only exasperate and inflame. They were also clearly of opinion that issuing such a proclamation would only be held in contempt and expose the weakness of the executive powers and that unsupported as we are and threatened from the next province they advised that no steps whatever should be taken but to represent a state of all their transactions and facts to Your Lordship. This is very *galling*!

Letters, pp. 183–184

One of the most effective propaganda weapons employed by the Liberty Men was the rumor that the King intended to unleash an Indian war upon disloyal backcountry people. Though untrue, the report spread like wildfire through the Carolinas and Georgia. Emotions were further inflamed by wild stories that Royal agents intended to instigate an uprising of slaves.

Gov. James Wright to Lord Dartmouth

June 20, 1775

My Lord: The Liberty People have now got another pretence for raising men. They assert that Mr. Stuart, the Superintendent, has been endeavoring to raise the Cherokee Indians to come down against them. This they allege that they have got undoubted proof of and all he can say will not convince them to the contrary. They sent some of their party here who have so inflamed and enraged our people that he did not think himself safe and His Majesty's armed schooner *St. John* having put in from Providence he went on board her and I suppose by this time is sailed for St. Augustine. And several boatsful of men from the Carolina side have been down at our inlet some days. The accounts differ as to number, some call them fifty, others eighty, all well and completely armed. Some allege their intention was to seize on Mr. Stuart, which very probably was part of their errand, but I believe they have another point in view and that is, three vessels being expected here from London and a considerable quantity of gun powder being on board for the Indian trade, they intend to seize on that and carry it to Carolina, and this is certainly in their power to do and it's not possible to prevent it.

One of these vessels arrived here on Saturday the 18th instant and the Captain, one Ash, informs me that several boats lay off a little way from him and that one with three or four men came on board and one of them inquired whether he had any gunpowder on board and on showing his cockets and their finding he had none they behaved very civilly and went away but made great inquiry after another ship, one Maitland, who has a large quantity of gunpowder on board, and it is said they intend to watch our inlet till the others come and take out all the gunpowder and if that is the case I am much afraid it will embarrass us with the Indians, for they have for some time [been] very impatient for their usual supplies.

Letters, pp. 189–190

John Joachim Zubly (1724–1781) was a Swiss-born clergyman who came to Georgia in 1745 and thirteen years later became the first resident minister of Savannah's Independent Presbyterian Church. He was also a scholar and rich planter. Zubly was elected to the Georgia Provincial Congress that met in July, 1775, and was one of Georgia's three representatives at the Second Continental Congress at Philadelphia later that same year. Zubly's *Law of Liberty*, from which the following paragraphs have been drawn, was presented to the opening session of the Georgia Provincial Congress in July, 1775, and published as a pamphlet. Though Zubly fought British taxation, he spoke out against separation from England. For this he was imprisoned and later banished from Georgia.

The Law of Liberty

When a house is in flames, every man is inexcusable that does not contribute whatever he may think in his power to their being extinguished. The question which now agitates Great Britain and America is whether the Parliament of Great Britain has a right to lay taxes on Americans who are not there represented and whether the Parliament has a right to bind the Americans in all cases. To bind them in all cases, the Americans look upon this as the language of despotism in its utmost perfection. To make the Americans hewers of wood and drawers of water, to oblige them to make bricks without straw, to deprive them of the enjoyment of their religion, it would, say they, be no more than a natural consequence of the right of binding them (unseen, unheard, unrepresented) in all cases. Nothing less than a claim destructive of all natural and national liberty could possibly have united all America in a general opposition or have aroused them to join like one man in their common defence.

The bulk of the inhabitants of a continent extending eighteen hundred miles in front on the Atlantic and permitting an extension in breadth as far as the South Sea look upon the claim to bind them in all cases whatsoever as unjust, illegal and detestable. With an unparalleled patience did the Bostonians bear the annihilation of their trade, the blocking up of their harbor and many other distresses till at Lexington an attack was made upon their lives. This attack convinced all America that the British ministry and troops were athirst after their blood. In the cause of liberty the Americans are not afraid to look regulars in the face. In an unjust and oppressive service, British troops are far from being invincible. The cannonading of New York without the least warning will stand as a lasting monument of cruelty as nations not remarkable for humanity would be ashamed of. The destroying of the New England fishery, the endeavor to stir up popish Canadians and savage Indians against the colonials, detaining the inhabitants of Boston after they had given up their arms, a proposal to put in the power of domestics [slaves] to cut the throats of their Southern masters can only exert the sense of injury. The Americans have been called "a rope of sand," but blood and sand will make a firm cementation, and enough American blood has been already shed to cement them together into a thirteenfold cord, not easily to be broken. The violence of present measures has almost instantaneously created a continental union, a continental currency, a continental army. The most zealous Americans could not have effected in an age what the cruelty and violence has effectually brought to pass in a day.

We are met, gentlemen, in a most critical time and on a most alarming occasion. You are chosen by the general voice of this province. To enforce some acts for laying a duty to raise a perpetual revenue in America, which the Americans think unjust and unconstitutional and some provinces have opposed, a fleet and army has been sent to New England, hostilities have been commenced, blood has been shed and many lives have been taken. From this other provinces have taken the alarm. How far and wide the flame so wantonly kindled may be permitted to spread none can tell, but in these alarming circumstances the liberty of this continent, the safety and domestic peace of this province will naturally become a subject of your deliberations. Our King can do no wrong, but may we not hope that when the truth of things, the tears of his suffering subjects, the distress caused by acts extremely ill advised once reach his notice a generous pity will command redress?

Never let us lose out of sight that our interest lies in a perpetual connection with out mother country. There are thousands in Great Britain that think with us and wish well to the American cause. Let us convince our enemies that the struggles of America have not their rise in a desire of independency, but let every step we take afford proof how greatly we esteem our mother country and that to the wish of a perpetual connection we prefer this only consideration, that we may be virtuous and free. Let me entreat you, gentlemen, think cooly and act deliberately. Rash counsels are seldom good ones. Let neither the frowns of tyranny nor the pleasure of popularity sway you from what you clearly apprehend just and right and to be your duty. Consider how much lies at stake—your religion, your liberty, your property, your posterity.

On July 6, 1775, the Georgia Provincial Congress resolved to adopt the Continental Association. Henceforth no goods from Great Britain or Ireland would be imported, no slaves from Africa or elsewhere, no East Indian tea, no wine from Madeira, nor any molasses, syrup or coffee from the British West Indies would be admitted. A concession was made to the exporters of deerskins; non-exportation would begin only on September 10, 1775. The revolutionary action of the Provincial Congress was to be enforced by local committees. Thus, for the first time political power devolved upon those men whom Governor Wright called "the lowest sort" of people. The governor's reports now took on a plaintive tone.

JAMES WRIGHT TO LORD DARTMOUTH

July 8, 1775

My Lord: I wrote Your Lordship that our inlet was guarded by boats with many armed men from Carolina, since which several have gone down there from Savannah, all waiting the arrival of a ship expected from London with gunpowder, it is said to seize upon the gunpowder, those from Carolina to take the gunpowder out belonging to the inhabitants of their province and those from hence to take out the powder belonging to the inhabitants of this province, at least this is what is given out. And Captain Grant in His Majesty's armed schooner having called in here, the Liberty Gentlemen have fitted out a schooner, some say with eight and some with ten carriage guns, many swivels and fifty men. Captain Grant is sailed and no vessel sent here yet by Admiral Graves. And when in Council on the 4th instant Mr. Baillie, the Commissary in whose charge the guns, &c. belonging to His Majesty are, came there and informed me that a great many people were taking and carrying away some of the guns, carriages, shot, &c.

My Lord, I have just been informed that Mr. Barnard Elliott, a Captain in the troops raising by South Carolina, is in the back parts of this province enlisting men without having made the least application to me or taking any notice at all. Am also informed that the Committee in Charles Town, or Council of Safety as they call themselves, it is not certain which, have appointed three persons as superintendents or managers of the Indian affairs in the Creek Country and also three to manage the Indian affairs in the Cherokee Country. Thus Your Lordship sees that the powers of Government are wrested out of my hands, that law and Government are nearly if not quite annihilated and a mere nominal Governor can be of little use and to me a most disagreeable situation and it's not in my power to support either any longer.

The Provincial Congress is now sitting here. I am informed delegates are chosen to proceed immediately to Philadelphia and that our ports and courts are to be shut up.

Letters, pp. 191–192

Acting under authorization of the Provincial Congress, Georgians seized a cargo of gunpowder intended for the Indian trade. South Carolina activists, who had been loud in their condemnation of their neighbors' lagging patriotism, now admitted Georgia into full partnership in return for a share of the powder.

JAMES WRIGHT TO LORD DARTMOUTH

July 10, 1775

My Lord: Since writing my last of the 8th instant, Captain Maitland arrived, the warlike schooner fitted out as mentioned before went to sea and met with the ship about four leagues from the bar, conducted her in and then took out all the gunpowder on board amounting to about six tons, as the Captain tells me, and which is now in the hands of the Liberty People here, who forcibly hold it against the owners. The Sandwich packet arrived at Charles Town on the 2nd instant, when Your Lordship's letters and those from Mr. Pownall and indeed every letter directed to me both public and private were seized upon and opened in Charles Town and on the evening of the 8th instant I received them sealed up again by the deputy postmaster general in Charles Town and endorsed thus, "Opened by the Committee of Inspection at Charles Town"!

A committee from the Provincial Congress now sitting here was sent to the post office, who ordered the deputy postmaster here not to send me any of my letters. But after the Congress had deliberated on the matter, a message was sent to the postmaster that he might deliver them, and I accordingly received them after about an hour's detention, so that Your Lordship sees there is an end of all correspondence and I cannot attempt to send any answers to Your Lordship's letters in future from hence by the post to Charles Town in order to go by the packet, for, were I to do it, they would certainly be intercepted. It being impossible, My Lord, for me to submit to these daily insults, I must again request His Majesty will be graciously pleased to give me leave to return to England.

July 18, 1775

My Lord: The Congress have agreed to send 2000 weight of gunpowder into the Indian country as a present from the people, and it's particularly agreed that the Indians be acquainted that it is not from the King or from Government or from the Superintendent or from the traders but from the "people" of the province, and I am much afraid this will raise strange ideas amongst the Indians and be attended with very bad consequences. They have appointed here what they call a Council of Safety and very nearly followed the example of the Carolinians except as to raising an army. It was proposed to raise 350 men, but after great debates that was carried in the negative and this province having now joined with the others I am well informed that the gentlemen who came from Carolina assured the Congress here that if they should on any account want assistance they should immediately have it to the amount of one thousand men.

Letters, pp. 194–195, 196–199

Before it adjourned, the Provincial Congress appointed a standing Council of Safety as an executive body with jurisdiction over the various local committees. In its first announcement to the people of Georgia on July 25, 1775, the Council of Safety declared, "A civil war in America has begun." Not even the radical Council of Safety was prepared to declare a separation from the mother country just yet, but the Council was correct in stating that a civil war had started. The local committeemen, calling themselves Liberty Boys, attacked people who refused to honor the Association.

GOV. JAMES WRIGHT TO LORD DARTMOUTH

July 29, 1775

My Lord: The Council of Safety, as they call themselves, have in a solemn manner forbid the rector of the parish to preach any more in the church, and he has been so much threatened that on the 25th instant he left the town. The reason given for this is because he refused to preach a sermon and observe a fast which had been directed by the Continental Congress to be observed throughout all the colonies and has reflected on the conduct of the Americans. And, My Lord, on the 24th instant, about 9 o'clock at night, I heard a very great huzzahing in the streets and on sending out found they had seized upon one Hopkins, a pilot, and were tarring and feathering him. And soon after they brought him in a cart along by my house and such a horrid spectacle I really never saw. They made the man stand up in a cart with a candle in his hand and a great many candles were carried 'round the cart and thus they went through most of the streets in town for upwards of three hours. On inquiring what he had done, I was informed that he had behaved disrespectfully towards the Sons of Liberty and drank some toasts which gave great offence.

[ENCLOSURE]

TESTIMONY OF JOHN HOPKINS

Savannah, Georgia
July 29, 1775

About 9 of the clock in the evening of the 24th instant as I was sitting at supper with my family there came to my house a number of persons (some were in disguise) and opened the door. Joseph Reynolds of Savannah, bricklayer, Captain McCluer and Captain Bunner, at present of Savannah, mariners, laid hold of me, without saying anything to me. As soon as the aforesaid people laid hold of me, a great number rushed in and hurried me out of my house and led me to the outside of the town. They consulted to tar and feather me, but the majority resolved to carry me to a more public place. Accordingly they led me into the middle of the square near to the dial in Savannah and stripped me of my jacket and shirt and with great reluctance left the rest of my apparel on me and then they proceeded to tar and feather me and immediately put me into a cart and carted me up and down the streets of Savannah for upwards of three hours in the above condition.

During the time they carted me to the Liberty Tree and there swore they would hang me. Bunner said he was rather fat but he would go up the tree and hang me. Bunner further said that unless I would drink "Damnation to all Tories and success to American Liberty!" I should be hung immediately, which request I was obliged to comply with. They continued to abuse me, gave me a great deal of ill language and upbraided me with my conduct. Some one or other said that if they could lay hold of the parson they would put him along side of me in the cart. I also heard said in the mob that Mr. Smith should be next and that they intended to continue on until they had tarred and feathered all the Tories, or words to that effect.

I saw in the aforesaid mob, together with the persons aforementioned, Thomas Lee, carpenter, John Spencer, carpenter, Alexander Phoenix, merchant, Ambrose Wright, planter, Samuel Wells, mariner, Francis Arthur of Savannah, surveyor, Oliver Bowen, merchant, John McCluer and Captain McCluer, Joseph Habersham and Francis Harris, gentlemen, Quintin Pooler, merchant, Captain Hawkins, mariner, and Thomas Hamilton, butcher, and several others that I cannot recollect. Between the hours of 12 and 1 of the clock they discharged me at the vendue house with orders "to beg all America pardon"!

Letters, pp. 200–203

MEMORIAL OF HADDON SMITH

After having for some time previously officiated as minister of Christ Church at Savannah in the province of Georgia, the prevailing distractions in America obliged me to flee from the violence of the people who had usurped the powers of government. Upon the first breaking out of the civil war in Georgia, several very inflammatory publications appeared in the *Georgia Gazette* against government. I, in order to counteract the evil tendency of those publications, did publish some papers in favor of government. When I was discovered to be the author, I was continually persecuted by the people calling themselves the Provincial Congress. The said Congress, in order to establish the authority of the Continental Congress within the province of Georgia, did appoint the 20th of July, 1775, to be observed as a general fast and required me to preach a sermon suitable to the occasion. I refused to comply. In consequence, I received a threatening letter from them. On the 22nd of July, 1775, a number of people—a deputation from the Provincial Congress—came to my house, declared me an enemy to America and forbid me doing any more duty in the town of Savannah. I went down immediately to them. I saw standing in the porch of the house Peter Farling of Saint John's Parish, Jonathan Cochran of Saint Andrew's Parish, planters, Edward Telfair of Savannah, merchant, George Walton of Savannah, and Oliver Bowen of Savannah, merchant, and some others. Peter Farling held a written paper in his hand and read from it the following words: "Sir, from your late conduct in disobeying the orders of the Congress, you are deemed an enemy to America!" The next day being Sunday, they fastened the doors of the church.

On the evening of the 24th of July, 1775, a number of people assembled together did seize upon John Hopkins and, having tarred and feathered him and otherwise cruelly treated him, did enter my house to seize me and use me in the same manner. Happening providentially to be out on a visit with my family, I escaped that intended violence. Informed that they had entered into a conspiracy to take me the following evening, I was obliged to retreat with my family in the night to a sea island about fifteen miles from Savannah, called Tybee Island, where I remained for several days, when an opportunity offered of a passage to Liverpool.

Colonial Records of Georgia, XXXVIII, pt. 1, pp. 531–532

A distraught Governor Wright begged the government to send troops to Georgia. He could no longer count on the loyalty of the militia, many of whom had taken the oath to uphold the Association.

James Wright to Lord Dartmouth

August 7, 1775

My Lord: It gives me great concern that every letter I now write to Your Lordship is to give you accounts of the very illegal, insolent and dangerous transactions of the Liberty People here. On the 2nd instant a complaint was made to the Chief Justice against Ebenezer McCarty, Florence Mahoney and William Davis. On taking affidavits against them, it appeared amongst other matters that the said McCarty had been enlisting men in this town for one of the Carolina regiments. On a warrant being issued and the parties being apprehended, the said McCarty was by the Chief Justice committed to jail as not bailable. On the 3rd instant a great number of people assembled together and went to the jail and forced it open and took out the said McCarty, who was immediately set at large. On the 5th instant he went through the town with a drum beating up for men and passed close by the Chief Justice's door, also came very near my house. Unparalleled insolence, My Lord! And this is the situation His Majesty's government is reduced to in the province of Georgia.

I omitted to mention before that they took possession of the public magazine to put the gunpowder in and appointed a guard to protect it, an officer who they call Captain, and, I am told, twenty men, and who still continue to guard it day and night.

Throughout the province every method has been used to compel the people to sign the Association. Those who decline they threaten to proscribe, and, for fear of that and losing their property or having it destroyed, great numbers have been intimidated to sign, and I suppose by far the greater part of the province have signed it. Indeed it is said there are few in the county who have not.

August 17, 1775

My Lord: I am now again constrained to write Your Lordship a farther disagreeable account of the proceedings of the Congress and Liberty People here. The Congress determined that no militia officers should remain but such as signed the Association and directed that the Captains of the militia should order musters throughout the province and that any of the officers that might refuse to sign the Association should not be suffered to act any longer but that the people should elect others in their places. Thus Your Lordship sees how they are going on here, and the scheme and attempt to wrest the command of the militia out of my hands, and it is said the Committee of Safety are to give commissions to the people who are to choose officers in the room of those who refuse to sign the Association.

My Lord, I mentioned in my last some means used to compel people to sign the Association and those, with tarring and feathering and the punishment of ordering any that refuse to quit their habitations on a few days' notice, are executed without any hesitation. One Mr. Brown, a young gentleman who appeared a little active in opposing the Liberty People, has been most cruelly treated in the town of Augusta. He, having threatened to get a party and take satisfaction, the offenders raised a number of men in the country and wrote to Savannah to the Council of Safety for assistance, and a party of the grenadier company and some of the light infantry company, who signed the Association, set out from hence to Augusta the 9th instant without any application to or authority from me, but I am well informed were ordered to do so by the Council of Safety and it's said they, by persuasions and threats, prevailed on a great number to join them as they went through the country and what outrages or acts of violence they may commit before they return it's difficult to say, though I am just informed Mr. Brown has retired into Carolina. My Lord, are these things to be suffered in a British government?

Letters, pp. 204–208

Thomas Brown, a young gentleman from Yorkshire, arrived in Georgia in November, 1774, with over seventy indentured servants. He was just the type of settler Governor Wright wanted and, as a gesture of approval, Wright made Brown a magistrate. People in the backcountry, impressed with Brown's apparent wealth and importance, whispered that he must be a natural son of Lord North sent to spy on Georgians. Brown was too bold for his own good. When the Augusta Sons of Liberty recruited signers of the Association, Brown organized a counter-association. In a letter to his father, Brown described what happened.

THOMAS BROWN TO JONAS BROWN

Charles Town
November 10th, 1775

Dear Father: 'Tis not with a little dejection of spirits that I sit down to transmit you an account of the extraordinary and unpleasing incidents of the last four months, during which I have had no opportunity of writing to you, my situation having subjected all letters to interception.

In my last, I expressed my apprehensions that a test oath would be administered, annexed to the Articles of Association. Shortly after, Mr. Gordon being at Brownsborough, near one hundred people waited upon several gentlemen for the above purpose, who, terrified at their formidable appearance, inconsiderately subscribed to the oath and fled. After which they waited upon me at New Richmond and tendered me a paper to sign. I desired their excuse, they asked me my reasons. I answered, my situation was peculiarly delicate, that I did not wish to take up arms against that country which gave me being.

On the other hand, it would be equally disagreeable to me to fight against those amongst whom, it was probable, I should spend the remainder of my days. They replied, as the oath required neither one nor the other what could be my objection to it? I answered that I had so far through life preserved my opinion free and I flattered myself that my conduct could not be considered criminal, as I acted no ways repugnant to the laws of the province or in prejudice of the good of society. But as they insisted upon my giving a definitive answer, I should mention the dictates of my judgement contrary to which I hoped I should never be compelled to act. I then gave the following reasons: "That though an obligation to take up arms was not particularly expressed in the oath, yet it was, I presumed, implied, as it enjoined a strict, implicit obedience to, and acquiescence in and an approbation of, every measure which might be pursued in America."

Wherefore as it was my particular desire to live in peace and tranquility without meddling with politics, to which I had neither time or inclination to attend, I did not wish to partake of the merit or demerit of the actions of others. Further that as I had so recently taken the oaths of allegiance to His Majesty at my entrance upon the office of magistrate, I could not, either conscientiously or consistent with the character of an honest man, take the oath they proposed, for being under a prior obligation yet legally valid I could not, in my opinion, annul it by any subsequent resolution. Thereupon they told me that matters were now come to such a crisis it became necessary to know whom they ought to consider as friends or foes; that those who were not for them were against them; and that they would not permit any to remain neuter, and if I did not subscribe what was tendered to me they would treat me as an enemy to the liberty of America.

I told them it was not in my power to prevent them using their pleasure but that it was impossible to deprive me of the privilege of thinking. On which I returned to my house and, seeing them determined to commit some outrage either upon my person or property, I put my pistols into my pocket and returning asked them their determination. They told me they would drag me down to Augusta and oblige me not only to take the oath but subscribe both it and the Articles of Association. I answered that whilst they were contending, as they informed me, for public liberty, I hoped their actions would correspond with their professions and that they would hold sacred the liberty and privileges of individuals, that as I had neither transgressed any provincial law or regulation of

161

the Continental Congress I requested them to suffer me to depart and live in peace. Thereupon about fifty of the company rode away and wished me a change of sentiments and a good morning.

The remainder now became more violent and threatened to use immediate force to compel me to compliance. Seeing no remonstrances could prevail, I declared that the first person who attempted to touch me might abide by the consequence. Hereupon six or eight with drawn swords rushed towards me. I presented my pistols and stood upon the defensive. A person coming behind seizing my left arm, I snapped my right pistol. Which missing fire, they poured in upon me and, pushing me down, I discharged my other pistol and shot their ringleader thro' the foot. Whilst their attention was engrossed in the seizure of the pistols, I fortunately disengaged myself and had recourse to my sword. I parried off their repeated lunges and kept them at bay for some time, until a cowardly miscreant came behind me and gave me such a violent blow on the head with a rifle as fractured my skull and brought me to the ground.

In consequence of this accident, I was deprived of my reason for two days, and, whilst in this situation, a committee, aided by its myrmidons, carried me off from my house about five miles and with unparalleled barbarity put me to the torture by tying me to a tree and placing burning lightwood candles under the soles of my feet. [Note by a contemporary copyist: "So soon as Mr. Browne was carried off in a state of insensibility the bandits plundered his house and took away upwards of twenty stand of arms with accoutrements and ammunition, part of his house and kitchen furniture, &c. And besides the ill treatment above described it seems he was also tarred & feathered, but by reason of the particular ignominy of this sort of discipline we suppose Mr. Browne did not care to make mention of it in his letter."]

A physician of my acquaintance having humanely attended me and by proper treatment restored the use of my reason, I had the good fortune so far to ingratiate myself with the guard placed over me as to be permitted to make my escape, and being furnished a horse by one of them, I fled into the back settlement of South Carolina and there raised near three hundred men, both for my personal safety and with the intention of bringing the offenders to consign punishment by the laws of the country. Matters being thus circumstanced, I deemed it further expedient to take some measures for the preservation of my property, and for that purpose I called together a number of my friends to consult with them what plan it was most prudent to adopt. By my persuasion they unanimously came to a resolution to the following purport of which I drew up a contract, namely: Not to take up arms against His Majesty's government, to live in peace with their fellow countrymen, to aid and assist each other voluntarily in case of an invasion by the Indians or an insurrection of Negroes or against any enemy whatever who might disturb the peace of the province. This resolution was subscribed by four thousand men.

So soon as this Association of Neutrals was made known at Charles Town, the Congress there assembled in order to counteract our purposes deputed an unprincipled quondam judge, with three Dissenting ministers and two lawyers, to ride the circuit and at every town to attempt to persuade and prevail upon the people to take up arms against government. This respectable tribunal ordered twelve notorious horse stealers to take me, dead or alive.

Notwithstanding this order for my apprehension, I was determined to risk my person for the service of the province and to support my friends, amongst whom were a Colonel Kirkland and a Mr. Cunningham, people of great influence in that quarter. Wherefore as I feared this deputation might by false arguments and specious reasoning draw away the people from their allegiance. I procured a proper escort and with unwearied diligence attended at all the places of their meeting, and after the judge and his coadjutants had addressed the people upon public grievances and the necessity of a firm union for the preservation of their liberties, I in reply harangued them on this side of the question and with such success as to procure in the circuit one thousand persons, exclusive of the number before mentioned, to subscribe the resolution not to take up arms against His Majesty.

The intentions of the judge and his assistants being thus defeated they had recourse to arms to effect that which they could not by false reasoning and misrepresentations. They therefore draughted fifteen hundred men from the militia and marched towards us with intent to reduce us to obedience and submission. Mr. Cunningham and I were not inactive on our parts, for the course of seven days we embodied twenty-five hundred men near a place called Ninety-Six. On news of our state of defense, the enemy halted. We continued under arms near ten days, but some of our ammunition being intercepted, we listened to some proposed terms of accommodation and having deputed six or eight of our officers to treat about this matter a suspension of hostilities was mutually agreed upon.

Under the security of this treaty and at the particular request of the governor, Lord William Campbell, I proceeded to Charles Town to confer with him on the measures to be adopted in future. On my arrival there I received the disagreeable information that His Excellency had been obliged to take refuge on board the *Cherokee*, armed ship. Being now left destitute of support, I was immediately taken into custody by the Council of Safety. I underwent a long and minute examination and must inevitably have fallen a sacrifice to their revenge but I resolutely informed them that I came to Charles Town under sanction of the suspension of arms lately agreed upon and that a breach of public faith on their part would be productive of fatal consequence, for if any injury was offered to my person I had firm assurance that my neutral friends in the interior parts of the province by way of retaliation would wreak their vengeance upon all provincial Associators contiguous to the district in which they lived.

Hereupon I was acquitted and dismissed with an express mandate to leave the town and quit the province immediately. In three or four days I shall leave this place and proceed to Savannah and continue my route to St. Augustine.

Private Collection, Oxford, England

Thomas Brown sought allies in South Carolina and found that there were many people willing to rally to the King. The Augusta Liberty Boys expected an attack by Brown and his friends and asked the Savannah Council of Safety for help. The Council ordered the militia to march up to Augusta to defend the place. The possibility of a British-instigated Indian war weighed heavily on the minds of Georgians. When a group of Liberty Boys demanded and received the surrender of the Georgia rangers garrisoning Fort James on the Broad River, the Council of Safety ordered the fort returned to the rangers. Governor Wright could only wring his hands helplessly.

GOV. JAMES WRIGHT TO LORD DARTMOUTH

September 16, 1775

My Lord: The Liberty People are still going on in the the same way. I am informed that officers have been chosen by every company of militia in the province. Some who had commissions have been elected, and many new ones chosen, so that these people having signed the Association will now be considered by the Provincial Congress and the other bodies as under their authority and direction and not the King's or mine. In short, My Lord, the whole executive power is assumed by them, and the King's Governor remains little else than nominally so. Your Lordship sees the great and criminal strides they are making in subversion of law and the King's government and establishing one of their own, and this new government seems to me to be on the following plan: The Provincial Congress, a kind of legislature in the respective provinces, subject to the control and direction of the Continental Congress, which is the supreme legislature and governing power over the whole continent. The Council of Safety seems to be the executive branch in each colony, subject to the Provincial Congress, and the general and parochial committees dispense law and exercise the powers of the several courts, just as it seems right in their own eyes.

September 23, 1775

My Lord: On the 17th instant a vessel arrived here from London, one *Rainier*, on board of which was 250 barrels of gunpowder. Great part of it, I am informed, is His Majesty's, being the annual present for the Indians sent out to Mr. Stuart, the Superintendent, and the rest is the property of persons concerned in the Indian trade, the whole of which immediately on the ship's arrival at Tybee was seized upon and taken out by the Liberty People here and brought up to town in great triumph and is forcibly kept from Mr. Stuart and the owners who meant to send it into the Indian country. I am well informed that the Council of Safety, as they call themselves, give out that they have received an answer to their talk sent to the Cherokees, by which those Indians declare that they will have nothing to do with the dispute between Great Britain and the colonies but that if they do interfere at all, it shall be in behalf of the people here, who they know, and not for the white people over the great water, who they know nothing about.

I must beg leave to add that from the situation of affairs here no time should be lost. It is really a wretched state to be left in and what it's impossible to submit to much longer, Government totally annihilated and assumed by congresses, councils and committees and the greatest acts of tyranny, oppression, gross insults, &c. &c. &c. committed and not the least means of protection, support or even personal safety, and these almost daily occurrences are *too much*, My Lord!

October 14, 1775

My Lord: Since my last a party of the backcountry people went armed to a small stockade fort on the ceded lands which was garrisoned by a party of the rangers and compelled the commanding officer to deliver it up to them, and they then immediately sent a messenger express to the Council of Safety here, to acquaint them what they had done and receive their directions, and those people ordered them to deliver up the fort again to the officer and return to their habitations. It is this day reported that another small fort on those lands has also been taken from the rangers who garrisoned it. In short, My Lord, the poison has infected the whole province, and neither law, Government or regular authority have any weight or are at all attended to.

November 1, 1775

My Lord: Things have remained tolerably quiet in this town, but the people in the back parts of the province, following the example of others, are forming cabals and setting up for themselves. They give out that there is a new government now and that no application is to be made to me but to the Council of Safety. And I am informed that a party of about thirty men are gone out against an Indian town on the Ocmulgee River. They say that those Indians have stolen several horses from them and they are gone to obtain restitution or satisfaction and that if the Indians do not give it or resist they will kill them.

December 9, 1775

My Lord: The Provincial Congress met here on the 16th ultimo and have sat every day since. The first material thing that was published was on the 30th of November when, with an intention to shut up the courts of justice, a resolve was sent 'round to all the attorneys at law. On Tuesday, the 5th instant, an edict was served on all the attorneys. Mr. Hume, the Attorney General, not paying obedience to the said mandate, was on the 6th instant served with an order to attend the Congress and, on not attending, a warrant was issued against him, and he was apprehended and carried before them, when, not acknowledging or submitting to their authority, he was dismissed. And it was some time debated whether he should not be delivered over to the mob to be, I presume, torn to pieces! However, at length, as a matter of great humanity and tenderness, they condescended to order him out of the province within a month. Thus, Your Lordship sees the distress the King's officers and friends of Government are drove to in this province. And no ship of war or any protection afforded as yet, and I am really of opinion, My Lord, that if no support or protection comes here very soon that every officer and friend of Government will either be forced out of the province or must submit to worse fate, and it is confidently reported, and I believe it to be truth, that the Continental Congress has ordered 3000 men to be immediately raised, 2000 to assist the Carolinians against any of His Majesty's troops when any come there and 1000 to be sent here, so that we shall be in a fine situation unless assistance should happily come before.

Letters, pp. 209–210, 212–213, 215, 218, 223–224

Georgia's three delegates to the Continental Congress, Archibald Bulloch, John Houstoun and John J. Zubly, returned to Savannah in December. Bulloch and Houstoun were ardent patriots, but events were moving too fast for Zubly. He stood for American rights but opposed a war with the mother country. He parted company with his associates when the Congress authorized the Georgia Provincial Congress to raise a regiment.

Gov. James Wright to Lord Dartmouth

December 19, 1775

My Lord: The people who went from hence as delegates are returned, and it is said they have brought blank commissions from the Continental Congress to be filled up by the Council of Safety here to officers for a regiment of what they called "Provincials" which is to be raised for this province to consist of eight companies of 75 privates, say 600 rank and file in a regiment. Thus, Your Lordship sees they are preparing throughout to support their usurped powers and to resist the King's troops when any may be sent. In this province, My Lord, we are more unhappily circumstanced than in any other, for there are very few men of real abilities, gentlemen or men of property in their tribunals. The parochial committee are a parcel of the lowest people, chiefly carpenters, shoemakers, blacksmiths &c. with a few at their head in the general Committee and Council of Safety. There are some better sort of men and some merchants and planters but many of the inferior class, and it is really terrible, My Lord, that such people should be suffered to overturn the civil government and most arbitrarily determine upon and sport with other men's lives, liberties and properties.

January 3, 1776

My Good Lord: Since the return of two of the delegates it is said as soon as their regiment is raised they will levy a tax of £50,000 Sterling on the inhabitants of this province, it being their quota of the general Continental expense already incurred, and that if any refuse to pay their proportion they will seize on their estate and sell them for anything they will fetch. This is publicly declared and if they are determined to do it, I don't see how it will be possible to prevent them. No troops, no money, no orders or instructions and a wild multitude gathering fast! What can any man do in such a situation? No arms, no ammunition, not so much as a ship of war of any kind and the neighboring province at the same time threatening vengeance against the friends of Government and to send 1000 men to assist the Liberty People! All these things, My Lord, are really *too much*!

Letters, pp. 227–230

THE NARRATIVE OF HENRY PRESTON OF SAVANNAH, JOINT PROTHONOTARY AND CLERK OF THE CROWN FOR THE PROVINCE

In the morning of the 23rd of January, 1776, about 7 of the clock, Adam Trick of Savannah came to my house and knocked at the door. I, being in bed, immediately got up, when the following message was delivered by the said Trick, "The Gentlemen of the Council of Safety" (I believe he meant Congress) "gave their compliments to me and begged the favor of [my giving them] all the keys of the courthouse, as the Assembly room was too small, the Congress was going to sit in the court room" or words to [that] purport.

I answered the said Trick, I had not the keys of the courthouse but the keys of my own office, which I was determined no man should have, for them I would keep.

The said Trick then further asked me if I knew where they were or who had them. To this I answered I had them not. He further asked if I had not a private or a back door key to go in when I pleased. To this I answered I had a back door key and some time ago could go in when I pleased, but if I had the keys of the courthouse I had orders not to deliver them. He then asked me if he should deliver the above answers to the Congress. I told him, yes. He entreated me a good deal to deliver the keys and hoped I would excuse him and went away towards the Assembly room.

Between the hours of 10 and 11 of the clock of the forenoon of the same day, there came to my house, Messrs. George Walton, William Ewen and John Wereat, all with swords, who desired to speak to me and we all retired into the back piazza of my house.

Mr. Walton said to me, we are informed you have got the keys of the Prothonotary's office. I answered, Yes, I had. He then said, They were come for them, and I think said, by order of the Congress (This I am not certain of) and must have them. I answered that I was sorry it was not in my power to deliver them, for, I told them, no man whatever should keep the keys of that office but myself. This I had also told the Chief Justice. Mr. Walton said they were come *via et amis* and by God they must [have] them! It was in vain to attempt to keep them. I told him that I would keep them be the consequences what they would. He also asked me if I had them about me. I answered, No, I had not. Mr. Ewen said, If they were in my waistcoat pocket, they could in a minute take that from me and would return my waistcoat again. He also entreated me to deliver the keys as it would be best for me, alleging that it would save the country the expense of new doors and locks, for they were determined to be into the courthouse at all events. Mr. Walton then spoke seemingly in a passion, that it was useless to evade any longer. They were come for them and have them they would! I told him I could not deliver them, it was contrary to my duty and my oath, that I could not even suffer any person to go into that office without my consent, that he well knew the oath of office I had taken as also the Oath of Allegiance [to the Crown]. And I thought it wrong to ask one to break that oath, which if I did give them the keys would certainly be a break of my oath. He said it could not be a break of my oath if they were [to] take them by force, which they intended to do, and also desired a final answer whether I would or would not give the keys or show them to them. If I did not I might depend upon it that the commanding officer would (or should) have orders to take me into custody with a file of musketeers and was going away. Mr. Wereat at first spoke nothing more, then entreating and recommending to me to let them take the keys, as it would be better for me, as they were going through the house, Mr. Walton again said in the hearing of Mr. Preston that a file of musketeers would take me into confinement, and all went out of the house. To this I answered that I must abide by the consequences, be what they would.

In the course of the foregoing conversation, I told the aforesaid gentlemen that if they did break open the office and take the records . . . that I would attend [as] a private person and direct them how and in what manner to take them down, so as not to be greatly injured or much mislaid, or words to that effect.

About an hour afterwards, Adam Trick came to me and told me that the gentlemen desired to speak to me at the courthouse. I sent word I would wait upon them in five minutes. Upon my entering the portico of the courthouse, I saw the front door open. I was stopped by a sentinel. I told him to call to some person in the courthouse to acquaint the gentlemen that sent for me that I attended, (not knowing who it was but rather apprehended it was the Congress, as Trick had told me, they were to sit there) and Trick, I think, told the sentinel to let me go in.

Upon my entering the courthouse I perceived my office broke open but by whom I know not, the padlock hanging to the staple, the staple drawn, and the lock of the door broke. And I believe, not one paper wrecked or removed until I went. Mr. Walton told me they had sent for me as a private gentleman to direct how to take the papers down from the cases where they were in proper order, which I accordingly did, also thinking it part of my duty to see them as much taken care of as I possibly could.

As one large trunk was already packed full, I told them that these papers in the trunk were the proper papers to begin with, which they did, and continued to pack in a large case until all the papers, books and other records in both the Office of Prothonotary and Clerk of the Crown were removed and packed up in two large cases near four feet square and one smaller trunk.

They behaved very politely and gave me every paper and other matters that I asked for that either belonged to myself or [Prothonotary or Clerk's Office].

The people that I saw active and who I believe were the Committee appointed by the Congress for the aforesaid business were George Walton, John Wereat, William Ewen and Ambrose Wright of Savannah, together with Adam Trick who acted as messenger.

In the evening of the same day, Mr. Fred Harris came to my house and asked me if I was going out of town. I told him, Yes. He then said he was sorry to prevent me, that he came to ask for my parole of honor not to go without the limits of the town without leave from the commanding officer. I promised I would not without leave or words to that or the like effect.

The foregoing narrative is as nearly as I can recollect, or at least the substance, of the whole conversation, though perhaps not verbatim, dated at Savannah the 25th January, 1776.

Henry Preston Papers, Georgia Historical Society

⌈ 21 ⌉

Their commissary-general called us poor, deluded wretches. I retorted that they could be misinformed by their leaders as well as we could be deluded by ours. This made him so angry he ordered me to be confined amongst the drunken soldiers and Negroes, where I was threatened to be run through or, as they termed it, skivered.

MORDECAI SHEFTALL, 1778

EVENTS took a dramatic turn with the sudden arrival of British warships off Tybee Island on January 18, 1776. The Council of Safety placed Governor Wright under house arrest, but the governor and other Royal officials fled to the safety of the British vessels. The British wanted the provisions aboard the merchant ships impounded at Savannah under terms of the Association, but militiamen, under command of Colonel Lachlan McIntosh, attempted to prevent the seizure of the rice cargoes by dismantling the rudders and finally setting the ships on fire. Despite the best efforts of the Georgians, the British made off with most of the rice and Governor Wright went with them.

GEORGIA COUNCIL OF SAFETY TO
THE SOUTH CAROLINA COUNCIL OF SAFETY

Savannah, March 4th, 1776

Gentlemen: Our dispositions on the evening of the 2d were such as appeared to our officers the most likely to prevent the landing of our enemy; and so as, if they should make their landing good, either above or below the town, to prevent their getting in; however, notwithstanding our vigilance, they, by collusion with the masters and others on board the merchant ships which hauled near the shore of Hutchinson's Island, in the night-time got on board these ships, about four o'clock yesterday morning, to the number, as far as we are competent to judge from the observations we made, and the intelligence we received, of between 200 and 300, where they affected to conceal themselves. We had our fears respecting these shipping, and therefore kept a good watch upon them; but it was impossible for sentinels on shore to descry them in boarding from the other, the vessels being betwixt. Captain Rice, who commanded a boat of observation, was sent on board the shipping about nine o'clock, to order the rigging on shore, and was, without any noise, or the smallest knowledge of us, kidnapped. This we did not know till about half an hour afterwards. Two sailors, under pretence of coming on shore for clothes, gave information of the troops being on board the shipping, and of Rice's being taken. About 300 men were then immediately marched to Yamacraw, opposite the shipping, with three four-pounders, and threw up a breastwork. The armed schooner *Hitchenbrook*, of [ ] guns, with a number of men on board, which, with others, went up the Back River in the afternoon of the day preceding, about this time set sail down the South River, with intent, no doubt, of covering the landing of the troops from on board the merchant shipping, but being continually fired at by two companies of riflemen, who were placed in ambuscade, she was obliged to come very slowly and often came to, and returned a very smart fire at every place where the riflemen fired from, until the tide was spent, and she could not go down. During the course of this firing, only one of our men got wounded, and that slightly, in the thigh; but on board several were seen to fall. In town, we had exhibited a still more interesting scene. We found the men and officers clamorous about the capture and detention of Rice; and two gentlemen, Lieut. Daniel Roberts, of the St. John Rangers, and Mr. Raymond Demere, of St. Andrew's Parish, solicited and were permitted to go on board to demand a surrender of Rice and his people. They accordingly divested themselves of arms, and were rowed by a negro on board a vessel in which were Captain Barclay, the Commodore, and Major Grant, and these officers, contrary to all principles which cement society and govern mankind, immediately arrested our deputies, and yet detain them as prisoners. We waited with anxious expectation for near half an hour, when we demanded our deputies, by the help of a trumpet, without getting any other but insulting answers. Whereupon we fired two four-pounders directly into them, and then they informed us that they would send an answer in writing; which they presently afterwards did, and signed by Lieutenant Roberts and Mr. Demere, purporting that if we would send two of the persons in whom the people most confided, they would treat with them. Capt. Screven, of the St. John Rangers, and Capt. Baker, of the St. John Riflemen, chagrined, no doubt, (the former particularly on account of his lieutenant,) by detention of our deputies, took about a dozen of the riflemen in a boat, and rowed directly under the stern of Captain Inglis, in whose vessel were a great part of the soldiery, and in peremptory terms demanded the deputies, and were informed, after one shot from Capt. Baker, by a discharge down directly upon them of near 200 shot, both from swivels and small arms, which were kept up while they were in reach; the captains and men in the boats not in the smallest degree confused, or even, perhaps, disappointed by the attack, fired three rifles, most of them three several times, as they say, not without execution; and wonderful to tell, not a man of them was killed—one man only received a slug in the fleshy part of his shoulder, which was immediately cut out, without the smallest inconvenience or danger. The spectators all declare, as we now do, that such a providential deliverance has not yet been known. The unmanly attack upon a few men in an open boat produced a general fire from our field-pieces and entrenchments, and as smart a return from two four-pounders and several swivels from the shipping, which lasted from about 12 o'clock to 4; and although they often fired langrage, which continually whistled about our men, not a single man was even touched, but we have no doubt a number of the enemy met with a worse fate, as they were seen frequently to fall. About 4 o'clock we called a council, and determined to have the vessels immediately burnt, and issued orders to Colonel McIntosh accordingly. Whereupon the *Inverness*, late Capt. McGillivray, loaded with rice and deer-skins, was set on fire and cut loose. Upon this, the soldiers, in the most laughable confusion, got ashore in the marsh, while our riflemen and field-pieces with grape-shot were incessantly galling them. The shipping were now also in confusion. Some got up the river, under cover of the armed schooner, while others caught the flame, and as night approached, exhibited a scene, as they passed and repassed with the tide, which at any but the present time would be truly horrible, but now a subject only of gratitude and applause. The ships of Captains Inglis and Wardell neither got up the river nor on fire; they were ordered on shore, and now are prisoners of Capt. Screven in the country, and their vessels brought down close into a wharf. They were permitted to write to Capt. Barclay in the evening, to inform them of their situation, and to request an exchange of prisoners, which the latter peremptorily refused.

We have thus given you a particular detail of things as they really happened, to prevent the belief of any erroneous intelligence, and from which you will be competent to judge of our situation.

Col. McIntosh laid before the Board a resolution of your Congress, to aid us, accompanied by a letter from Mr. Lowndes; and we are very glad that you have determined to afford us further assistance. We wish it may arrive in time.

George White, *Historical Collections of Georgia* (New York, 1854), pp. 88–89

Meanwhile, the Provincial Congress met in the comparative safety of Augusta and issued Georgia's first constitution, a simple document of thirteen paragraphs called *Rules and Regulations*, on April 15. The political connection with the King was not broken until Georgia delegates George Walton, Lyman Hall and Button Gwinnett voted for independence on July 4, 1776. Georgia's first governor under the *Rules and Regulations* was Archibald Bulloch.

The Continental Congress created the Southern Military Department in February, 1776, and appointed Major General Charles Lee to command. Lee arrived in Charleston in time to defend that city against a British naval attack in July. Georgians informed Congress about their situation and their needs.

Jonathan Bryan, John Houstoun, Lachlan McIntosh to Congress

[August, 1776]

The deputies sent from Georgia by the desire of His Excellency General Lee conferred with him upon the state of that colony in order to devise the best method of putting it in a proper posture of defence, beg leave to represent that from the weak and defenceless situation of the colony, surrounded as it is with enemies, it stands in immediate need of assistance from the general Congress. However small the colony may be itself in a comparative point of view, yet from the great plenty of provisions, numerous stocks of cattle and excellent inlets, harbors and rivers (perhaps equal to any upon the continent) with which the colony abounds and, above all, the firm attachment of its inhabitants to the American Cause, they are led to trust that the protection and security of that colony will be held an object of considerable importance. No one of the thirteen United Colonies is so weak within, so much exposed without, to the east the inhabitants suffer the danger of British cruisers, their Negroes are daily inveigled and carried away from their plantations, British fleets may be supplied with beef from several large islands well stocked with cattle, which line their coast and sound[s] where large ships may sail. To the south, they have the province of East Florida, the inhabitants and soldiery of which must of necessity make inroads upon Georgia for the article[s] of provision with which they have heretofore been chiefly supplied. Georgia now stands as a barrier to South Carolina and effectually excuses that province from the like depredations. The southern parts of Georgia contain vast stocks of cattle and our most valuable rice plantations lie that way. By some late computations there are said to be upwards of 30,000 head of black cattle in the province and hogs, &c. without number. We have certain accounts of there being at this time upwards of 1000 British troops in St. Augustine. To the west and almost down to upon the Georgia line are the most numerous tribes of Indians now in North America, to wit: the Creeks, Cherokees, Choctaws and a number of small tribes, in the whole at least 15,000 gunmen. All these Nations have been much tampered with by the emissaries of government and without the utmost exertion of prudence on our side, it is feared may be brought to act against us. They are so situated as to make it extremely convenient for our enemies to supply them from East and West Florida with ammunition and everything else they want. Our last accounts from the

Indians are rather unfavorable, and when we consider their natural principles of infidelity and how much more able our enemies are to purchase their friendship by presents, &c. than we are, there seems to be the greatest reason to apprehend a rupture with them. In such a case, the fate of Georgia may be easily conceived. Add to all these considerations the vast number of Negroes here, perhaps of themselves sufficient to subdue us. In point of numbers the blacks exceed the whites and the ready channel of supply and secure retreat which St. Augustine affords render them much to be dreaded.

The conquest of Georgia would doubtless be considered as a great requisition by Great Britain. It is a most excellent provision country, abounds with ship timber and lumber of all kinds and is most conveniently situated as a place of rendezvous to their shipping. Under all these circumstances, it must certainly appear indispensably necessary that measures be immediately taken for the defence and security of that province, but the low situation in point of means or ability of its inhabitants put it out of their power to do so of themselves, more especially as they have been already put to a very great expense in consequence of the late descent upon them. The great objects seem to be more fortifications and a good understanding with the Indians.

We would therefore beg leave to propose: First, that His Excellency General Lee be requested to state the peculiar situation of the province of Georgia to the General Congress and to obtain directions from them to raise and take into Continental pay so many men as may be considered to be sufficient to defend that province, in our opinion less than six battalions will not answer the purpose. But as we don't conceive any of these men can be recruited in Georgia, we would apprehend it full as eligible (if that can be done) to order some of the regiments already raised to march thither, and farther that the four troops of horse already raised be augmented to a regiment and put upon the Continental Establishment. Part of these battalion troops may be so situated as to serve equally for the protection of Georgia and South Carolina against the Indians and above all may entirely shut up the communication between them and our enemies to the southward, which will certainly be the most effectual means of preventing an Indian war.

Secondly, that the sum of £[ ] be granted by the General Congress for building four fortifications and guard boats in the province of Georgia. The reason why we conceived this ought to be a general charge is because it is evident the same will serve against attacks from the south and for cutting off the communication between East and West Florida and the Indians upon which the peace of the back inhabitants of Georgia, South Carolina, North Carolina and Virginia depends. Besides it seems to be a part of the plan of administration to throw forces into the Indian country where they expect to be joined by considerable numbers of the savages and in the event there is no province or place through which they can so conveniently pass as through Georgia.

Thirdly, It is a fixed principle with the Indians to be paid for their good offices and in this controversy we conceive they will expect to be well paid even for neutrality. The articles they prefer will doubtless be ammunition and clothing, but these we have it not in our power to give them. We would then propose cattle as a substitute and are inclined to think if the communication between them and our enemies were cut off they would soon be brought to be well satisfied with a present of this kind. It is therefore submitted to the General Congress whether it would not be worthwhile to give directions that a number not exceeding 5000 head of cattle be purchased and distributed among the Indians by the commissioners. We are of opinion this step would answer many valuable purposes and would have a tendency not only of attaching them to our interest from gratitude but would also be a means of civilizing them and by fixing the idea of property would keep them honest and peaceable with us for fear of reprisals.

Papers of the Continental Congress, National Archives

A convention met in Savannah in October, 1776, to draft a permanent constitution for Georgia. Button Gwinnett returned from Congress in time to be elected chairman of the committee which drew up the constitution. The document, adopted on February 5, 1777, was one of the most democratic in America. The one-house legislature elected the governor and the state judges. Because the radicals dominated the convention, conservatives found fault with their work. Lachlan McIntosh, promoted by Congress to the rank of brigadier general, said that the constitution-makers were merely multiplying jobs for themselves. He wrote, "Some I fear, lust after the old flesh pots." McIntosh's friend John Wereat complained that the constitution was the work of a small clique "at a nightly meeting in a tavern."

The rift between radicals and conservatives grew wider after a second attempt to invade Florida. Button Gwinnett was elected to replace Archibald Bulloch when the latter died under mysterious circumstances. Gwinnett, who had aspired to the brigadiership occupied by McIntosh, insisted on the invasion of Florida and went himself as commander-in-chief of the militia. McIntosh and the Georgia continental troops marched separately. Gwinnett refused to tell McIntosh his plans, and their quarrel caused the Council of Safety to recall them both. Gwinnett left the militia under command of Colonel John Baker, while McIntosh's continentals were led by Colonel Samuel Elbert. The two bodies of troops were supposed to rendezvous at Sawpit Bluff on the St. John's River. Colonel Baker reported the ensuing events to General McIntosh.

COLONEL JOHN BAKER TO GENERAL LACHLAN MCINTOSH

Jericho, May 22, 1777

Sir: I should have waited on you in person and had set out with that view from my fort but called at Jericho in my way to see my family when I had the misfortune of losing my horse, which has retarded my going down.

I am now therefore to acquaint you of my return from our southern expedition and a melancholy one it has turned out to be. I was ordered by Colonel Elbert to march to Fort Howe the 27th of April in order to proceed on from thence to the southward, but before I marched I went to Sunbury where Colonel Elbert and myself agreed to meet each other at a place known by the name of Saw Pit Bluff about twelve miles distance from the mouth of St. John's River. A calculation was then made what time it would take us to march to said bluff. It was agreed twelve days.

Wednesday, the 30th April, I march[ed] from my fort for Fort Howe, where I arrived Thursday evening and there found Colonel Sumpter who I expected was to proceed on with me. But to my great surprise was informed by him he had orders from you to return to Carolina and accordingly he marched from Fort Howe the next day. However as I had agreed to meet Colonel Elbert I was determined to proceed and did with all the expedition possible. Colonel Sumpter thought, as the river was exceeding high, I would not get over under eight days but we got over in two days with everything safe and arrived the 13th day at Saw Pit Bluff. We met with no interruption on our way, only a few Indians over Altamaha River where we had a small skirmish and lost Lieutenant Fraser and Lieutenant Robinson wounded, which I imagine you had an account of before this. Your letter per Mr. LeConte came to hand the day this skirmish happened and had answered it before it happened, which was Sunday the 4th instant. Monday I took forty men and went as far as Pinholloway in search of the Indians (which was the course they steered) but could make no discoveries of them. Therefore returned to our camps. Tuesday morning marched for Saw Pit Bluff where I arrived on Monday, the 12th May, and there expected to have found the galleys, but I have not seen or heard anything of them since.

The day after my arrival at Saw Pit Bluff which was Tuesday, I sent my brother with forty men towards the Cow Ford in order to make what discoveries he could. In his way he called at Rolphe's place on the main road, where he found one Barfield living at said place, who acquainted him that the evening before he was out horse-hunting a little way from home and that fourteen Indians rose up and surrounded him, but on finding who he was they let him go about his business. Barfield further told him that James Moore and another man had passed the same evening and informed him that he saw our tracks going towards Saw Pit Bluff. My brother could get no other intelligence (only that they heard of our coming) nor no discoveries could be made. He returned the same evening to the camps. Thursday following about 10 o'clock at night, one of our sentries fired, as he says, at two men without hats on. He first hailed them, but on hailing they ran off. We had no mistrust of enemies being about at that time. However, early next morning I had the horses got up and found near forty head missing. I immediately ordered twenty men that had horses to equip themselves and turn out with me. We had not gone far before we came across their tracks which we followed near four miles, where we found the horses and most of them hobbled and strung along a swamp side. By the horses being placed in that manner we were apprehensive they were waylaying us and so it happened. But as there was no way of getting them, we ventured up and got most of the horses unhobbled and just as we were driving them off they fired on us and shot one man through the thick of his arm. We rode off and drove the horses off but they followed us and shot four or five horses from under the men and shot one of the volunteers in the belly, which I was obliged to leave at one Dr. Pearson on an island in the neck between Wassau and St. John's.

Our men behaved very cowardly in this action. All I could say and do could not get them to stand and fight. Some would now and then get down and fire at the Indians, by which means we got our horses off and killed one Indian. We retreated to the camp and got reinforced and returned to immediately where we had the skirmish and found the woods on fire, which gave us reason to think we had killed some of them or they were afraid we should pursue them. We reached the swamp near where they had fired and soon found one hid in a hollow log. The number of Indians I believe did not exceed fourteen and I believe they were the very Indians Barfield told my brother of. The Indians made off immediately for the Cow Ford and I suppose by the behavior of our men the Indians and scout were encouraged to pursue us, which they did the next day. But on finding we were discovered in that neck, I thought it prudent to retreat out as quick as possible or we should not have made as good a retreat as we have done. For it was really a dangerous place. Saturday morning as we were marching of[f] from along the swamp that made the neck and where we encamped the night before, we saw a number of men just ahead of us seeming to be going towards Joseph Rains's, the way we were going. I immediately rode towards them and found they were the scout and Indians and as soon as they discovered us they fired a gun which I imagine was to give the regular troops notice that was behind them. As soon as they fired, I ordered every man to get down and hitch their horses and take to trees, but, instead of obeying orders, many of them never got off their horses or even attempted to follow me. Some there was, I believe between twenty and thirty, that behaved very well and for four or five minutes seemed as if we should make the scout and Indians give way to us. But behold all on a sudden the regulars made their appearance on the left of us and those on horseback and near their horses fled immediately on the sight of them, which occasioned those [who] had attacked in front to fly also or they would have been surrounded and taken and killed. I was very near being taken, owing to a man's taking my horse and riding off, but luckily I called to him to quit my horse or I should shoot him, which he did in the nick of time or I should have been in Augustine with my commission, which they have got.

We were obliged to make a very hasty retreat, owing to our men being scattered. Many took to the swamp that made the neck we came out off. My brother rode after them and stopped between fifty and sixty of them from going across the swamp or imagine we should have lost many more of them. I am afraid they have taken some that took to the swamp. Seven of the men that took to the swamp overtook us before we arrived at Altahama and says they saw twelve or fifteen more that went over the swamp and were going down in search of the galleys. Captain Few, Captain Williams, Mr. Bryant and Mr. Joseph Johnston and twenty-nine privates are missing, Lieutenant Fraser killed, Sergeant McGowen ditto, Lieutenant Robinson wounded. A. Trowell wounded, Samuel Mason died with a violent fever, Thomas Coleman drowned crossing Satilla River. The number of men march[ing] from Altamaha including officers and volunteers is 109, out of which there is thirty-eight missing, killed and wounded.

On our retreat we came across one of the regulars which we have brought along with us. He is a Dutchman and speaks but little English but understand by him there is two armed vessels lying at the mouth of St. John's. One is Mobury's sloop of fourteen guns, the other a ship of fourteen or sixteen guns. He further says there is a guard of thirty men at Esther's Bluff and a strong guard at the Cow Ford and many armed boats about the creeks on St. John's. He also says he heard there was more troops arrived in St. Augustine. I have acquainted Colonel Scriven with the above that he may acquaint Colonel Elbert. I could not learn from the person who commanded the regulars only that one Captain Woolf was with them and another Captain and a Major but did not know their names. It seems the prisoner was but the day before we were attacked brought from on board Mobury's sloop. I do not at present recollect any other particular. I shall wait on you next week.

Library of Congress, Manuscript Division

Back in Savannah, the Georgia Assembly exonerated Gwinnett of any responsibility for the failure of the expedition. McIntosh took violent exception to Gwinnett's version of events and blurted out that Gwinnett was a scoundrel and a lying rascal. Gwinnett challenged McIntosh to a duel. At unusually close range, both men were shot in the thighs. Gwinnett died of his wound, McIntosh recovered. Gwinnett's followers set up such an outcry against McIntosh that the general was transferred to the Northern Department.

The exiled Thomas Brown, now lieutenant colonel of the Florida Rangers, made mischief for

Georgia by employing Indians and staging raids along the frontier. In 1778, he sent word to South Carolina Loyalists to join him in Florida. The migration of hundreds of these people through the backcountry startled and confused Georgians. The state legislature met in Augusta to address the problem. The clerk, James Whitefield, reported to Congress that yet another Florida invasion was underway.

JAMES WHITEFIELD TO CONGRESS

[Augusta,] May 6, 1778

Sir: I have in command from the General Assembly now sitting to acquaint Congress with the distressed situation of this state and represent in some measure the urgent necessity which requires immediate exertions from your respectable council in its behalf. Although invaded by sea and land and surrounded by a multitude of enemies who commit daily depredations, the people still retain an unabated ardor to uphold and maintain that sacred cause which has for its object the civil and independent rights of the United States.

About five weeks since a large body of disaffected persons amounting to about 600 men by the most accurate information embodied themselves in the back parts of the state of South Carolina and forced a march through the upper settlements of this state to the province of East Florida and formed a junction with the tyrant's forces and adherents there. Measures were immediately pursued to obviate their designs, but proved ineffectual. Since the above mentioned period, several other large parties of the disaffected attempted to cross Savannah River and pass through this state to East Florida, but the guards on the Georgia side and the close pursuit made by a party of the Carolina militia have as yet frustrated their attempts. These are the men who caused such trouble at the commencement of this war in South Carolina and with whom a treaty of neutrality was then made.

On the other hand, General Prevost with an army of about 1200 men composed of regulars and Florida scouts, which latter are chiefly made of small parties of the disaffected that passed from Carolina during the last winter, left Augustine and has established strong posts, one on the River St. John's and another on the south side of St. Mary's River, where he was joined by the above mentioned multitude from Carolina, besides a number of savages who commit the greatest barbarities. I must add to this that the enemy formed a further design of establishing a post at Frederica, but the gallant behavior of the officers and men belonging to the galleys in the service of this state and the troops under the command of Colonel Elbert prevented it by taking three of the enemy's vessels of war, viz. the *Hitchenbrook* of sixteen guns, the *Rebecca* of fourteen, and a brig of six guns, which are fallen into our hands. Had not the Almighty so signally interposed in our behalf the state must have probably fallen before now as it would have been entirely surrounded by its foes. If anything can increase that aggravated appearance of the many ills that threaten us it is the almost certain accounts which we daily receive that Cameron with a numerous party of Indians intends an immediate attack on the western frontiers of both this state and South Carolina. These movements of the enemy evidence a settled system of subduing this state at least if not Carolina also and breaking the glorious chain of the general independency of the United States. The best accounts which are received of their designs tend to confirm this principle.

This, sir, is a just description of our situation and no doubt will merit the utmost attention of Congress, a situation which we are determined to change as far as in our power lies. As the greatest exertions are necessary for that purpose, we have concluded on an expedition against the province of East Florida, which is now forwarding with all possible dispatch. To speak in terms of positive truth the question must shortly be decided whether Georgia will be free or not.

The expenses attendant on a service so essential to the safety of the United States will certainly be great, but we hope Congress will view them as inconsiderable when compared with the object in question. Indeed the emissions of money heretofore made for the support and pay of the Continental troops and other expenses have depreciated the value of the currency of this state in such a manner as to threaten ruin to its public credit, a ruin which our internal enemies have artfully combined to hasten on and promote.

The alarming complexion of things induced the Assembly to request the Governor to take the field in person, which he has accordingly done with a body of militia and with the assistance from South Carolina to cooperate with the Continental troops under the command of General Howe. The Assembly is now sitting in Augusta, where its presence was thought necessary to raise the spirits of the inhabitants of the back parts and encourage them to oppose any further attempts of the disaffected of South Carolina who are now gathered in large bodies from crossing the river and pursuing the former multitude which passed to East Florida.

The innumerable evils arising from our large emissions of paper currency render it a matter of necessity that Congress should assist this state with the means of redeeming itself. I am therefore commanded by the Assembly to request that Congress would immediately furnish us with one million of Continental dollars for the purpose of supporting the credit of our former emission made for Continental services and defraying the expenses of the present expedition. A supply of this nature forwarded with dispatch would raise the spirits of the distressed people whose critical situation is such as not to admit of any delay. It is a frontier state, sir, far removed from the immediate eye of Congress, laboring under the weight of internal and external oppressions. She appeals to Congress and if by Heaven's permission it should happen that the resources of her support are interrupted on this occasion she is determined to distinguish her fall by every seal of martyrdom for her religious and independent rights.

Papers of the Continental Congress, National Archives

The third descent into Florida was different from the first two only in that it was a larger failure. Georgia Governor John Houstoun refused to cooperate with General Robert Howe, and a third army of South Carolinians under Andrew Williamson added to the confusion of command. There were some exciting skirmishes with "Burntfoot" Brown himself, but nothing important was accomplished.

Now the British high command decided to shift the focus of the war to the South in the expectation that there were large numbers of Loyalists waiting for the sight of redcoats to declare themselves. Lieutenant Archibald Campbell was charged with the responsibility of reclaiming Georgia. Eager to become the first British officer to "rend a Stripe and a Star from the Flag of Congress," Campbell's force captured Savannah in the last days of December, 1778.

JOHN HOUSTOUN TO THE CONTINENTAL CONGRESS

Georgia, January 2, 1779

Sir: It is with great concern I now sit down to inform you that Savannah is in the possession of the enemy and their army is at this moment in full march towards the westward. A fleet of thirty-seven sail arrived at Cockspur on the 24th of last month, where they lay till the 28th. They then came up and the day following effected a landing at Brewton's Hill about two miles below the town. In less than two hours after they landed, they began their march for the town and having made a show of bringing their principal force on in the direct road filed off through the woods and came in at the south side of the town, where only a handful of militia, eighty-five in number, were stationed. Their numbers being greatly superior, they soon forced this small party of militia, though not without receiving and returning several smart platoons in which some of our citizens fell, and they also lost some men. The particular list of either I am not yet furnished with, but find Colonel Walton amongst the wounded. The Continental troops being placed at the eastern quarter of the town, they had to make their retreat through the enemy who attacked them in flank as they marched for about half a mile. The South Carolina brigade under Colonel Huger kept the edge of the town and aimed directly for the Broad Road leading westerly from the spring. They effected their point with the loss of a few men killed, wounded and taken prisoners. The Georgia brigade under Colonel Elbert struck through the [illegible] of the town, but being intercepted by a large

181

creek that makes out of the river a little above the town, the greatest part of those who could not swim were taken prisoners. I can with great [illegible] assure you the small party of militia which I have before mentioned behaved to admiration and were it not for their efforts opposed to at least 1000 men, I am firmly of opinion very few of the troops would have got off. Indeed the two brigades, too, considering the peculiar circumstances under which they happened to fall, conducted themselves as well as men could do. The enemy's force is thought to be from 1500 to 2000 men already landed, but it is said there are as many more remaining at Cockspur. How this may be I can't say, for it is very remarkable. We have not had any single deserter or indeed any sort of certain intelligence since they came in. General Lincoln is now at Purisburg, I am informed, with a respectable force. What a pity he did not arrive a few days sooner. I think he would have saved our state. However we do not despond, well knowing from the first favor of Congress what her future exertions will be to reinstate us. Most people in and about the town have lost their all, and the spirit of rapine, insolence and brutality indulged in [by] the soldiery exceed description. Colonel Campbell commands by land and Admiral Hyde-Parker by sea. People who have got out of town since the action say both these officers profess great humanity and totally disavow many horrid acts committed by their people. How that may be, a short time will show us, but for my part I wish to leave nothing to their humanity and as little to their justice. I will write Your Excellency more particularly on this subject as soon as further information puts it in my power to do so. I am now endeavoring to rally and collect what militia I can.

Continental Congress Papers, National Archives

NARRATIVE OF MORDECAI SHEFTALL

This day [December 29, 1778] the British troops, consisting of about 3500 men, including two battalions of Hessians, under the command of Lieutenant-Colonel Archibald Campbell of the 71st regiment of Highlanders, landed early in the morning at Brewton Hill, two miles below the town of Savannah, where they met with very little opposition before they gained the height. At about 3 o'clock P.M. they entered and took possession of the town of Savannah, when I endeavored, with my son Sheftall, to make our escape across Musgrove Creek, having first premised that an entrenchment had been thrown up there in order to cover a retreat and upon seeing Colonel Samuel Elbert and Major James Habersham endeavor to make their escape that way. But on our arrival at the creek, after having sustained a very heavy fire of musketry from the light infantry under the command of Sir James Baird during the time we were crossing the common, without any injury to either of us, we found it high water. And my son, not knowing how to swim and we, with about 186 officers and privates being caught as it were in a pen and the Highlanders keeping up a constant fire on us, it was thought advisable to surrender ourselves prisoners, which we accordingly did and which was no sooner done than the Highlanders plundered every one amongst us except Major Low, myself and son, who, being foremost, had an opportunity to surrender ourselves to the British officer, namely Lieutenant Peter Campbell, who disarmed us as we came into the yard formerly occupied by Mr. Moses Nunes.

During this business, Sir James Baird was missing, but, on his coming into the yard, he mounted himself on the stepladder which was erected at the end of the house and sounded his brass bugle horn, which the Highlanders no sooner heard than they all got about him, when he addressed himself to them in Highland language, when they all dispersed and finished plundering such of the officers and men as had been fortunate enough to escape their first search. This over, we were marched in files, guarded by the Highlanders and York Volunteers, who had come up before we were marched, when we were paraded before Mrs. Goffe's door on the bay, where we saw the greatest part of the army drawn up. From there, after some time, we were all marched through the town to the courthouse, which was very much crowded, the greatest part of the officers they had taken being here collected and indiscriminately put together. I had been here about two hours, when an officer, who I afterwards learned to be Major Crystie, called for me by name and ordered me to follow him, which I did, with my blanket and shirt under my arm, my clothing and my son's, which were in my saddle bags, having been taken from my horse, so that my wardrobe consisted of what I had on my back.

On our way to the white guard house we met with Colonel Campbell, who inquired of the Major who he had got there. On his naming me to him, he desired that I might be well guarded, as I was a very great rebel. The Major obeyed his orders, for, on lodging me in the guard house, he ordered the sentry to guard me with a drawn bayonet and not to suffer me to go without the reach of it, which orders were strictly complied with, until a Mr. Gild Busler, their Commissary-General, called for me and ordered me to go with him to my stores that he might get some provisions for our people, who, he said, were starving, not having ate anything for three days, which I contradicted, as I had victualled them that morning for the day. On our way to the office where I used to issue the provisions, he ordered me to give him information of what stores I had in town and what I had sent out of town and where. This I declined doing, which made him angry. He asked me if I knew that Charles Town was taken. I told him no. He then called us poor, deluded wretches, and said, "Good God! how are you deluded by your leaders!" When I inquired of him who had taken it and when, he said General Grant with ten thousand men and that it had been taken eight or ten days ago. I smiled and told him it was not so, as I had a letter in my pocket that was wrote in Charles Town but three days ago by my brother. He replied, we had been misinformed. I then retorted that I found they could be misinformed by their leaders as well as we could be deluded by ours. This made him so angry, that when he returned me to the guard house, he ordered me to be confined amongst the drunken soldiers and Negroes, where I suffered a great deal of abuse and was threatened to be run through the body or, as they termed it, skivered by one of the York Volunteers, which threat he attempted to put into execution three times during the night, but was prevented by one Sergeant Campbell.

In this situation I remained two days, without a morsel to eat, when a Hessian officer named Zaltman, finding I could talk his language, removed me to his room and sympathized with me on my situation. He permitted me to send to Mrs. Minis, who sent me some victuals. He also permitted me to go and see my son, and to let him come and stay with me. He introduced me to Captain Kappel, also a Hessian, who treated me very politely. In this situation, I remained until Saturday morning, the 2nd of January, 1779, when the commander, Colonel Innis, sent his orderly for me and my son to his quarters, which was James Habersham's house, where, on the top of the step, I met with Captain Stanhope of the *Raven* sloop of war, who treated me with the most illiberal abuse and, after charging me with having refused the supplying the King's ships with provisions and of having shut the church door, together with many ill-natured things, ordered me on board the prison ship, together with my son. I made a point of giving Mr. Stanhope suitable answers to his impertinent treatment and then turned from him and inquired for Colonel Innis.

I got his leave to go to Mrs. Minis for a shirt she had taken to wash for me, as it was the only one I had left, except the one on my back, and that was given me by Captain Kappel, as the British soldiers had plundered both mine and my son's clothes. This favor he granted me under guard, after which I was conducted on board one of the flat boats and put on board the prison ship *Nancy*, commanded by Captain Samuel Tait, when the first thing that presented itself to my view was one of our poor Continental soldiers laying on the ship's main deck in the agonies of death and who expired in a few hours after. After being presented to the Captain with mine and the rest of the prisoners' names, I gave him in charge what paper money I had and my watch. My son also gave him his money to take care of. He appeared to be a little civiler after this confidence placed in him and permitted us to sleep in a stateroom—that is, the Rev. Moses Allen, myself and son. In the evening we were served with what was called our allowance, which consisted of two pints and a half and a half-gill of rice and about seven ounces of boiled beef per man.

Historical Collections of Georgia, pp. 340–342

The "Great Itinerant" George Whitefield had established a school for orphans outside Savannah in the late 1730's and called it Bethesda. Whitefield attempted to promote the school into a college in 1764, but his adherence to Methodism ended any hope of a Royal charter. When Whitefield died in 1770, he willed his school in Georgia to Selina, Countess of Huntingdon, a patron of English Methodists. She hired the Rev. William Percy to administer the school. Margaret Floyd reported to Lady Huntingdon on the fate of the school.

Margaret Floyd to Lady Huntingdon

[undated]

Dear and Honored Madam: I write this and hope it may get safe to your hands, for I am sure you have not had the true state of the Orphan House represented unto you. I therefore think it my duty as a faithful servant to let you know the truth as far as in my power, if it pleaseth God to spare me, for I am very infirm at times.

Dear Madam, I make no doubt but you heard that Savannah was taken by the British, December the 29th, 1778, which was the ruin of the Orphan House. Mr. Piercy and his family went to Charles Town about a month before and left my husband and me to take care of the Orphan House, which we did while it was in our power. Mr. Piercy wrote me a letter, informed us that he expected to return in three weeks' time, which, poor gentleman, he was disappointed [in doing], for the British came and took all the best of the things at the Orphan House, both yours and his. And if he had been there the officers of the army told me they would have put him to death, I understood, for nothing but preaching the gospel in the Dissenting way.

February, the Hessians came out first and plundered the house of all the poultry and meat and likewise sugar, tea, coffee, candles and everything of that kind. The 11th, came out Colonel Hamilton and one Mr. Stuart and took an inventory of the things at the Orphan House, and I showed your name and mark on the sheets and table linen and other things, of which there was a great plenty. But they did not mind it. They came out again the 13th and brought the Hessians' Guard, a Lieutenant and twenty-five men, and left them there and would not suffer one of us to go into one of the rooms where the furniture was. The 28th, came out General Provost's men and brought the two wagons and loaded them with the Orphan House things. I could only stand at a distance and behold the soldiers loaded with sheets, table linen, pillow cases and the best of the things

185

that was in the house. February the 26th, came out Captain Moore and Major Lowrey and took the ox cart belonging to the plantation and loaded it with the things belonging to the house. All this while the Hessians' Guards was a-destroying the cattle, both milch cows and other stock, both at the house and plantation.

In the meantime, my husband got liberty to stay in the school house till further orders from Mr. Lewis Johnson, superintendent of the police. We had as yet the keys of the store of the plantation tools till Mr. Lewis Johnson put another overseer and then turned away the one Mr. Piercy left there. He gave his new overseer orders to take all the plantation tools that was in the store which we had in care. This was in March, the 28th. All this while we had no provision from the plantation till April 6th. We got an order from Mr. William Telfair, one of the commissioners of claims for to take ten bushels of corn that was at the house. There was a crop at the plantation almost beat out when they turned the overseer away.

Then Mr. Bailey, being one of the commissioners of claims, got the charge of the Orphan House and plantation and then we had no more to do with the house for that time, though we stayed in the school house, still not knowing what to do. Mr. Bailey and his family came to the Orphan House to live in May the 13th and then the Hessian Guard was taken away and then the crop began to be destroyed. He and Mr. Reid joined in shares and made tar with their Negroes on your land, cut staves and clapboards and whatever they wanted and lived on the Orphan House provisions the most of the time, which was from July the 1st till the last of March, 1780, in which time we strove for a living and my husband worked in the garden and sold what Mr. Bailey did not want for to support our poor family, which was in distress till December. Then the Governor and the head men sent out three hundred soldiers to stay at the Orphan House and then more trouble began. They put some of the soldiers in the house with us. It could not be possible that we could live with them. [They] continued their stay till April the 1st, destroying the buildings and everything they could come at. Mr. and Mrs. Bailey supplied them with what they could of the Orphan House things that was left with beds and bedsteads, tables and chairs and other things.

We stayed but twelve days with the soldiers but that time afforded us a great deal of trouble. I [saw] myself the good books gave to their children to play with and other things. Mrs. Bailey cut up one of the feather beds to make herself pillows, belonging to the Orphan House. We was obliged to move to a little hut about a mile of[f], where we stayed till we received a letter from Mr. Piercy dated August 5th, acquainting us that he had committed the care of Bethesda Estate to Mr. Glen, Mr. Tattnall and Mr. Hall and that he intended to go to England and requested us to return back to the Orphan House again to take care of it in the same manner as when he left Georgia in the room of Mr. Bailey, whom he heard had greatly injured the place, and he did not doubt but the gentleman would grant us every privilege to make us live comfortable and happy. This was in August.

Mr. Tattnall sent for my husband and we agreed to go to the House again, but he would not disturb Mr. Bailey till he should move himself. So we waited till October the 29th. Then Mr. Tattnall let us know Mr. Bailey was removed. My husband went to the House and found a man there that Mr. Bailey left with orders not to suffer him to come into the yard nor House by no means. So he returned and went to Mr. Tattnall and told him, but he did not get the man removed till November the 29th. By that time Mr. Bailey had all the plunder he wanted from the house and plantation. There was two crops. One was made before he came, and another after, all which he moved away and left one crop just gathered in. We could not tell how much was made, not being at the place some time before. But we knew the poor Negroes to be obliged to quit work and go in the woods to gather huckleberr[ies] to eat, for they was almost starving part of the time we lived at the house.

The time of the siege of Savannah and there was nothing troubled but five or six head of cattle, which the British left. Mr. Tattnall came out to see us the first and last time, though he went often to the plantation, but there was no rice at the house. We told him of some of the things that Mr. and Mrs. Bailey had took from the house, but he put it off and said he would look into it, saying that the times was so troublesome now to trouble a friend to government. We showed him the buildings that was destroyed by Mr. Bailey and the soldiers. He said when money was made at the plantation he would have them repaired. But we found no repair but letter after letter to accommodate the refugees with rooms for their families till there was an hundred and fifty! All the rooms was full but three, which was reserved for us. And the few things that was left then, the buildings was destroyed worse than before. He sold all the potatoes and rice to supply them and had to buy corn to supply the Negroes, so little of it that they was at half allowance till the other crop was made.

This was in 1781. We got a little provision from the plantation till it was all sold and then we was obliged to buy corn for the support of our family and to help the poor old Negroes that was at the house with us. We could do nothing for a living now, only take care of the poor remains of the Orphan House and [see] that they did not burn the buildings. As for the garden, they destroyed everything in it. We could not raise a fowl nor hog, but lived on the little wages Mr. Tattnall was please[d] to give us, that was little by little, till the first of the next year. Then he cut us short of £10 of our wages and said Your Ladyship would not allow it and paid us the remainder of £30, which was not our agreement. But we was obliged to put up with it, though we had no privilege but the wages to depend upon. He told us he had wrote to Your Ladyship the state of the Orphan House was in and that he had sent to inventory of the things that was left. He expected you would send somebody over to take the charge of the place.

We continued still, expecting to hear from Your Ladyship, taken what care we could, in which time my husband was very ill and laid eleven weeks sick, in which time I sent to Mr. Tattnall for a little money to supply our distress. But he would not give us a farthing, though he had all the other crop carried to town and I suppose sold it, for he said he sent Your Ladyship money. The poor Negroes had to go all the way to town for their week's allowance.

My husband departed this life in June the 13th, 1782. Mr. Tattnall went away in the middle of July. The refugees went away the same time. He left nobody to take charge of the plantation and I had nobody at the house but a poor blind sister. The Americans came into Savannah and there was orders given that half the Negroes on every plantation should go to town to pull down the works the British had made up. But the man that was sent out took all that was able to work. The Negroes applied to me but I could do nothing for them till my son came to see me and then I got him to go to town and to intercede with Mr. Clay to take charge of the plantation till orders came from Your Ladyship. We got the Negroes all back to their places again. I continued at the house above a year, till I was likely to starve. Mr. Clay had no orders to pay me and Mr. Tattnall would not, so that I am deprived of my [wages], though I have [had] the care of the house ever since and what things is left.

For I go every now and then and air the house and things. I do not live far from the house. It is about a mile by water so that I can't go there by myself, which makes it very troublesome to me. I would be glad of a discharge, though not without [unless] it came from yourself. There is two old Negroes stays at the house, Sue and Abigail, and they plant a little provisions for themselves. Dear Madam, I would have wrote before but the gentlemen that had the charge of the place told me they had sent the true state of the place to Your Ladyship, so I waited with patience. I could tell you more by word of mouth and better than I can write. Dear Madam, I remain, with God's assistance in what I can, your humble servant.

Location of manuscript unknown

Acting under standing orders, Lieutenant Colonel Campbell marched to Augusta where a number of Loyalists were presumed to be waiting. Thomas Brown and his rangers rode in the van. Except for a skirmish at Burke County Courthouse, in which Brown was wounded, the

British were unopposed and Campbell occupied Augusta on January 31, 1779. He described the town as consisting of "a number of straggling Houses, arranged in a long Street lying parallel to the River." The British strategy seemed to be working as eleven hundred men came in to take an oath of allegiance to the King during the first week. But the sudden arrival of an army of North Carolinians under General John Ashe caused Campbell to retreat from Augusta on February 14, 1779. On the same day, Whigs under Andrew Pickens and Elijah Clarke defeated a body of Loyalists at Kettle Creek in Wilkes County.

Campbell retreated only as far as Brier Creek, where he gave command to Lieutenant Colonel James Mark Prevost, brother of General Augustine Prevost, who brought his Florida troops up to occupy Savannah. The Whig army under John Ashe, grown careless in pursuit of the British, was surprised and routed by Prevost on March 3, 1779. British occupation of Georgia now extended into the backcountry as far as Brier Creek. Burke, Richmond and Wilkes counties remained free of British control, but in constant fear of British-instigated Indian raids. Members of the legislature assembled in Augusta and reported to Congress on the perilous state of the province.

SUPREME EXECUTIVE COUNCIL TO CONTINENTAL CONGRESS

Augusta, July 10, 1779

Sir: The present unhappy situation of this state calls aloud for the serious attention of all those that it ought to concern, it being one-half in full possession of the enemy and the other half having been ravaged and plundered by them and what adds more to our calamities is that we have not a proper representation at Congress, which is the only motive that now prompts us to put pen to paper in order to speak to the Honorable Congress in this manner. When the enemy approached our country, the first place they took into possession was the seat of our government with the three lower counties.

The inhabitants being chiefly contained in six, the representatives of the other three, rather than give up or let government fall, met at Augusta agreeable to the time pointed out by our constitution and went through all the ceremonial part of it in order at least to keep up a show of government, by which means we hope and flatter ourselves that we have rendered the common cause some (though but small) service as well as the keeping some better order among ourselves than what might have been had it been otherwise, but you must think that it could be but a bare shadow of government that we could keep up, when we inform you that our treasurer moved out of the state when the enemy came in and our affairs have bore such a gloomy aspect ever since that we have not as yet thought it prudent to order him back, so that we have no money at our command to answer any purpose whatever.

In short, our money affairs is in a very bad situation, at present our Georgia currency in a manner quite sunk and we at this time incapable of calling those to an account that have received Continental money for the use of this state. Mr.

Telfair indeed informs us of some he paid into the treasury but says that he has been since informed that it is of those dates that are forbid to pass. But we must here acknowledge our obligations to that good and worthy gentleman, General Lincoln, who has had a fatherly care over us and we believe has done all that lay in his power for us. Yet there are many things that cash are necessary to keep up government with that does not come in the line of his duty to take notice of.

Our great fear at present is that as we are not properly represented at Congress you will be apt to entertain a bad opinion of us. True it is we must [tell] Congress with shame and sorrow that too many have joined the enemy, but we must do them that justice to say we believe that the major part of the inhabitants of this state that has joined the enemy have done it more through compulsion than real desire. And as for our not being represented [it] is owing to the desperate situation our delegates have been reduced to by being drove from their homes and some losing near or quite all their fortunes, which reason they assign for their not attending, and we at the same time not having it in our power to furnish them with money and although numbers have joined the enemy others left the state while many are hiding about and will take up arms of neither side. Yet we believe we can raise 700 good men as well as bold warriors, such as we think are not afraid to [call] themselves "the sons of Liberty" and defend it with their arms at the risk of their lives!

A few days ago we received the following intelligence from one of our spies, who being in Savannah about two weeks since and being looked upon as a particular friend to government, says he was invited to breakfast with Colonel Provost who is appointed acting governor of that place and waiting on the governor rather early for breakfast found him in his apartment where he writes and does business and while the governor was busy he pretended to amuse himself with some books that lay about in the room and in the meantime discovered two letters that had been just wrote and still open, the one directed to A. Gilvery, commander in East Florida, the other to Paress, commander in West Florida. He says he glanced his eyes over the two letters and found them to be both of one purport and the chief contents was for them to hold themselves in readiness to join the Creek Indians at the shortest notice. He says as he wanted to be further satisfied in this matter, [he] raised the discourse at breakfast by beginning an exclamation about the people's taking up arms against the King in the upper parts of Georgia (he himself being an inhabitant of that place). On which the governor told him freely that he plainly saw the upper parts of Georgia must be made a sacrifice of before they would be brought to proper subjection, which he intended to effect by bringing the Indians on them. The spy answered that that would be a pity too, for that they had some good subjects in that part and for his own part he did not know what he should do. The governor answered that those things could not be stopped in such cases, but that he would have him and all their good friends move within their lines. The spy told him that that could not be done but by being much [to] their prejudice as they had all crops growing which they depended on for the support of their families, but how long did he think it would be before the matter would be effected? The governor answered that that would depend upon circumstances, though he did not imagine it could be brought about in less than two or three months, but that he should certainly be informed of it before it happened.

Papers of the Continental Congress, National Archives

Governor James Wright returned to Savannah on July 14, 1779, and announced the restoration of Royal government. Georgia thus had the unique distinction of being the only rebellious colony to be restored to the mother country and exempted from taxation. Before the end of the year, two groups of unreconciled rebels, one radicals led by George Wells and the other conservatives led by John Wereat, established rival governments at Augusta. Poor, strife-torn Georgia presented to the world the spectacle of three governments, one in Savannah and two in Augusta, when it could hardly afford one.

John Wereat to Benjamin Lincoln

Augusta, August 18, 1779

Sir: After several fruitless attempts to establish a government in this state agreeable to the Constitution thereof, a number of the members of our Assembly met at this place on the 24th ultimo, but, finding themselves inadequate to proceed to business as a House of Assembly, they elected nine persons as a superior executive council and delegated to them competent powers and authority to act as such. This measure they did not conceive they had sufficient power to establish but recommended it to the inhabitants of the state and it has been adopted by a very large majority of them. The choice having fallen upon John Wereat, Joseph Clay, Humphrey Wells, John Dooly, William Gibbons, Myrick Davis, Joseph Habersham, William Few and Seth John Cuthbert, we beg leave to offer you our sentiments on such matters as may immediately occur to us on the subject of the public disputes of our country.

A considerable part of the state having been in the immediate possession of the enemy ever since its invasion by them, those counties which have held out against them have been constantly subject to their incursions and depredations and of course the few militia there of much harassed with duty but their spirits have been kept up with the idea of support from the Continent and our sister state otherwise we apprehend a total evacuation would long since have taken place by those who have firmness enough to sacrifice everything to the cause of America, whilst the wavering would have joined the enemy and assisted them in their operations against Carolina. The arrival of the advance of General Scott's army under Colonel Parker and Major Jamieson at a very critical juncture has had the most salutary effect that could be expected, for it has infused new spirits into the militia who are now all cheerfully under arms to oppose the concerted invasions of the enemy's irregulars and Indians, who are at this time making different inroads upon us. General McIntosh has sent out a part of the Continental troops to support our militia, and we hope that for the present we shall be able to repel the enemy and to keep them from reaping any considerable advantages from the attempts of small parties, but we presume, sir, that we need not endeavor to impress your mind with an idea of the feeble resistance we should be able to make to any serious attempt of the enemy to subjugate the upper parts of the state, even with the assistance that General McIntosh can at this time afford us.

We believe it is generally allowed that unless the enemy are considerably reinforced, they will not make another attempt upon Charles Town and from a variety of circumstances we are led to hope that they will not receive such reinforcements. Should this be the case, there can scarce remain a doubt but that they will aim at a total [subjugation?] of Georgia this fall, for we cannot in reason suppose that they will keep a considerable body of troops inured in Savannah, whilst the back country, so necessary to their quiet and subsistence as well as to their future designs, remains unconquered. The large quantities of grain that will be made in the vicinity of this place and the numerous herds of cattle through all the upper parts of the country must be very considerable objects with them, particularly as we know that they cannot even now get sufficient supplies of cattle without coming upwards and then fighting for them. The frequent skirmishes of our militia with their irregulars, who are employed as drovers, evinces the truth of this observation and should they gain the upper parts of the state we are bold to assert that Carolina would be in a very dangerous situation.

The great defection of the upper parts of that country is well known—a circumstance on which the enemy found the most sanguine hopes, and we have every reason to believe that they continually receive encouragement from these people to invade the back country nor could the enemy wish for a more favorable situation to be joined by them than that of Augusta or anywhere above it where the river is shallow and the swamps all passable. Add to the circumstances already mentioned which might induce the enemy to progress upwards in force that of having no obstructions to their intercourse with the Indians a very capital one and which will immediately be the case should they effect an entire conquest of this country, and unless they should do this their intercourse will be very precarious and uncertain and we shall always have it in our power to give the most considerable interruption to it. We think this point worth paying the most particular attention to, as we are informed that Indian goods are now imported at Savannah and that the Creek Indians have had no late supply from the Floridas.

Should the trade from this country with the Indians be once open and un-interrupted, the enemy will find not the least difficulty whenever they have a mind in bringing the savages upon the frontiers of Carolina. Besides our appre-hensions on the above heads, we are fearful that in case the British troops should move up this way, the greatest part of the inhabitants worn out with fruitless opposition and actuated by the fear of losing their all, would make terms for themselves and as the human mind is too apt to be led by a natural gradation from one step of infancy to another, we have not the least doubt of their joining the enemy against their countrymen in any other state. But even should the British commander not bend his force this way, a great many families, ha-rassed and unsupported, would remove far northwardly, for which they are already thinking of preparing and this dangerous migration nothing but the appearance of support can prevent.

With minds forcibly impressed by the operation of such powerful reasons, we beg leave, sir, to solicit you in the most serious manner to order General Scott, who we understand is on his march southwardly with the rest of his troops, im-mediately to this place. We cannot think that the lower parts of Carolina will be endangered by such an order, for we may reasonably presume that the enemy will never penetrate far into that part of the country while a respectable force remained in their rear which would be the case if General Scott and his troops were in Georgia.

The expenses incurred by the militia in the Quartermaster General's depart-ment in this state since the invasion of it are at present on a very disagreeable footing. Individuals are distressed for moneys due them by the public, whilst they know not who to apply to for redress. The persons who have had the man-agement of these matters have not been so regular as could be wished in their proceedings, on which account Colonel Wylly thinks he is justifiable in not settling them unless he has particular orders to that purport. We therefore re-quest that you will direct him to assimilate them, as nearly as may be, to the Continental charges and expenses and to discharge them. The accounts of the late expedition of Colonel Dooly down the country by your orders are in the same predicament and equally want settling.

We are particularly struck with the necessity of a measure which we are much at a loss to put in execution. This is the augmentation of the pay of our militia. It is exceedingly hard on and discouraging to them to know that the militia of

Carolina receives $30 a month while they get but $6, which is so perfect a trifle that they scarcely think it worth receiving. We think, considering the very particular situation of the country, that they ought to receive this pay and that it ought to be a Continental expense and make no doubt but that Congress will see into the expediency of the measure and acquiesce accordingly in it, but we have been unhappily a long time without a representation in that body and although we think we are invested with sufficient authority to do this matter, yet the low state of our finances puts it out of our power. We would willingly negotiate a loan in behalf of the state if we knew how to obtain it, until delegates whom we mean to elect and send off immediately could arrive at Philadelphia, when it should be repaid in case that Congress should not make it a Continental expense. We flatter ourselves that you will see fully into the necessity of this step and that you will back our applications to Congress on the subject and in the meantime request that you will give us all the advice and assistance in the matter that may lie in your power.

At the same time that we gratefully acknowledge the attention which you have already paid us, we cannot from a most serious view of our truly alarming situation refrain from repeating our solicitations with respect to General Scott and trust that your own good judgement will sufficiently enforce the arguments we have offered and your impartiality and philanthropy lead you to do everything in your power at least to preserve the remains of one of the links of the American chain.

We are informed that James Lambert, David Rupell and Henry Ferguson are on board the prison ships in Charles Town. These men were citizens of and owe allegiance to this state, the former having been a member of the House of Assembly and a Captain of a company of militia, is charged with deserting with his whole company to the enemy and crimes of a like nature are alleged against the other two. As a court is about to be held [with] the trial of criminal causes, we have made [application] to the state of South Carolina for those persons and request the favor of you to order a guard to receive them and conduct them to Augusta, that they may be dealt with according to law.

We have also applied to the Assembly of Carolina for the loan of some money in the present distressed situation of our affairs. If our application shall prove successful, we shall be glad if the money could come with the same guard.

Benjamin Lincoln Papers, Duke University

I was every moment in danger of being smashed to pieces with a shell or shot in two with a cannon ball. I watched the flashes of the mortars and guns. A house was no security, for the shot went through many houses. When I heard the whistling of a shot or shell, I fell on my face.

ANTHONY STOKES, 1779

THE BRITISH having recaptured Savannah in December, 1778, the King's government was restored along the coast in the following March and Governor Wright returned to Savannah in July. In October, 1779, a grand French fleet, which had been operating in the West Indies protecting the French sugar islands, sailed north. The French admiral, Count Charles Henri d'Estaing, with twenty-two ships and four thousand soldiers, expected to make quick work of recapturing Savannah. But a textbook siege, a slow starving of the city by surrounding it, then battering it into subjection with a four-day bombardment followed by a direct assault, cost hundreds of lives and was a failure. King George ordered cannon salutes and fireworks at St. James, and Savannah remained in British hands till the end of the war. But for the inhabitants of Savannah, who spent most of the siege hiding in cellars, and even for the Franco-American attackers, who realized they were killing citizens of their would-be nation, fear and regret outweighed the glory.

JOHN JONES TO HIS WIFE

Camp before Savannah
7th October 1779

This letter, my dear wife, will be handed you by Ismael, I expect. I am sorry 'tis not yet in my power to congratulate you on our safe arrival in Savannah. The enemy still continues very obstinate and a more cruel war could never exist than this. The poor women and children have suffered beyond description. A number of them in Savannah have already been put to death by our bombs and cannon. A deserter is this moment come out who gives an account that many of them were killed in their beds. Amongst others a poor woman with her infant in her arms were destroyed by a cannon ball. They have all got into cellars but even there they do not escape the fury of our bombs, several having been man-

195

gled in that supposed place of security. I pity General McIntosh his situation in particular, the whole of his family is there. We have burnt as yet only one house, but I expect this night the whole will be in flames, Count d'Estaing being determined they shall now surrender. We keep up a most [constant?] cannonade and bombardment and this evening we shall carry on our approaches within pistol shot of the enemy's lines. We are hourly expecting that they will strike, though many with myself are of opinion they will not until we compel them by storm. Their investment is complete and the siege a regular one. I think the matter so near a conclusion that I must doubt if Ismael will return from Mrs. McPherson's in time. The want of thick clothes has been the means of my taking a great cold and am at present very unwell, having, too, a small touch of the gout, which I much fear will increase. We have been very unlucky with respect to the weather —a continual rain and 'tis now very cold. I wish you might have Ismael to send me a bottle of gin.

Seaborn Jones Collection, Duke University

ANTHONY STOKES TO HIS WIFE

Savannah, November 9, 1779

Soon after my arrival, I made application to the barrack-master to be provided with apartments; but Savannah was so full that it was with difficulty I got two rooms in a house in which the town adjutant and his wife were quartered; and those worthy people showed me great civility, doing every thing in their power to make my life comfortable. After some time my health was so much impaired with living in town, that I proposed going to my house in the country, which is on the salts. With the assistance of friends and a good deal of trouble, I at last moved my baggage and some provisions to the country, where I soon grew better; but I had not been many days, and had scarcely completed the removal of my baggage, when (on the third of September) the Count d'Estaing, with twenty-two sail of the line, and fourteen frigates, and a number of transports, appeared on the coast, and a descent being preconcerted with the Rebels in South Carolina, the latter had sent parties within ten miles of Savannah, and taken several prisoners, negroes, and horses.

I now moved into town, and ordered my negroes to bring in my baggage; but before that was completed, the French landed on the twelfth of September, and came into my neighborhood, by which means I lost the wine, provisions, furniture, some books, and other articles that were left behind. Several of my negroes were also left at the plantation, and Fanny, that was just delivered, ran into the woods to avoid being taken.

The house in which I was quartered, was that in which Mrs. Lloyd formerly lived; and under the house there was a cellar, which a merchant desired the town adjutant and myself would permit him to apply to the barrack-master for the use of, and we accordingly consented to it. This merchant lent his cellar to two others, who, without the knowledge of the town adjutant or myself, inhumanly put twenty-five puncheons of rum into the cellar, after the town had been invested, and Count d'Estaing had demanded the surrender thereof to the arms of France.

The French and Americans had invested the town, and the French had entrenched themselves up to the chin, about two hundred yards from our lines, some time before their artillery and ammunition came up from their ships; and as a slight cannonade had passed over, many began to flatter themselves that the enemy would go away without any further effects.

But in this they found themselves much mistaken; for at midnight of the third of October, when all the women and children were asleep, the French opened a battery of nine mortars, and kept up a very heavy bombardment for an hour and a half, in which time those who counted shells found that they fired one hundred, which were chiefly directed to the town. I heard one of the shells whistle over my quarters, and presently afterwards I got up and dressed myself; and as our neighborhood seemed to be in the line of fire, I went out with a view to go to the eastward, out of the way; but a shell that seemed to be falling near me, rather puzzled me how to keep clear of it, and I returned to the house not a little alarmed.

I then proceeded to the westward, and then the shells seemed to fall around; there I soon joined a number of gentlemen who had left their houses on account of the bombardment, and, like me, were retiring from the line of fire to Yamacraw; here we stayed till between one and two in the morning, when the bombardment ceased. Fortunately for us, there was no cannonade at the same time, and in the night shells are so discernible that they are more easily avoided than in the day.

Being indisposed, I had not slept a wink from my going to bed at nine till the bombardment began at twelve; and before I returned again, it was near three in the morning, when from fatigue I soon fell asleep; but at five I was awakened with a very heavy cannonade from a French frigate to the north of the town, and with a bombardment and cannonade from the French lines in the south, which soon hurried me out of bed; and before I could get my clothes on, an eighteen-pounder entered the house, stuck in the middle partition, and drove the plastering all about.

We who were in the house now found ourselves in a cross fire; and notwithstanding the rum in the cellar, we thought it less dangerous to descend there than to continue in the house, as the fall of a shell into the cellar was not so probable as the being killed in the house with a cannon ball; for the cellar being under the ground, a shot in its usual direction would not reach us. The cellar was so full of rum and provisions that Mrs. Cooper, the negroes, and myself could hardly creep in; and after we had descended into it, some shot struck the house, and one passed through the kitchen, from which the negroes had then lately come down; and had they not luckily moved away, it is probable that several of them would have been killed. Whilst we were in the cellar, two shells burst not far from the door, and many others fell in the neighborhood all around us. In this situation a number of us continued in a damp cellar, until the cannonade and bombardment almost ceased, for the French to cool their artillery; and then we ascended to breakfast.

As the cannonade and bombardment were chiefly directed to the town, no mischief was done in the lines that I heard of; but Mr. Pollard, deputy barrackmaster, was killed by a shell in that house on the bay which was formerly inhabited by Mr. Moss; and the daughter of one Thomson was almost shot in two by a cannon ball, at the house next to where Mr. Elliot lived. I am told there were other lives lost, but I have not heard the particulars. Fortunately for us, after breakfast the town adjutant's wife and myself went over to Captain Knowles, who is agent for the transports, and to whose cellar Mrs. Prevost, the general's lady, and several gentlemen and ladies had retired for security. This house was directly opposite to my quarters, and about thirty or forty feet distant.

The general's lady and Captain Knowles invited us to stay there, which invitation we accepted, and we continued in the cellar, with several others, as agreeably as the situation of matters would admit of, until three o'clock on Tuesday morning. During the whole of this time the French kept up a brisk cannonade and bombardment; the shot frequently struck near us, and the shells fell on each side of us with so much violence that in their fall they shook the ground, and many of them burst with a great explosion. On Monday night we heard a shot strike my quarters, and in the morning we found an eighteen-pounder had entered the house and fallen near the head of my negro, Dick, who providentially received no hurt.

Most of the houses in the town had banks of earth thrown up, and those that had cellars secured them as well as circumstances would admit of. Captain Knowles, for the security of the ladies in his cellar, had in some places thrown up a bank of sand on the outside, and in other places put large casks filled with sand; he also propped up the floor over the cellar, and put such a quantity of sand on it that it was bomb-proof. This worthy man and able officer had been taken prisoner by the Rebels in Carolina, and was on parole unexchanged; he therefore could not go into the batteries, which was a loss to His Majesty's service.

The guns seemed to approach on each side, and about three o'clock on Wednesday morning a shell whistled close by Captain Knowles's house. Soon afterwards another came nearer, and seemed to strike my quarters, and I thought I heard the cry of people in distress. We all jumped up, and before I could dress myself, my quarters were so much in flames that I could not venture further than the door, for fear of an explosion from the rum. George and Jemmy were over with me in Captain Knowles's cellar; the others were at my quarters. George ran over before me, and fortunately for me drew out of the flames the two black trunks with some of my apparel, &c., that I brought out with me, and then removed them over to Captain Knowles's passage, which was all the property I saved, except a little black trunk that was put into one of the large ones by accident; for I momentarily expected that the explosion of the rum would blow up the house, and kill every one near it; and as soon as the French observed the flames, they kept up a very heavy cannonade and bombardment, and pointed their fire to that object to prevent any person approaching to extinguish the flames.

I retired to Captain Knowles's, where, in vain, I called out for some of my negroes to help me save my two trunks, for I expected that Captain Knowles's house, and the commodore's next to it, would be destroyed. No negro came to my assistance, and I was informed that mine, who had slept at the quarters, being frightened at the shell, had ran away; but unfortunately that information was not true. Being in the direction of the French fire, I was every moment in danger of being smashed to pieces with a shell, or shot in two with a cannon ball; and as each of the trunks were too large for me to carry off, I thought it safest to abandon them, and retire to a place of safety, than to run the risk of losing my life as well as my property.

I had some distance to go before I got out of the line of fire, and I did not know the way under Savannah Bluff, where I should have been safe from cannon balls; and therefore, whenever I came to the opening of a street, I watched the flashes of the mortars and guns, and pushed on until I came under cover of a house; and when I got to the common, and heard the whistling of a shot or shell, I fell on my face. But the stopping under cover of a house was no security, for the shot went through many houses; and Thomson's daughter was killed at the side opposite to that where the shot entered.

At last I reached an encampment made by Governor Wright's negroes on the common between Savannah and Yamacraw, and it being dark I fell down into a trench which they had dug. I proposed to stop at the house of a Mr. Tully; but a soldier, who was on guard at the Hessian hospital at Yamacraw, advised me to go further from the line of fire, and conducted me to the house of Mr. Moses Nones, at the west end of Yamacraw, which was quite out of the direction of the enemy's batteries.

This place was crowded, both inside and out, with a number of whites and negroes, who had fled from the town. Women and children were constantly flocking there, melting into tears, and lamenting their unhappy fate, and the destruction of their houses and property. Several of them I helped out of a chair, which was immediately despatched to fetch more from the danger they were threatened with.

The appearance of the town afforded a melancholy prospect, for there was hardly a house which had not been shot through, and some of them were almost destroyed. Ambrose, Wright, and Stute's, in which we lived, had upwards of fifty shot that went through each of them, as I am informed; and old Mr. Habersham's house, in which Major Prevost lived, was almost destroyed with shot and shells. On the streets, and on the common, there was a number of large holes made in the ground by the shells, so that it was not without some difficulty the chair got on; and in the church, and Mr. Jones's house, I observed that the shells came in at the roof, and went through to the ground; and a number of other houses suffered by shells.

On the seventh and eighth of October, at night, the French fired carcasses on the town to set it on fire; but by the vigilance of those who were appointed by the general to act as firemen, only one house was burnt. The enemy finding that their artillery did not make such an impression on the town as to bring about a capitulation, at half-past four on the morning of Saturday the ninth of October, marched up in columns, and attacked two redoubts on the west; but the principal attack was made on a redoubt built by the spring near the edge of the road that goes out to Mr. McGillvray's plantation. The enemy showed themselves in parties all round the lines, and were, by the blessing of God, repulsed everywhere. But the principal slaughter was at the redoubt near the spring, where their loss was very great.

The troops in the lines were much safer from the bombardment than the people in town. Those who pitched marquees [tents] on the common to the southwest of the town were quite out of the line of fire; and some of the militia officers' ladies and several other women, repaired to the lines for safety, and not one of them were hurt. Many of the inhabitants went on board the ships in the river, and others retired to Hutchinson's Island, opposite the town, which you may remember is a rice swamp, and very unwholesome, particularly in the fall.

I twice took a stroll to that island, and at Mr. McGillvray's rice barn the ladies told me there were fifty men, women, and children. Other places seemed to be equally crowded; but neither the ships nor island were places of security, for many shells fell into the river, and some into the shipping, and it required only a greater elevation of the French mortars and more powder to throw the shells among them on the island. One of their brass cannon threw a great number of balls into a point of Hutchinson's Island that lay next the town; besides, a descent on the island was expected from the French frigate and galleys in the Back River; and at one time, some gun-boats from the French ships landed there, but a party of armed negroes drove them off.

In short, the situation of Savannah was at one time deplorable. A small garrison in an extensive country was surrounded on the land by a powerful enemy, and its seacoast blocked up by one of the strongest fleets that ever visited America. There was not a single spot where the women and children could be put in safety; and the numerous desertions daily weakened that force which was at first inadequate to man such extensive lines; but the situation of the ground would not permit the able engineer to narrow them. However, with the assistance of God, British valor surmounted every difficulty, and the siege has rendered famous a sickly hole which was in woods and had only one white man in it at the time General Oglethorpe landed. But insignificant as some may think it, this place is the key of the southern provinces, and the Gibraltar of the Gulf passage; for to the south of this province there is not a port on the continent that will receive a sloop of war.

On the side of the British troops only one captain and seven men were killed. However, I do not mean to be particular on this head, as his excellency the general's account will be exact and authentic. I shall only observe that some who were taken prisoners by the French, and afterwards exchanged, said that the French acknowledged that they embarked twenty-five hundred men less than they landed. Even the people at Charleston admit that twelve hundred French and Rebels fell on the ninth. Amongst the slain were Charles Price, formerly prothonotary, who was killed in the governor's plantation, nearly opposite his own house; young Baillie and John Jones, who formerly lived out at Sunbury, and some others from Carolina and Georgia, whom you did not know.

The French behaved with great bravery, and several of them got on the top of the redoubt; but they all accuse the Rebels of backwardness, and the French officers mentioned them in the most contemptible manner to the British officers that went out with flags. The affair of the ninth made such an impression on the enemy that their fire was afterwards very slack, and they were chiefly employed in removing their cannon and stores. On the nineteenth of October, the French quitted their lines, on the twenty-first of the same month they embarked, and two or three days ago the last of their ships quitted this port.

You will naturally wish to know what the amount of the forces were that acted against us. I have it from good authority that about forty-five hundred men landed from the French ships; and although the number of Rebels is not known, yet they are generally agreed to have amounted to about twenty-five hundred at least; some say a greater number. The French fleet consisted of twenty-two sail of the line and fourteen frigates, as I mentioned before, besides a number of Carolina galleys and privateers; and the French took from us the *Experiment* of fifty guns, Sir James Wallace commander, and the *Ariel* of twenty, commanded by Captain McKensie. The British regulars in the lines never amounted to two thousand effective men; the militia that came in were about three hundred and fifty; and the sailors hardly exceeded that number.

Many who did not think so much of religion before now acknowledge that our deliverance was miraculous, and arose from the immediate interposition of God in our favor. Had the French marched up to town immediately, or had they prevented Colonel Maitland joining us with the troops under his command, I will leave you to judge what the consequences must have been. At first I found numbers in despair; but I did all that I could to support those who desponded, and I would not suffer the language of fear to pass my lips. Colonel Maitland died on the night of the twenty-sixth of the month, October, regretted by all that knew him.

The French and Americans plundered the country in the most shameful manner. Not content with taking away provisions and stock, they even robbed poor people of their bedding and clothes. Colonel Mullryne came in before the siege, as did most of His Majesty's well-affected subjects; but Mrs. Mullryne was at her own house all the time, and it would shock you to hear her relate how basely the French and Americans treated her. They pillaged the house of every thing but the furniture of one room. Many of those who had taken the oaths to government after Colonel Campbell's arrival, and had obtained His Majesty's protection, thought the French and Rebels were so sure of taking the town that they joined them. Several of these false brethren are now in jail.

Rivington's Royal Gazette, November 20, 1779

⌈ 23 ⌉

So great is our terror that we dare not keep a bridge standing within a mile of town. There is no prospect of any planting except upon a few islands. The country people must soon throw themselves upon the mercy of the rebels. Indeed we may truly say, "The Glory is departed!" I could weep to think of our situation.

THOMAS TAYLOR, 1782

DURING THE MONTH after the Siege of Savannah a remarkable drama played out in the Whig portion of Georgia. On October 13, 1779, George Walton was exchanged for a British officer on parole. General Benjamin Lincoln ordered Walton to proceed to Augusta and arrange for the election of a constitutional government. Lincoln did not share John Wereat's opinion that the ad hoc "Supreme Executive Council" had a legal right to represent Georgia or to claim the funds appropriated by Congress. Walton's call for a new government was greeted with enthusiasm by George Wells and the radical critics of the Wereat regime. Delegates were assembled, a legislature elected, and George Walton chosen as governor. Lincoln recognized the Walton administration and released to it the congressional subsidy.

The most famous, or infamous, action of the Walton government consisted of a request to Congress to transfer General Lachlan McIntosh out of the state. The report was signed by the Speaker of the House but, in a later investigation, that worthy denied signing the document. McIntosh's friends, including John Wereat, blamed Walton for the forgery. Actually, Walton had sound reasons for requesting McIntosh's transfer, for the General had been known to be sympathetic to Tories. Walton admitted signing the Speaker's name but explained that the resolution was voted by the legislature but the Speaker had left town before the clerk copied out the letter to Congress. As his blistering letter to McIntosh of January 19, 1780, reveals, Wereat was furious at Walton. He referred to Walton, Wells and Richard Howley as "the Triumvirate that rules this poor state."

JOHN WEREAT TO LACHLAN McINTOSH

Augusta, 19th January 1780

Dear Sir: I well know your attachment to the real interest of your country, your unremitted endeavors to promote it as well in the line of your profession in the field as in the councils of the colony when you was there and the ungrateful, ungenerous and unjust returns you have received.

203

How gladly would I get the base proceeding you mention reversed was there the least probability, but, alas! we are hastening from bad to worse with great rapidity. Can you expect justice after you know the Triumvirate that rules this poor state. If you do I fear you will be greatly disappointed. This is poor consolation to a friend, but it is the truth and must not be suppressed.

New plans for persecution are formed and will be pursued with unrelenting malevolence against some men who will be convicted of having pretty good possessions acquired by many years' industry and on which some of our boisterous *patriots* look with evil and longing eyes. I have been told that one of them made use of the following expression, "Campbell and M[cCartan] possess too much property in this place! I have bled in the service of this country and by God must have part of it." Can you expect justice from one who is capable of making use of such an expression or is such a one fit to be entrusted with guardianship of the lives, liberties and property of the good people of the state? Ought not such men to be as carefully avoided as the pestilence and be abhorred and detested by all such as have the least respect for justice, humanity and the rights of mankind?

Will not J. Houstoun, H. Cuyler, James and Joseph Habersham, William Bryan, Doctor Jones, A. T. Brisbane, Doctor Brownson, Doctor Dinwiddie and some others have reason to reproach themselves when they see their country involved in distress and ruin, honest men persecuted and probably destroyed with every other concomitant evil which their presence would have certainly prevented. They have left a few men in the lurch who were hopeful to see justice, mercy, harmony and good understanding prevail in the state to check and discourage the wicked and designing whose principles and policy is to raise themselves to wealth and opulence on the ruin of honest and inoffensive individuals and of the whole state to effect which they hold nocturnal combinations, mislead the ignorant and unwary and league with the wicked and daring.

A remarkable instance of tyranny happened here this day. Two gentlemen were arrested and ordered to give bail for their appearance at the next Superior Court to be held for this county to answer such charges as should then be exhibited against them. When they appeared to enter into recognizance before the chief justice they demanded a copy of the charge against them, which was denied and they now remain prisoners as they refused to become bound 'till they knew for what. This is a specimen of the justice that may be expected in the course of the current year. How greatly, my dear sir, have you and I been deceived in the opinion we entertained of one man whom we esteemed as a real patriot who would never lose sight of justice and the natural and legal rights of mankind. Can you believe that this wretch has a heart as callous as adamant and to the last degree avaricious that he would sacrifice and destroy his best friends to accomplish any favorite point he had in view and in short that Nero of infamous memory was not a greater tyrant than G[eorge] W[alton]!

I assure you that I am seriously thinking of a retreat (at least during this year) over the river in a state remarkable for its public justice, not thinking myself secure here. To show you that this is not barely an imaginary evil believe me when I tell you that a resolve is entered on the minutes little short of proscription to any person holding any office and to any member of the House who shall hold any conversation, associate or hold any intercourse with persons *suspected* of being inimical to the independence of America and gives a power to the governor to suspend all public officers who are guilty of the above offence. I expect at least to be expelled [from] the House in the course of a few days, which I shall look upon as far from being in the least disgraceful.

The popular cry at the beginning of this session and which was repeatedly bellowed forth upon all occasions was true: Whigism, love of country, public virtue, independence and disinterestedness. But today the tone is changed. Your public officers must be supported in affluence. They must be held in the highest veneration and respect and put out of the reach of Tories for which purpose large salaries must be annexed to their officers and which were voted accordingly. We grant away money without having any possible means of raising it unless it is by borrowing of our neighbors or the United States who, if they knew into whose hands it was to fall, would be unwise to advance it. Ought not men in this time of general distress to step forth in the service of their country disinterestedly and not run it to any unnecessary expense? The late executive council (that Walton has damned by the lump) did not run the state to a shilling expense but several of them came a great distance and at a considerable expense with no other motives but to serve a distressed and almost deserted country at a time that some of our now blustering, noisy heroes choose to keep themselves at a proper distance and out of harm's way.

The only chance a man who is obnoxious to the reigning powers can have in my opinion will be in the courts of justice unless a mode should be adopted to abolish trial by jury. This I think they will scarcely be hardy enough to attempt after vehemently crying "Constitution, Constitution, Constitution! We support the Constitution!" I have a high opinion of the integrity of the gentleman who is at the head of the judiciary department and believe he will endeavor to do whatever he thinks is right. After all the disagreeable truths that I have told you let me entreat you to come and resume the command here if possible where you will find friends glad to see you in spite of malevolent calumniators.

Manuscript Division, Library of Congress

The in-fighting between the Whig factions subsided when Charleston fell to General Henry Clinton's army in May, 1780. Whig resistance collapsed over most of Carolina and Georgia. Richard Howley gave up the office of governor to become a delegate to Congress along with George Walton. George Wells served briefly as governor but that hot-tempered patriot was killed in a duel with John Wereat's young friend James Jackson. Then Stephen Heard became governor in transit as he fled to the mountains in the face of the advancing British force. The new commander in Augusta was none other than Lieutenant Colonel Thomas Brown of the King's Rangers, now also serving as Superintendent of Indians. Brown invited the Indians to return to Augusta for the distribution of presents. With the willing cooperation of the Creeks and Cherokees, Brown controlled the vast frontier from his post at Augusta.

The lure of Indian presents drew Lieutenant Colonel Elijah Clarke and his loyal followers to Augusta. British reinforcements from Ninety-Six rescued Brown after a four-day battle and chased Clarke back to the North Carolina mountains. A British contingent under Major Patrick Ferguson tried to intercept Clarke, but instead was caught by Clarke's friends on King's Mountain in a battle that has been called the turning point of the war in the South.

General Nathanael Greene assumed command in the Southern Department and the tide of war gradually changed in favor of the American cause. After the climactic Battle of Guilford Courthouse, British General Charles Cornwallis invaded Virginia and left only scattered outposts to hold the Carolinas and Georgia. Greene turned his attention to these isolated garrisons. Greene's best man, "Light Horse Harry" Lee, opposed Thomas Brown in a two-week battle of Augusta. On June 5, 1780, Brown surrendered and Lee sent him to Savannah under protective custody as a paroled prisoner.

After retaking Augusta and supervising the restoration of a Whig government, Nathanael Greene dispatched one of his best known generals, "Mad Anthony" Wayne, to take charge of the campaign against Savannah. Governor Wright's frantic appeals for help were ignored. Cornwallis surrendered at Yorktown in October, 1781, and the British began to scale down the war. In fact, British General Alured Clarke had enough men under his command to wage a vigorous campaign against Wayne, but he read the mood in London and did nothing. Dr. Thomas Taylor, who had come to Georgia in December, 1775, reviewed events for John Wesley, whose own sojourn in Georgia had proved equally unhappy. Gloomily, Taylor wrote, "The Glory is departed."

DR. THOMAS TAYLOR TO JOHN WESLEY

February 28, 1782

Revd. and dear Sir: I am not quite certain whether I have wrote to you since my unfortunate journey up the country last summer, the particulars of which I will therefore recapitulate.

About the beginning of April last, soon after the affair at Guilford, which was generally believed to have settled the peace of the backcountry, I set off for Augusta, having previously sent off by water an assortment of medicines which I had just received and which cost me near £80 in London. Before I reached Augusta I was informed that a party of rebels had a few days before crossed the river and were spreading devastation all around. However, I happily arrived in safety. Col. Brown, who commanded, had detached a considerable part of his force to escort several large boats then on their way from Savannah. In the meantime, the rebel army moving thru' the country without molestation increased from one hundred to three hundred and then took post between him and the boats so as to prevent a junction.

Things were in this situation when Gen. Greene, having obliged Lord Rawdon to retreat to Moncks Corner and captured all the small forts on the Congaree and Santee rivers, found himself at liberty to detach Col. Lee towards Augusta who, arriving about the end of May, immediately took possession of the small post at Silver Bluff about fourteen miles down the river where the boats had been detained upwards of a fortnight. He there found a most seasonable supply for the rebel army, consisting of the very articles they were in the utmost want of, viz. arms, ammunition, rum, salt, saddles, blankets, medicines, &c. Had Col. Brown had proper information of the state of things in Carolina he would certainly have destroyed the boats and brought up the small escort to Augusta, which could have been done with great ease by a night march, but there appears to have been an unhappy deficiency in this respect.

Col. Lee, immediately after this success, appeared in force at Augusta and, having obliged Col. Grierson who commanded the Royal militia to evacuate his post about half a mile from Col. Brown's, he laid close siege to that of the latter, named Fort Cornwallis. In the abrupt retreat of Col. Grierson, in which we lost sixteen killed, several wounded and about forty prisoners, I had a very narrow escape indeed, for which I trust I shall always feel a proper sense of gratitude to my Maker. After a close siege of fourteen days, Col. Brown was obliged to surrender on the 5th of June. The whole garrison were to be sent prisoners on parole to Savannah, but the very next day at noon Col. Grierson was basely murdered in the very midst of the rebel troops. A sham pursuit was made for a few minutes after the murderer, but he was permitted to escape. Col. Lee and his officers expressed abhorrence of the fact, but to my certain knowledge he refused to prevent it, for that very morning I went to see that gallant, unfortunate man and upon my carrying him a drink of water some of the miscreants about bestowed on us with the most bitter curses. He told me that his life was threatened and if not removed from the place where he then was he was certain the threat would be executed. He therefore begged me to represent this matter thru Col. Brown to Col. Lee, which I did but in vain. It would transcend belief were I to recount the murders committed by these wretches upon the unhappy Tories all over the country. The patriots at home may exclaim and with some justice on the impropriety of employing Indians, but their cruelties in this part of the continent have been exceeded in number at least fourfold by those of the rebels. Putting a man to death in cold blood is very prettily nicknamed "giving a Georgia parole."

Here in Georgia Col. [Alured] Clarke with 1000 regular troops and 500 or 600 refugee militia besides inhabitants and Indians and seamen is blocked up by Gen. Wayne. . . . So great is our terror that we dare not keep a bridge standing within a mile of the town so that tho' the planting season is at hand there is no prospect of any except upon a few islands near the town. The country people, unless something is done, must soon, to avoid perishing, return and throw themselves upon the mercy of the rebels. Indeed we may truly say, "The Glory is departed." I could weep to think of our situation. May the Almighty soon disperse the cloud that at present looms over us and restore peace once more, but I fear that is not yet near. A good old Quaker up the country used often to say to me, there can be no peace before this people are humbled.

William L. Clements Library

The British evacuation of Savannah in 1782 and the Treaty of Paris in 1783 ended hostilities but failed to quiet internal dissension in Georgia. The Revolution had provided frontier people the opportunity to shoulder aside the pre-war "establishment" of low-country merchants and planters. Now the frontiersmen defended the radically democratic Constitution of 1777 against the objections of the conservatives, who tended to be lenient to repentant Loyalists, less interested in frontier forts and opposed to the issuance of paper currency. But these two enduring factions were brought together by frustration over western lands when it came time to ratify the new American Constitution.

In 1783 and 1785 several minor Creek chiefs agreed to cede land beyond the Ogeechee, Georgia's limit of settlement for the previous twenty years. But the brilliant chief Alexander McGillivray refused to let eager Georgians occupy the new counties of Washington and Franklin and launched a war against trespassers. Democratic frontiersmen and conservative low-countrymen now united in favor of a strong central government that could deal with the Indian problem and provide a better climate for business. In late 1787 John Wereat was chosen to preside over a state convention called to consider the new American Constitution. In the midst of the general chorus of approval, the old warrior Lachlan McIntosh raised a cautionary warning that would prove prophetic seventy years later. The Constitution of the United States was ratified in Augusta on January 2, 1788, after only one day of debate.

LACHLAN MCINTOSH TO JOHN WEREAT

Skidaway, December 17, 1787

My dear sir: I hear you are chosen one of the convention which I am glad of and flatter myself you will not think it either impertinent or officious in a fellow citizen to give his opinion in a business of so high importance to ourselves and our posterity as the new Federal Constitution now offered to your consideration and more especially as our legislature have thought proper to enter upon it rather precipitately before the opinions of the other states are known.

Some of the men who framed this Constitution are the wisest and best that this or perhaps any other nation ever produced. Yet with all their good intentions and abilities if we thought them infallible there would be no occasion to appeal to the states and people at large who in Republican Government ought at all times to think themselves the ultimate and best judges of their own grievances and conveniencies.

The popularity of the Framers is so great that the public voice seems to be for adopting the Constitution in the lump on its first appearance as a perfect system, without inquiry or limitation of time or matter. Such hasty resolutions have occasioned all the misfortunes that ever happened in governments and it is really astonishing to see people so reluctant lately to trust Congress with only five percent duties upon imports for a short time to pay the national debt expressly and so jealous of the sovereignty of their respective states so eager now to yield these and everything else into their hands forever and to become the state instead of United States of America.

It is indeed generally agreed as we might have expected that this Constitution discovers great judgement and abilities and that the pressing exigencies of our national affairs requires some speedy and effectual remedy. If therefore we reject the whole or any part of it I fear we will remain for a considerable time at least without remedy in the same unconnected state we now are in, as it appears to be so constructed that the whole or none of it must stand or fall together and should it be found necessary to call another convention of the United States to amend it we cannot expect the last illustrious members will serve again and the determination of any other less dignified will not have the same general influence and may miscarry also.

Upon the other hand, the objections made to this Constitution by Mr. Gerry of Massachusetts, the sentinal of Pennsylvania and others who dare express their mind upon it so early though perhaps overcautious, appear nevertheless to be very weighty and if the remedy should prove worse than the disease what reason will their constituents and posterity have to reflect upon the convention of Georgia in whom they confided and in whose option it was to adopt or reject it for them. In either of these determinations, there appears to me the greatest difficulty and as I had a wish to be in this convention I drew up the compromise as a memorandum for myself which I had some hopes might meet with the wishes of all parties either with or without the annexed condition and be adopted not only by our own but some other states, especially the Southern states who are more particularly interested as they are and ever will continue from their extent and other circumstances the minority in Congress. Therefore it may be thought prudent at least for them at this time to avoid the rock on both sides of the question instead of binding ourselves and posterity forever to adopt the constitution only for a certain period of time, during which they will have a fair trial of its effects and at the expiration of that time be at liberty and have it in their own power to adopt it again if they please for another period either without or with any amendment they may find necessary which probably will hereafter be done by conventions as the precedent is now set which is a new and far better method of settling public differences than the old way of cutting one another's throats. If we bind ourselves and our posterity now by adopting this Constitution without any conditions or limitation of time any efforts made thereafter for redress of grievances must be termed rebellion as it will be impossible to obtain amendments in the mode proposed when the majority which is observed will ever be against the Southern states find it [in] their interest to continue them and men of influence are once fixed in their saddles.

It is known to have been long the intention of the Eastern and Northern states to abolish slavery altogether when in their power, which however just may not be convenient for us so soon as for them, especially in a new country and hot climate such as Georgia. Let us therefore keep the proper time for it in our own power while we have it. This Constitution prolongs the time for twenty years more, which is one reason for fixing upon that period in the enclosed hint as well as to pay off our individual encumbrances which it is conceived may be done in that time when we have given up all our purse strings for that purpose without regard to our own particular engagements.

Bevan Papers, Manuscript Division, Library of Congress

Index

With a few exceptions, persons who are mentioned without first names
are not included in this index.